FILMMAKERS SERIES
edited by
ANTHONY SLIDE

Peckinpah's Women

*A Reappraisal of the Portrayal
of Women in the Period Westerns
of Sam Peckinpah*

Bill Mesce Jr.

Scarecrow Filmmakers Series, No. 90

The Scarecrow Press, Inc.
Lanham, Maryland, and London
2001

SCARECROW PRESS, INC.

Published in the United States of America
by Scarecrow Press, Inc.
4720 Boston Way, Lanham, Maryland 20706
www.scarecrowpress.com

4 Pleydell Gardens, Folkestone
Kent CT20 2DN, England

British Library Cataloguing-in-Publication Information Available

Library of Congress Cataloging-in-Publication Data

Mesce, Bill.
    Peckinpah's women : a reappraisal of the portrayal of women in the period Weste
    Sam Peckinpah / Bill Mesce, Jr.
        p. cm.—(Scarecrow filmmakers series ; no. 90)
    Includes bibliographical references and index.
    ISBN 0-8108-4066-9 (alk. paper)
    1. Peckinpah, Sam, 1925–1984—Criticism and interpretation.
    2. Women in motion pictures.   I. Title.   II. Filmmakers series ; no. 90.
    PN1998.3.P43 M47   2001
    791.43'0233'092—dc21   2001031102

∞ ™ The paper used in this publication meets the minimum requirements
of American National Standard for Information Sciences—Permanence of
Paper for Printed Library Materials, ANSI/NISO Z39.48-1992.
Manufactured in the United States of America.

Contents

To the best part of me—
Gaby and Cathy

Acknowledgments

Special thanks to Kathleen Bryant-Turitz, Richard T. Jameson, Bill Maass, Maribel Padilla-Mesce, Bill Persky, Mark B. Peters, Esq., Sean Michael Rice, and Dr. Suzanne Trauth.

art: 1: skill acquired by experience, study, or observation, 2a: a branch of learning: (1) one of the humanities (2) *pl* LIBERAL ARTS, b: *archaic:* LEARNING, SCHOLARSHIP, 3: an occupation requiring knowledge or skill, 4a: the conscious use of skill and creative imagination esp. in the production of aesthetic objects; *also* works so produced

syn: ART implies a personal, unanalyzable creative power. (*Webster's Ninth* 1990, 105)

Introduction

Reappraising a Reappraisal

Basil Ransom's companion privately remarked how little men knew about women, or indeed about what was really delicate, that he, without any cruel intention, should attach an idea of ridicule to such an incarnation of the pathetic, should speak rough, derisive words about it.

—*Henry James,* The Bostonians (1885)[1]

$\mathcal{I}$ was fifteen, crowded with five friends in Big Randy's dad's mammoth Chevrolet Caprice in what was one of the few remaining drive-ins in that part of New Jersey. I don't remember what movie we had gone to see, but the second feature (those were still the days of second features) was a Western that opened with a Main Street shoot-out the likes of which my John Wayne–cultivated sensibilities had never seen. Blood spurted, people spun under bullet impacts, slow motion mingled with real-time jump cuts to create a ballet of death both repellent and hypnotic. Even at that young age—or, perhaps, precisely because I was at such an unfinished, malleable age—I was struck by the singular vision at work on screen, even though I didn't quite have the maturity to understand all of what I was seeing.

But I could respond to the overturn of traditional Western iconography and ideals. The familiar—dusty streets, men in celluloid collars and woman in ankle-length skirts, listless horses standing at hitching posts—collided with the new—.45 automatics, soldiers in olive drab instead of Federal blue, machine guns, "Tin Lizzie" automobiles, and pump-action shotguns. The expected moral topography became violently inverted as a squad of American soldiers turned out to be masquerading railroad robbers, and the ragtag company of thuggish snipers waiting in rooftop ambush turned out to be a posse representing the law. Viscerally and aesthetically, one couldn't help but feel the chill of something dark and new as the opening credits climaxed with a close-up of William Holden, his flat, hard order—"If they move . . . kill 'em"—and the muted thrum of Jerry Fielding's final note of the opening music. And then the shooting started. . . .

A parade of temperance marchers were caught in the crossfire, used as shields by the robbers, ruthlessly shot out of the way by the ambush team. The robbers trampled over them to escape while the bounty hunters flitted about the bodies, bickering over claims like vultures squabbling over carrion. Those were not just the bodies of innocents strewn about the street, but Innocence itself. The Western I had known—white hats versus black hats, "Aw shucks, Ma'am"—died in that fly-blown street, then resurrected reconceived and recreated.

I didn't know the name of that movie. There'd been too much horseplay in the car to allow any attention to the opening credits. It had begun to rain and between the weather, the air conditioning Big Randy kept running to keep the windows defrosted, and the din inside the car, Randy had developed a headache and called an early halt to the evening. But those opening scenes stayed with me. I very much wanted to know what story could possibly have spun out from such an opening.

A few years later in college I chanced across a network-butchered version of that same film on my roommate's ten-inch black-and-white portable TV. It was only then I learned the title: *The Wild Bunch*. Even in truncated form on the small TV screen, the movie still intrigued, its characters compelled, its finale retained its air of inevitable tragedy and apocalyptic cataclysm. As it happened, just a few months later, the university's theater screened an intact version of the film. This time I watched every title of the opening credits and I set a waving flag by the director's name in my memory: Sam Peckinpah.

The word "aficionado" carries a more sophisticated air than the common parlance "fan," but they are, essentially, the same thing, and by any other name I now was one. I looked for Peckinpah's name on films, began to nose around the university's library stacks to see where this cinematic firebrand had come from, watched every new effort to see where he was going. I read every article and review, each of them as much a discussion on movie violence and sexuality and the morality of the man behind their depiction as an evaluation of a piece of moviemaking. I exercised my growing passion for his work in a paper for my film study class. As Peckinpah's career began to falter, I shared the common view of other devotees in seeing him as the archetypal film *artiste* victimized and ultimately martyred by the crass and insensitive studio executives more than one filmmaker has disdainfully referred to as, "The Suits."

When I first began work on this project seven years after Peckinpah's death in 1984, I saw it as an opportunity to redress some of the injustices visited on one of my favorite filmmakers by both the industry and his most vehement critics. I would complete the critical redemption that was already in process over his work and that would reach a peak with the huzzahs that greeted Warner Bros.' re-release of a restored *The Wild Bunch* on the film's twenty-fifth anniversary.

Among his various crucifixions, Peckinpah had—in my view—been a whipping boy for feminist film criticism, and that was an element of his work that had yet to receive a serious revisitation. I would be Peckinpah's self-appointed respondent on that score. In academic thesis terms, my work would constitute an apologia.

But what I have since come to understand is that apologias—when applied to creative works—are tricky things because *any* evaluation or analysis of a creative work is a tricky thing. This is, after all, art we're talking about and "Art," as Peter Falk reminds us in *Tune In Tomorrow* (1990), "is not just some guy's name."

*   *   *

The dirty little secret of film criticism—whether it's of the heavy-minded *Sight & Sound/Cahiers de Cinema*/Siegfried Kracauer brand, or the town wit's glib three-inch column in the local biweekly—is that "good" movies are whatever a critic likes. This is not meant to be as dismissive as it sounds, but unless one presupposes there exists somewhere an objective artistic gauge, some defined aesthetic compass point to which the critic can reference on aesthetic matters, it's not an unreasonable claim.

Art is, by nature as well as by definition, "unanalyzable." Art, whatever the medium—painting, sculpture, photography, theater, music, performance pieces carried out on subway platforms—is a subjective experience for both creator and audience. Art can't be judged by numbers any more than it can be created by coloring by numbers. Film analysis offers justification for an opinion, but cannot offer proof for something that is unproveable.

Critical evaluations are informed opinions, value judgments, intellectual exercises, and as such are, ultimately, arbitrary. One person's Jackson Pollock is another person's drop cloth. Where one sees a Hudson School riverscape another sees motel art. Other than a critical consensus (which have been known to change over time), there's no definitive proof for either case. And even if the consensus is that a painting adorning a wall in a Motel 6 may be hackneyed, slapdash, and puerile, that doesn't necessarily mean it's not art—it may just be *bad* art. Or is bad art still art? One can argue the case in any direction, but one will only ever be arguing opinion.

Perhaps that subjectivity is nowhere more evident than in film criticism, especially when it is applied to commercial feature films, for even the best films are the product of an equivocating alliance of art, popular entertainment, and commerce. Pity the poor, serious film critic trying to divine whether or not he or she is responding to a film because of its aesthetic power, or because the filmmaker, working in the most base, manipulative Hollywood manner, knows how to move an audience (though, in the process, perhaps incidentally producing great cinema). Sometimes the "art" in a film may be a happy accident, a product not of some auteur's grand design, but of conflicting and coincidental demands from the creative and commercial side of a production (is accidental art still art? Is the creator of accidental art still an artist?). This is, after all, a business where a production company's marketing chief may have a voice in creative decisions.

The point? "I don't know much about art, but I know it when I see it." The problem is we all see things differently.

★   ★   ★

As I began my research for this work, I realized I was just as capable as anyone else of confusing affection with appreciation, of imposing what I wanted to *be* on what *was*. That troubling insight came to me years ago on that first undergraduate Peckinpah paper while I was sourcing Paul Seydor's *Peckinpah: The Western Films.*

Seydor is an articulate, insightful appraiser of Peckinpah's work, and his book was—and remains—an invaluable source for anyone writing about the filmmaker, or even Westerns in general. Even when disagreeing with his analyses, Seydor provides a firm basis for discussion. But it is also clearly evident that he is a loyalist and one who feels he's the opposite number of Molly Haskell, one of the premier crop of feminist film critics (and who never met a frame of Peckinpah film she's liked): he's never met a frame of Peckinpah film he *didn't* like.

That slant initially struck me reading Seydor's section on Peckinpah's Civil War saga *Major Dundee* (1965). Seydor goes to some length to address the oft-cited major flaw in the film: the character of Teresa Santiago played by Senta Berger. He presents a perfectly valid dramatic justification for the inclusion of the character and also uses her to counter the misogynist label often applied to the director. While I generally agreed with Seydor's portrayal of Teresa, I also had to agree with the plaint that aesthetically validating her didn't change the widely held view that *Dundee* dies on its feet the minute she appears.

While such apologias from disciples are understandable, they actually do a disservice to the artist, and certainly for a case made in defense of the artist's work. If one assumes at least one purpose of an apologia is to deflect and/or convert criticism, once the author's bias is so clearly manifest, the case is lost: "Of course that's what *he* thinks! He *loves* that stuff!"

Webster's lists, as synonyms, "apology, apologia, excuse, plea, pretext, alibi," and too often in film criticism I came to feel apologias were just that: excuses and alibis by fans against most commonly raised criticisms, or sometimes elaborate justifications for enjoying fluff.

There are critics and schools of criticism whose goal it is to hold art accountable to some sort of social standard, to judge it by its morality. In her groundbreaking 1974 book *From Reverence to Rape: The Treatment of Women in the Movies,* feminist film critic Molly Haskell applied the then *au courant* standards of the women's movement to the body of American film. Similarly, Robin Wood and Vito Russo, in the 1981 work *The Celluloid Close,* looked at American film through the lens of gay culture.

There is nothing wrong in such historical film surveys. They are not only important in the academic sense but also provide, at the very least, the basis of a reexamination of how we, as a people, view and think about things and people often marginalized by the American mainstream. Like a child who only learns from a rap on the knuckles and an admonishing, "No! Bad baby!" there is a value to being reminded of our missteps and being held accountable for them. If nothing else, it is a process that reminds our self-congratulatory selves that perhaps we haven't grown up as much as we think we have.

But at the same time, that subjective factor can blur the line between aesthetic appreciation and moral castigation; a film is decried not because it is bad filmmaking, but because the critic considers it "wrong." Such a blurring is understandable. How does one separate one's outrage over a film's content from one's judgment over the piece as a creative work?

It is a tidy enough statement to say that filmmakers should be held accountable for the moral import of their work, but on what moral basis do we begin the judgment? Morality—at least in some matters at some levels—can be a surprisingly fungible commodity. Fifty years ago people in this country thought Joseph McCarthy served a moral cause, and a hundred years earlier it was not considered immoral to displace and/or slaughter Native American populations.

In the arena of film criticism, a distinction has often been drawn between a filmmaker's artistry and the filmmaker content. There is nary a mention of D. W. Griffith's *Birth of a Nation* (1915) that does not position the film as a milestone in world cinema. At the same time, there is usually a caveat regarding the virulent racism riddling the film, usually with an apologetic codicil along the lines of, "In the context of the times . . . ," or, "One has to understand Griffith's background . . . ," none of which I'm sure makes the film any less offensive to some, particularly to African Americans.

Leni Riefenstahl's *Triumph of the Will* (1935) and *Olympia* (1936) are also acknowledged works of filmic art, though both were made in direct service of one of the greatest evils the world has ever known.

Perhaps the ability to make such a separation is a product of time; as years pass, appraisal can become more dispassionate. Or perhaps it is because the majority of the critical community is rarely a member of the constituencies marginalized or persecuted in such works. Or maybe the power of the films as films is so evident, we look for some balm to cushion their more unpalatable aspects.

My highly subjective point of view is that next to the Ku Klux Klan and the Nazis, Sam Peckinpah's cinematic sins, despite the felony caliber indictments against him, seem of misdemeanor quality.

$\star$ $\star$ $\star$

When I first began work on this project in the early 1990s, it seemed a singularly appropriate time for the subject. *The Wild Bunch* was about to be resurrected, echoes of the Anita Hill/Clarence Thomas affair still hung in the air bringing a greater awareness of gender issues, and people were taking vehement offense at what they saw in the movies:

Ridley Scott's *Thelma and Louise* (1991) was decried by men as antimale, while women complained it depicted Women's Lib gone rabid;

Paul Verhoeven's *Basic Instinct* (1992) managed to offend both gays and heterosexual women;

John Avnet's adaptation of Fannie Flagg's novel *Fried Green Tomatoes* (1991) drew applause from some gays for including a lesbian couple, while other gays bemoaned the softening of the more overt aspects of the relationship;

Jonathan Demme's *Silence of the Lambs* (1991) was protested by homosexuals, transvestites, and transsexuals who considered the film's villain (a serial killer making a female "suit" from the skins of his victims) typical Hollywood homophobia; although the film, and more explicitly Thomas Harris's source novel, made the point several times that the killer was neither a transsexual nor a homosexual;

Demme's *Philadelphia* (1993), while acclaimed for bringing the AIDS crisis to middle America, was also declaimed by gay activists like Larry Kramer who, like the *Fried Green Tomatoes* gadflies, felt the film gutted the main character's gayness to appease mainstream tastes;

The deservedly forgettable *Shakes the Clown* (1991), a film which disappeared almost immediately upon release, did last long enough to draw flak from America's clown community who resented the attempted black comedy's depiction of one of their profession.

If anything, we are in more fractious times now. At this writing, some Italian Americans are in their second season of complaining about Home Box Office's acclaimed crime series *The Sopranos;* mental health professionals and interest groups protested ABC's short-lived *Wonderland* series set in a Bellevue-type mental hospital; African American groups were highly vocal in their disappointment over the 1998 TV season in which not one network series premiere had a black principal in its cast; and the British have logged in with offenses over the Mel Gibson starrer *The Patriot* (2000) for its distortions regarding the Revolutionary War, over the WWII actioner *U-571* (2000), which turned a true-life British intelligence coup into an all-American affair, and even over Steven Spielberg's highly lauded *Saving Private Ryan* (1999) for ignoring the British contributions to the D-day landings.

One of the positive bits of fallout from the tempests of the 1960s was that groups that had felt oppressed or marginalized socially, culturally, economically, and politically found they had a voice—a *loud* voice. They learned that acting in concert gave them the power to affect their treatment by the status quo.

One of the negative bits of fallout from the same time was that some elements of these newly enfranchised groups evidenced an intolerance for offense that rivaled the intolerances of the status quo. Often disparagingly referred to as "political correctness," it is a sensibility that *in extremis* can mute, censor, and even repress that which is found somehow offensive. As Kathleen Murphy put it in a piece about Peckinpah's *Straw Dogs* (1972):

> [a] belief currently gaining more and more credence that if we just aren't reminded too often . . . of the dark underside of the mind, it will all go away, and we'll all be polite and peaceful together.[2]

Political correctness can be interpreted as an attempt to redress a past unfairness with a new one. It may very well be simply the pendulum compensating with a swing from one extreme to the other. Nevertheless, it is an extreme swing, not the pendulum hanging true.

★   ★   ★

I have spent eighteen years with Home Box Office, most of that time in the area of the pay-TV service's organization that deals with consumers. In that time I have sifted through literally hundreds of thousands of viewer letters, phone calls, and—of late—e-mails. My professional opinion is that everybody is offended by something.

Sometimes it's a matter of taste, sometimes ideology, sometimes religious conviction, but it's always *something*. In the year or so preceding this writing, I have seen complaints from those offended by graphic violence, strong sexual content, and profanity. Targeted shows have included *The Sopranos* (for perpetuating negative stereotypes of Italian Americans), *Sex and the City* (for the characters' fondness for fur coats), and *Real Sex* (simple immorality). Aggrieved constituencies have included women, African Americans, Latinos, Italian Americans, the mentally and physically handicapped, political conservatives, hunters, antifur protestors, gays, antigays, animal rights people, antismokers, antiabortionists, Catholics, policemen, firemen, Baptists, Muslims, and Jews. And those are just the ones I can remember off the top of my head.

In those eighteen years I've learned that despite their disparate views, most of these voices of protest share several tenets:

> They believe they speak with the voice of reason;
> They believe they represent a larger constituency;
> They believe that most right-thinking people would agree with them (and if they don't agree, that's only a sign of the moral degradation and general insensitivity of American society);
> They believe that no group is mistreated by the media as much as theirs, and that the suffering of no other group is comparable;
> They believe in the First Amendment and freedom of expression, but that freedom shouldn't extend to whatever it was that offended them.

If Sam Peckinpah were alive today, he would be in his antagonistic glory.

*   *   *

It was not long into those first days working on this project when I felt I'd run aground. In part, it was from a sense of disillusionment.

Sam Peckinpah, I was learning, was not quite the martyred maverick I had come to hero worship. Many of his professional problems seemed to be of his own making. And, on the personal level, he seems to have mistreated nearly every close acquaintance at one time or another, even his best friends. He was something of (and there's no academic way to put this) a bastard.

Eventually, I salved my bruised loyalist heart with the understanding that he was neither hero nor complete bastard, just a man as conflicted and flawed and talented as the flawed and talented characters he'd rendered on the screen.

But I was also stumped. I'd learned what I've belabored here: that Peckinpah's work—like any creative work—required no defending. Any piece of art is what it is. I could mount a credible apologia, I thought, even cite historical credibility for what Peckinpah had put on film. But people who disliked his movies wouldn't like them any better because I told them they should; people who were offended by his work wouldn't be any less offended because I told them they shouldn't be.

So, what was the point?

I had learned the lesson long ago in my first writing classes: When art and inspiration fail, fall back on craft. The academic craft called for the question—the justification for sitting at the keyboard— "What do we learn?"

There are things to learn, though they're as much about us as the films of Sam Peckinpah.

Maybe, as with *Birth of a Nation,* enough time has passed for us to look at this one element of Peckinpah's work more dispassionately than it had been viewed in those tumultuous years of his highest profile. Certainly his work would benefit from not having the filmmaker's own gratuitous posing clouding the issue. I always thought that some of the criticisms leveled against his work came from knee-jerk reactions and out-of-context interpretations. Maybe we could now finally separate social agenda from cinema aesthetics.

When Henry James first published *The Bostonians* in 1885, his story of suffragette Verena Tarrant and her insistent, patriarchal suitor Basil Ransom was panned. Seventy years later, it was rediscovered but viewed as a satire disparaging the women's movement. Still a few decades later, feminists gave the story yet another interpretation, faulting Basil who whisked the book's heroine off to marriage at the climax of the book and considering Verena's capitulation a martyrdom.[3] Creative works—even those considered mere entertainments—are like prisms throwing off different colors as the light of the passing day changes. I think enough of the day has passed to look at Peckinpah in a different light.

As I learned more about Peckinpah's career, I also came to believe that whatever his sins—and there were many—there were some laid at his door that were properly not his. Therein lies something to be learned about how film criticism oversimplifies and undervalues the complicated process that is commercial moviemaking.

And perhaps there is also this: that this is no last word. For any creative work, there is never a last word. There will come a later part of the day when the light will change again and someone may find yet some other color that I and the lookers who've come before me may have missed.

If there is any craftsmanship at all to a piece of entertainment, it will always find a way to attract a new audience; if there is any honesty to a piece of art, each generation will find something in it that touches them.

NOTES

1. Henry James, *The Bostonians* (New York: Vintage Press, 1991), 296.

2. Kathleen Murphy, "The Ballad of David Summer: A Peckinpah Psychodrama," *Movietone News* (January 1972): 24.

3. Alison Lurie, introduction to *The Bostonians* (New York: Vintage Press, 1991), xii.

· 1 ·

Ladies and Gentlemen: Mr. Sam Peckinpah

I don't want to destroy you, any more than I want to save you. There has been far too much talk about you, and I want to leave you alone altogether. My interest is in my own sex; yours evidently can look after itself.

—*Henry James,* The Bostonians (1885)[1]

$\mathscr{I}$n his heyday, from 1969 into the early 1970s, Sam Peckinpah was, arguably, among the most controversial and important American film directors working in mainstream film.[2] His lasting impact is evident in the literature of film that has appeared over the last thirty years. Hardly a published overview of the films of the 1960s and 1970s has appeared without citing at least some of his works as touchstones of style and content. In those pieces that examine the Western, Peckinpah has held especially high prominence since his first feature film releases in the early 1960s.

"Sam Peckinpah on a bad day," wrote critic Garner Simmons, "was a better director than ninety percent of those who have aspired to that title. On a good day, he was the best."[3] Critic Andrew Sarris, who, in the early 1960s dismissed Peckinpah as "too intellectual to tell a story . . . it remains to be seen whether he will be forceful enough to develop a theme,"[4] had come around by 1969, saying of the violent imagery of *The Wild Bunch,* "Though I prefer directors who make beautiful things look easy rather than directors (like Peckinpah) who make beautiful things look hard, not all that many directors can do beautiful things at all, and Peckinpah has done enough beautiful things in his short, stormy career to qualify as an authentic

1

original."[5] Film director Martin Scorsese looked at *Bunch,* Peckinpah's commercial breakthrough, and saw "savage poetry."[6] Even during Peckinpah's long decline, *Newsweek* reviewer Jack Kroll compared the filmmaker's work to that of Hemingway.[7]

Peckinpah's artistic status during his peak years of 1969–1972 is colorfully illustrated by an occasion when, while in Europe to direct *Straw Dogs,* he met David Lean on a Spanish movie lot. The revered director of such epics as *Lawrence of Arabia* (1962) and *The Bridge on the River Kwai* (1957) dubbed Peckinpah his equal, telling him, "Sam, you and I are the only real ones left."[8]

But as much as Peckinpah was praised was he also reviled.[9] His graphic depictions of violence and his stories of physical, psychological, and emotional brutality have had a resonating impact on moviemaking in this country and a polarizing effect on the critical community, particularly with regard to the issue of motion picture violence.[10] Yet, if his name does not stand quite as tall as other practitioners of the Western such as John Ford or Howard Hawks, or even "cult" directors like Anthony Mann and Budd Boetticher, it is no doubt partly due to the faltering quality of the films made during the latter part of his career. By virtue of his horrible relationships with producers and studio managements, as well as his own vices, and the decreasing commercial viability of the genre, Peckinpah's career was channeled far from the Western settings that served him best and into areas like spy thrillers *(The Killer Elite* [1975], *The Osterman Weekend* [1983]) and war films *(Cross of Iron* [1977]) with questionable results.[11] If Peckinpah had disappeared from the film scene in 1973, his reputation as a filmmaker would not require qualifiers to explain his last ten years of erratic filmmaking.

Peckinpah's name has also had to carry the weight of a host of pale imitators. Slow-motion violence had been depicted before Peckinpah (in Akira Kurosawa's *Seven Samurai* [1954], for example, or more relevantly *Bonnie and Clyde* [1967]), but his extensive use of the technique popularized it, and in less capable hands "it soon degenerated into a cinematic cliché."[12] Even with Peckinpah at the helm, though he used the technique as smoothly as any director, the device seemed tired and de rigueur in films like *The Killer Elite* and *Convoy* (1978).

So-called macho directors like Walter Hill and John Milius

would take superficial elements from Peckinpah's best films and re-gurgitate them sans the particular resonance with which Peckinpah imbued them. Hill's *The Long Riders* (1980), for one, is almost a pas-tiche of *The Wild Bunch,* even including such specific images as horse-men crashing through store windows in slow motion. His *The Driver* (1978) is a virtual—and empty—remake of his own script for Peckin-pah's *The Getaway* (1972), and he would return again to the same material in a marginally rewritten script for Roger Donaldson's glossy but failed 1994 remake. Milius improbably adapted *Bunch* into his surfing film *Big Wednesday* (1978), transforming, in the process, a gang of aging Western outlaws into a trio of surfers, and the Bunch's dra-matic walk to their final shoot-out into a march down a California beach to face, instead of the Mexican army, The Big Wave.

Peckinpah's poetry about the dying West, and Westerners who had outlived their time, would become rehashed time and again with various degrees of success (i.e., William Fraker's *Monte Walsh* [1970], Blake Edwards's *Wild Rovers* [1971], Don Siegel's *The Shootist* [1976], and Hill's *Geronimo: An American Legend* [1993] among others), but such *homages*—while keeping an impression of Peckinpah alive—rarely attained the same level of critical and commercial success. Like a game of telephone, the original message diminished with each re-telling.

Whatever questions there may be over Peckinpah's value as a filmmaker in general, his stock among aficionados of the movie West-ern is less arguable. A notorious self-deprecator, Peckinpah often said that his selection of material had been less out of choice than by the fact that the movie industry had "typed" him as a Western director. He once explained his cinematic raison d'être with characteristic glib-ness, saying, "I have five children and three ex-wives and I have to work for a living."[13]

Still, it was the genre in which he displayed his greatest strength. Of his fourteen directorial efforts, six are period Westerns (*The Deadly Companions* [1961], *Ride the High Country* [1962], *Major Dundee* [1965], *The Wild Bunch, The Ballad of Cable Hogue* [1970], *Pat Gar-rett & Billy the Kid* [1973]). Four others, by dint of their setting and themes, pass muster as contemporary Westerns *(Junior Bonner* [1972], *The Getaway, Bring Me the Head of Alfredo Garcia* [1974], *Convoy*). His three produced screenplays, which he did not direct ("The Authentic

Death of Hendry Jones" made as *One-Eyed Jacks* [1961], *The Glory Guys* [1965], *Villa Rides!* [1968]), were also period Westerns. With the possible exceptions of *Straw Dogs* and *The Getaway,* his period Westerns remain his most remembered and/or respected works.

A poll by *Take One* magazine of film critics put two of Peckinpah's Westerns—*The Wild Bunch* and *Pat Garrett & Billy the Kid*—on their 1978 "Best American Films of the Decade" list.[14] Film critics wrote of him that he was "one of the Western's new masters"[15] and that, "More than any other American director, [Peckinpah] was involved in the reshaping of the screen Western during the sixties."[16] A 1973 cataloguing of prominent Western directors summed up Peckinpah's place in the ranks saying, "In a ten-year career containing five Westerns, he has displayed a deeply felt personal interest in the West . . . and an original approach based on a mixture of romanticism, heroism, violence, death and losing out."[17] It would seem inevitable, then, that as the Western genre's popularity dimmed after 1973, so did Peckinpah's fortunes as a filmmaker. Though nearly always a hired hand, no longer at his disposal was the vehicle that most prominently displayed his abilities.

That change in the course of his career, and the consequent deteriorating quality of his work and dimming of his reputation, is cause enough to revisit his peak works. Was the earlier praise inflated? Or have the earlier works been unfairly devalued in light of his latter, inferior work? Or were judgments—both good and bad—too touched by the temper and tastes of the times? In 1969, when *The Wild Bunch* brought Peckinpah's name to mainstream prominence, the debate over cinema violence was a heated one. It was not solely a subject of film aesthetics and tastes, but a vitriolic social debate. Even coming after the controversies over the violence and morbid themes of Robert Aldrich's *The Dirty Dozen* (1967) and Arthur Penn's *Bonnie and Clyde* (1967), Peckinpah's graphic, slow-motion images of bullet impacts and spurting blood remained unprecedented, and the majority of major critics turned their reviews of *Bunch* and subsequent Peckinpah works into discussions about cinema violence. Andrew Sarris, for one, would always maintain that Peckinpah's violence had a direct effect on those years, reflecting, glorifying, and even contributing to the violence of an era marked by street protests, urban riots, and the Vietnam War.[18] That impression flavored writing about Peckinpah for years to come, and extant film book references still refer to him as a director particularly noted for cinematic bloodshed.

Yet, with that in mind, to watch a Peckinpah movie today is a revelation. Its graphic quality has long been eclipsed by everything from low-budget direct-to-video slasher films to big-budget big studio features with A-list stars. The *Halloween, Friday the 13th, Nightmare on Elm Street,* and *Hellraiser* horror film series; Stephen King adaptations; and the *Alien* films—all routinely offer up more grotesque forms of bloodletting than the most vicious Peckinpah scenes. Mainstream offerings like Jerry Bruckheimer–produced "testosterone fests" such as *Con Air* (1997) and the *Lethal Weapon* series boast higher body counts, as do the three *Die Hard* films (particularly *Die Hard 2* [1990], which gave viewers both massive killing—a jetliner crash—and macabre bloodletting—Bruce Willis stabbing an assailant through the eye with an icicle). There is Paul Verhoeven's *Total Recall* (1991), which had one villain plummet to his death after having both arms amputated by an elevator lift, his *Basic Instinct* (1992) with its ice pick murders, his *Starship Troopers* (1997) with futuristic soldiers impaled and torn apart by ten-foot-high alien insects, and his *Hollow Man* (2000) with Kevin Bacon's agonizing transformation into an invisible man, the viewer being treated to exposed sinew and organs.

Even films that aspire to be more than simple "popcorn" pictures now include physical actions that out-gore anything Peckinpah perpetrated: Mel Gibson's Oscar-winning *Braveheart* (1995) boasted impalements, hackings, and a head crushing; Michael Mann's acclaimed adaptation of James Fenimore Cooper's *Last of the Mohicans* (1992) had its share of bludgeonings; and Jonathan Demme's rendering of Thomas Harris's macabre thriller *Silence of the Lambs* (1991) featured a disembodied head in a jar of preservative, a partially skinned female corpse, an evisceration, and Anthony Hopkins as serial killer Hannibal Lecter escaping by wearing the sliced-away face of one of his guards (Hopkins won an Oscar for his performance). Steven Spielberg's *Schindler's List* (1993) and *Saving Private Ryan* (1998) featured some of the most horrifying acts ever put on film, all the more disturbing as they are re-creations of real-life events.

Still, Peckinpah's violence has impact but less because of an indulgence in gore than because of an effective style: an artful use of slow motion, composition, story context, and a style of editing reminiscent of the frenetic cutting of Sergei Eisenstein's *Potemkin* (1925) and *Strike* (1924).If time has ameliorated the shock value of Peckinpah's violence, it may, if anything, have exacerbated the view of another aspect of his work. Critic Richard T. Jameson touched on that aspect in 1981 when, writing of Peckinpah during one of the director's fallow periods, he said, "There are . . . people it would suit right down to the ground if Peckinpah never made another film. . . . Some are feminists."[19] In conjunction with his reputation as a movie screen violence-monger, Peckinpah had, in some eyes, become identified with "brute machismo (where the view was) women as sex objects (preferable for raping and punching out)."[20]

Peckinpah's misogynistic reputation was already so established by the early 1970s that he became a touchstone for critic Molly Haskell in her 1974 work *From Reverence to Rape: The Treatment of Women in the Movies,* the first major work of feminist film criticism. To Haskell, the perceived macho ethic that is the engine behind the violence in Peckinpah films also manifests itself in Peckinpah's cinematic portraits of women. In her eyes, it is bad enough that Peckinpah's male characters cater to masculine myths of tough-skinned men solving their problems in a blaze of gunfire, but the brutalizing treatment that code of behavior enforced on women was unforgivable.

Haskell brands Peckinpah a "neurotic . . . 'auteur' . . . whose sexual anxieties spilled over into [his] treatment of women,"[21] a filmmaker whose "kindly indifference" to women in his early films grew into "violent abuse and brutalization" in his later works,[22] and who was "[bathing] his twilight years in the blood of 'macho' fantasies."[23]

Critics like Haskell and Pauline Kael found elements in Peckinpah's violence-ridden film ethos they felt evidenced a repressive, brutal misogyny that both reflected Peckinpah's own retrograde view and a general male oppressive sensibility toward women. The reaction of Haskell et al. is understandable. Consider that in the fourteen films directed by Sam Peckinpah, five feature a rape or attempted rape; five feature the murder of a woman with at least thirteen women killed on screen, six of them in *The Wild Bunch* alone; men are betrayed—or feel betrayed—by their women in four films; and prominent female characters in five Peckinpah films are prostitutes, another is a coke-snorting nymphomaniac, another is so sexually aroused by violence she deserts her husband for the thug who's been tormenting him.

★   ★   ★

This is a particularly appropriate time to revisit this aspect of Peckinpah's work. The forceful feminist standards that called him to account have since changed. Or, it might be more accurate to say, remain in a state of flux.

After more than three decades of social progress, women still remain shortchanged in American society. Betty Friedan calls the woman's movement a revolution "still not finished . . . stalled, stuck, stopped in its tracks."[24] The American male-dominant myth that portrays men as beings of decisive action, stoic in the face of physical suffering and emotional duress, is still potent in our society.[25] Women suffer subtly and overtly from male dominance in every field from business to sports and medicine.[26, 27]

The relative disparity in cultural roles, despite an expansion of civil rights guarantees for women, was, to many, never better illustrated than during the 1991 Senate hearings on Clarence Thomas for a seat on the Supreme Court, and the subsequent allegations of sexual harassment by Anita Hill. The 98 percent male Senate investigated Hill's charges with a completely male panel. *Time* described the proceedings this way:

> The questions came from a group of Senators who had been disfigured by a failure of both intellect and empathy. Faced with a wounded woman, 14 men merely turned their heads.[28]

Then California congresswoman and Senate candidate Barbara Boxer observed:

> If there were more women in the Senate, [the investigating committee] wouldn't need to rely on spouses to tell them what's important to 51% of the American population.[29]

The social gains of women may be tentative but still surpass their deteriorating status in the media. Haskell maps a downward course for women in films beginning with the sexually repressed films of the 1950s and reaching a nadir at the time of her writing in the late 1960s and early 1970s.[30] Increasing violence against women on screen was, and continues to be, viewed by a number of observers as:

> A hysterical response to sixties and seventies feminism: The male spectator enjoys a sadistic revenge on women who refuse to slide neatly and obligingly into his patriarchally predetermined view of "the way things should naturally be."[31]

Susan Faludi, in her 1992 book *Backlash: The Undeclared War Against American Women,* posits a male reaction against the women's movement that, in part, manifests itself in the poor quality of female images on television and in film.[32]

Yet, at the same time, there is hardly a consensus on what a positive media image for women should be. The controversy that surrounded Ridley Scott's *Thelma and Louise* "mirrored the complicated mood of the last decade."[33] Some considered the film a promilitancy feminist tract.[34] Other saw an antimale tirade. Few seemed to hear screenwriter Callie Khouri's more innocuous synopsis of her own film when she said it simply depicted "what can happen when one unexpected event leads to another."[35] In another example, Paul Verhoeven's thriller *Basic Instinct* was condemned by several gay rights groups as symptomatic of Hollywood's on-screen prejudice against homosexuals. At the same time, the National Organization of Women (NOW) also protested the film because it was, according to NOW president Tammy Bruce, "targeted against women."[36]

It was in a similarly conflicted, clouded environment that Peckinpah's most controversial works were exhibited. The circumstances that allowed him to tell the stories he told the way he told them, and that created around him the air of a woman-hating macho fantasist, were created by a unique confluence of industry and social trends. To fairly reexamine the filmmaker's message, we have to also look at those trends: a change in the way motion pictures were produced and its concomitant impact on the allowable content of movies and particularly the on-screen opportunities afforded women; a newfound energy in the women's movement, which produced more vocal, sometimes more militant, social critiques; and the role of auteur theory in assigning an author's responsibility to a film's director.

Within that context, it is also necessary to review Peckinpah's total career, as it dictated a dwindling number of options. Circumstance may have put Peckinpah at a point in cinema history where he could fully express himself at just the time that expression would attract the most criticism, but his inability to navigate this environment as well as studio corridors of power was a result of his own personal failings. Ironically, the same personal history that infused his Westerns with such a unique flavor also made him the worst possible spokesperson for his own work.

This reexamination focuses on Peckinpah's period Westerns for particular reasons. Raised in the ranch and mining country of northern California, Peckinpah felt a special relationship with the truth and legend of the American West, which combined with his artistic abilities to bring a distinct voice to the movie Western. For whatever reasons Peckinpah was engaged for the films cited here—Peckinpah was obviously right in saying he'd been "typed" as a director of Westerns—the consensus seems to be that this genre with which he is most closely associated holds the films closest to his creative soul.

It was, after all, his growing stature as first a writer, then producer, and finally a director of television Western series that established him in Hollywood. His proficiency in the genre on TV earned him his first theatrical film directing assignment, also a period Western: *The Deadly Companions.* It was *Ride the High Country* that first established his theatrical artistic reputation, and still another, *The Wild Bunch,* that made him commercially successful. Peckinpah's first five feature directing jobs were on period Westerns. In an arc that perfectly reflected his career, it was yet another period Western, the disastrous *Pat Garrett & Billy the Kid,* that marked the beginning of his decline.

"[A] whore" is how Peckinpah often referred to himself, who, working for hire on films he did not originate, "tries to slip in a few comments on the side."[37] The exercise here is to discern his whoring from his more heartfelt commentary; to divine Peckinpah's "comments" from both his whoredom as well as opinionate perception. Nearly thirty years after he completed his acknowledged best work it would seem time to again try to discriminate the message he was hired to purvey from the true legacy he left in his work.

NOTES

1. Henry James, *The Bostonians* (New York: Vintage Press, 1991), 311.

2. David Weddle, "The Making of *The Wild Bunch*," *Film Comment* (May/June 1994): 44.

3. Garner Simmons, "The Peckinpah Tapes," *American Film* (May 1985): 59.

4. Andrew Sarris, *The American Cinema* (New York: Dutton, 1968), 219.

5. Quoted in *Filmfacts* XII (June 1969): 219, 220.

6. Marshall Fine, *Bloody Sam: The Life and Films of Sam Peckinpah* (New York: Donald I. Fine, 1991), 153.

7. Fine, *Bloody Sam*, 305.

8. Chris Hodenfield, "Last of the Real Ones," *American Film* (March 1990): 4.

9. Weddle, "The Making of *The Wild Bunch*," 44.

10. Simmons, "Tapes," 59.

11. Joel W. Finler, *The Movie Director's Story* (New York: Crescent, 1985), 224.

12. Louis D. Gianetti, *Understanding Movies*. 2nd ed. (Englewood Cliffs, N.J.: Prentice-Hall, 1976), 129.

13. Pat Berman, "A Strange Fascination for Violence," *Columbia Record* [Columbia, S.C.] (February 1,1975, Sunday edition), 1–B.

14. "The Best American Films of the Decade," *Take One* (July 1978): 27.

15. John Baxter, *Sixty Years of Hollywood* (Cranbury, N.J.: A.S. Barnes, 1973), 228.

16. Finler, *Movie Director's Story*, 224.

17. Michael Parkinson and Clyde Jeavons, *A Pictorial History of Westerns* (London: Hamlyn Publishing, 1973), 182.

18. Fine, *Bloody Sam*,156.

19. Richard T. Jameson, "Sam Peckinpah," *Film Comment* (Jan/Feb 1981): 34.

20. Jameson, "Peckinpah," 34.

21. Molly Haskell, *From Reverence to Rape: The Treatment of Women in the Movies* (New York: Holt, 1974), 326.

22. Haskell, *From Reverence to Rape*, 323.

23. Haskell, *From Reverence to Rape*, 364.

24. Betty Friedan, "The Dangers of the New Feminine Mystique," *McCall's* (November 1991): 80.

25. Charles U. Larson, *Persuasion: Reception and Responsibility*. 5th ed. (Belmont, Calif.: Wadsworth Publishing, 1989), 237.

26. Amy Engeler, "*New York Woman*'s Second Annual Roundup of Worst Places to Work," *New York Woman* (November 1991): 72–77.

27. Mary Bruno, "Bad Sports," *New York Woman* (November 1991): 64–66.

28. "An Ugly Circus," *Time* (October 21, 1991): 35.

29. Margaret Carlson (reported by Hays Gorey and Nancy Travers), "The Ultimate Men's Club," *Time* (October 21, 1991): 51.

30. Haskell, *From Reverence to Rape*, 38.

31. Robin Wood, "Beauty Bests the Beast," *American Film* (September 1983): 63.

32. Nancy Gibbs (reported by Ann Blackman, Priscilla Painton, and Elizabeth Taylor), "The War Against Feminism," *Time* (March 9, 1992): 53.

33. Alice Hoffman, "*Thelma & Louise*," *Premiere* (October 1997): 69.

34. Friedan, "The Dangers," 80.

35. Kevin Phinney, " 'Thelma,' 'Silence' Wow WGA," *Hollywood Reporter* (March 23, 1992): 49.

36. Kevin Phinney, "NOW Denounces *Basic Instinct*," *Hollywood Reporter* (March 19, 1992): 3.

37. Berman, "Strange Fascination," 1-B.

· 2 ·

Context: Wrong Man, Wrong Place, Wrong Time

If, when women have the conduct of affairs, they fight as well as they reason, surely for them too we shall have to set up memorials.

—Henry James, The Bostonians (1885)[1]

$\mathcal{S}$am Peckinpah's parallel reputations as filmmaker and topic of controversy jelled when his career was at its peak spanning the years between the releases of *The Wild Bunch* in 1969 to *Bring Me the Head of Alfredo Garcia* in 1974. The popular impression that developed of the filmmaker was the product of a unique conjunction of circumstances both cultural and professional. To better understand the view in which his feminist critics held him, it is necessary to look at the sociological backdrop that colored his time, as well as the dynamics of the motion picture industry, which granted him a certain amount of creative latitude, yet simultaneously limited him in certain defining ways, and the concept that awarded him responsibility for everything that appeared on the movie screen under his name.

UNDECLARED CIVIL WAR

The period from the assassination of President John Kennedy in 1963 through the Watergate scandal of the early 1970s represented arguably the greatest social upheaval for the United States since the Civil War. Like the first charge in a demolition series, the catalyst for what *Life* termed "A time of tumult . . . an era marked by conflict and tragedy" was the Vietnam War.[2]

Following the commitment of American ground forces in 1965, each subsequent escalation in a war increasingly thought of as vague of purpose and endless brought more and more vehement protests. Campus demonstrations became epidemic.

As the country reexamined the values that had embroiled it in Southeast Asia, its people began to question the nation's entire moral spectrum:

> The war was not the only thing dividing Americans in the spring of 1968. The agony of racial violence, the hostility between the generations, and the growing isolation of the white working class all threatened to unravel the social fabric of the nation. For blacks, students and workers alike the war acted as a powerful irritant, exacerbating their sense of powerlessness and inflating their discontent.[3]

An element in this caldron of social unrest was the women's movement. Discontent over traditional female roles had reached a critical mass in the late 1960s and into the early 1970s. Writers like Betty Friedan and Gloria Steinem were leading a highly public and highly vocal movement of women redefining themselves.[4] The year 1970 saw a nationwide rally of women protesting discrimination.[5] At street protests, women would burn their bras, a symbolic destruction of a harness that they felt enforced male standards of attractiveness. In 1973, Norma McCorvey, the Jane Roe of the Supreme Court's *Roe v. Wade* decision, won a decision legalizing abortion. To women, this meant they now had control over their own bodies. Putting the gender war in a lighter but nonetheless illustrative light, self-described tennis "hustler" Bobby Riggs, boasting of the innate superiority of men, sought to make his case by taking on tennis star Billie Jean King in a televised match watched by millions (Riggs lost).[6]

This time of foment when women, with the vigor of the newly enfranchised, made public their dissatisfactions and their ambitions, ushered in a new era in the social history of American women. Over the ensuing decades, women would gain unprecedented opportunity economically, culturally, and politically.

At the same time, ironically, it was one of the worst periods to be an actress in Hollywood.

SECOND BILLING

We may have female megastars like Julia Roberts and Barbra Streisand today, A-list directors like Nora Ephron and Mimi Leder, industry executives like Kathleen Kennedy and Dawn Steel, but there have always been women of impressive stature in Hollywood. The teens had Lilian Gish; the peak years of Metro-Goldwyn-Mayer had Judy Garland; Columbia Pictures had Rita Hayworth. Frances Marion was one of the highest-paid screenwriters in Hollywood through most of her career under the old studio system; Mary Pickford brought her enormous box-office muscle to bear on the business side of the industry as one of the founders of the United Artists (UA) studio; Dorothy Arzner was directing features in the 1920s; and in the 1940s Ida Lupino formed her own production company, in the process providing herself the opportunity to direct such brawny features as *The Hitch-Hiker* (1953).

But these were the exceptions. Throughout the old studio era executive suites at the major studios, even at Mary Pickford's UA, were male bastions. Except for costume design and makeup shops, craft department heads were normally male, as were the bulk of the rank and file. Behind-the-camera talent—directors, writers, editors, cinematographers—were overwhelmingly male, and even in front of the camera men dominated.

There is a somewhat sentimental view that during the heyday of the old studio system actresses fared better than in contemporary times. In part, this was a simple result of quantity. Studio output was much greater during the old studio era than it is today, providing more work—and one presumes a greater variety of roles—for women performers.

The Hollywood appellation "Dream Factory" is accurate in more ways than one, for Hollywood was not only a purveyor of fantasies, but did so on a factorylike basis. The old studios maintained enormous physical plants including postproduction facilities, costume and set construction shops, and extensive backlots, which could readily supply settings for almost any imaginable product from medieval epics to dusty Westerns, gay '90s musicals, or tales set in quaint European villages or Smalltown USA. The studios also kept large stables of craftsmen and talent—of both the in-front-of and behind-the-camera variety—on salary. With all these on-hand resources, running six and sometimes seven days a week the major studios could pump out enormous numbers of A and B features, newsreels, shorts, serials, and cartoons at a controlled cost. In 1934, for example, the average cost of a full-length film was only $250,000.[7] Even adjusted for inflation this would be only a fraction of what Mel Gibson was paid to star in *The Patriot* (2000). During the industry's peak year, 1939, the major studios—Columbia, MGM, Paramount, RKO, Twentieth Century Fox, Universal, and Warner Bros.—were releasing a combined total of fourteen to fifteen features *per week*![8]

The studio-exhibitor relationship was a closed loop adding still more stability to the process. Each of the major studios, with the exception of RKO, owned chains of theaters. This meant that every studio film was guaranteed exhibition, and theater box offices provided the studio with a steady revenue stream. The regular output of films meant that theatergoers had a new film to see nearly every week, a factor that helped maintain healthy attendance. It also meant that films faring poorly at the box office could be quickly replaced and their impact on the studio balance sheet thereby minimized.

In distributing so many films, the studios programmed their output much like a television network might, trying to offer a variety of titles throughout the year, some of which were intended to attract the widest possible audience while others were designed for what today's programmers call a "niche audience." Consequently, along with big-budget spectaculars like a *Gone With the Wind* (1939), there would be Westerns, detective stories, period pictures, musicals, adventures, adaptations of literary classics, and so-called women's pictures, which were usually some kind of romance or melodrama. The sheer bulk of annual studio titles meant that a large number of popular actresses worked steadily in both genre pictures and high-profile films and continued to do so until their box-office appeal waned.

Yet the idea that women had it better under the studio system is not completely true. Even during the best years of the system women never attained broad-based professional parity with their male counterparts. Joel Finler, in his 1988 book *The Hollywood Story,* canvassed the performer stables of the seven major studios from their rise in the teens until the collapse of the old-style studio system in the 1950s. That canvass shows that among the ranks of major and important stars, the Columbia, Paramount, and Universal rosters heavily favored males throughout that time. Warners tipped the scale more moderately but toward men stars nonetheless. Only at Fox, MGM, and RKO (the smallest, junior member of the studio club) was there an approximate even distribution.

Outside the category of "women's pictures," actresses were rarely considered strong enough to carry a picture without an equally strong male lead. Joan Crawford could topline *Mildred Pierce* (1945), *Flamingo Road* (1949), *The Damned Don't Cry* (1950), or any number of the torrid romantic melodramas she did for Warners, but she was not granted that weight—or even many opportunities—outside the genre; Bette Davis could hold the lead in "meller" like *Dark Victory* (1939), but in *The Private Lives of Elizabeth and Essex* (1939) she had to share billing with Errol Flynn. If the marquee carried Rita Hayworth's name, there was sure to be Glenn Ford's right alongside. Barbara Stanwyck? Gary Cooper. Katherine Hepburn? Cary Grant or Spencer Tracy. It was a standard industry practice, for the sake of offering broad box-office appeal, to team male and female stars and the bulk of studio features from the period show such pairings. But when not doing so, a man was more likely to be allowed to carry a picture than a woman, at least outside certain genres (it's a mark of the times that simply by having a female lead a picture would be considered a "women's picture").

One has to consider that there may be a certain element of self-fulfilling prophecy at work here. If studio heads believed women couldn't carry pictures, they were less inclined to give them the opportunity to try. But whether they were correct in their judgment, or simply created the circumstances that came to verify it, studio execs could point to box-office numbers to make their case.

Finler's book lists the major box-office performers at certain periods in the industry's history from the teens through the late 1980s. These lists include such features as *Birth of a Nation,* the Valentino version of *The Four Horseman of the Apocalypse* (1921), the Western *Duel In the Sun* (1946), the Roman Empire epic *Ben-Hur* (1959),

Grand Hotel–styled disaster picture *Airport* (1970), and most of the George Lucas/Steven Spielberg spectaculars (*E.T. the Extraterrestrial* [1982], and the *Star Wars* and *Indiana Jones* films, for example). But over eight decades only two blockbuster successes can be said to have been carried by a woman in the lead role: *The Wizard of Oz* (1939) starring Judy Garland, and *The Sound of Music* (1965) with Julie Andrews.[9] There have only been two other blockbusters where a woman held costar status: *Gone With the Wind* costarring Clark Gable and Vivien Leigh, and James Cameron's *Titanic* (1997) with Leonardo DiCaprio and Kate Winslet.

Even outside the circle of "A" features, the status of women under the studio system rarely matched that of men. The comic shorts that featured the likes of W. C. Fields, Edgar Kennedy, and Leon Errol had no female counterparts. Teamed with her husband George Burns, only Gracie Allen had any comparable prominence. Each of the studios also produced several long-running movie series such as the Andy Hardy movies with Mickey Rooney and Judy Garland, the Thin Man mysteries with William Powell and Myrna Loy, and Westerns starring the characters of the Cisco Kid and Hopalong Cassidy, just to name a few. Of these myriad series only six were anchored around a woman character:[10]

> There was Lupe Velez's "Mexican Spitfire," a cartoonish character that, by today's standards, would be considered terribly politically impolitic;

> Spinster schoolteacher Hildegarde Withers who, in the Miss Marple vein, doubled as a sleuth;

> The Nancy Drew movies which showed a supposedly independent young lady who could never quite close a case without the help of her father and doting boyfriend;

> And the Blondie movies which, while presenting Penny Singleton's Blondie as the brains in the Bumstead household, nevertheless kept her in the home and focused most of the comic action around her husband Dagwood.[11]

Only two series showed women as being wholly in control of their own destinies: Torchy Blaine, a rough-and-tumble newswoman in the Hildy Johnson mold, and the Maisie movies top-lined by Ann Sothern. Maisie was "an emancipated girl who took no nonsense from men."[12] But, while Torchy Blaine continually pined after a male colleague, only Maisie managed a male-comparable independence for though each installment brought a romantic interest into the heroine's sphere, the stories would end with her continuing on her solo way.[13]

Second-class status was the norm on screen during the studio period. Granted, it's dangerous to make such a sweeping generalization for there are numerous exceptions. Hardly a year of the industry's output doesn't contain several examples of women demonstrating a mobility and independence comparable to men. Director George Cukor evidenced a special strength in this regard, being "ahead of his time in his treatment of his female characters, outspoken and independent-minded ladies" in films like *The Women* (1939), *The Philadelphia Story* (1940), and *A Woman's Face* (1941).[14] There were also:

> Rosalind Russell's brassy newswoman Hildy Johnson in *His Girl Friday* (1940), Howard Hawk's distaff version of *The Front Page;*
>
> Madeliene Carroll as a gunrunner's daughter, shrewdly navigating China's internecine warlords in *The General Died At Dawn* (1936);
>
> Barbara Stanwyck's tough-talking chorine in *Ball of Fire* (1941);
>
> Myrna Loy's poised sitting municipal judge in *The Bachelor and the Bobby-Soxer* (1947);
>
> And a series of Garson Kanin/Ruth Gordon screenplays from the late 1940s into the 1950s that pitted Spencer Tracy against Katherine Hepburn as flip, cunning, and skilled equals, whether as sports manager and athletic star (*Pat and Mike* [1952]), efficiency expert and research department chief (*Desk Set* [1957]), or, in true professional parity, as battling husband and wife lawyers (*Adam's Rib* [1949]).

Such independent, strong-minded women were, however, depicted as outside the American mainstream. Female reporters, adventuresses, chanteuses, molls, and so on hardly represented the general celluloid female population. Comparatively few movie women were pictured in the professions, or maintaining a business, or holding down a job other than clerical work. In the main, they held traditional archetypal roles: housewives, teachers, secretaries, matriarchs, and the like. This did reflect, though in adamant fashion, a real-life demographic basis at a time when the country was still resolutely patriarchal. At the same time, it was also a reinforcement of an idealized version of the stable American home and family.

Even during this country's most unstable times, Hollywood offered ideals rather than truths. While among the majors only Warner Bros. concertedly mined Depression-era headlines for story material (i.e., *I Was a Fugitive From a Chain Gang* [1932]), most of the majors eschewed the grim realities around them.[15] It may have been the era of breadlines on the street, but the world on screen was mostly grand musicals and screwball comedies staged among the horsy set.

During the years of World War II, the industry showed a similar disconnect between real life and life in the celluloid world. Approximately one third of Hollywood movies made from 1942 to 1945 were pictures dealing with the war.[16] These included action pictures, wartime romances and dramas, and espionage thrillers. Movies dealing with the homefront, and particularly the women waiting out the safe return of husbands and lovers, such as *Since You Went Away* (1943) and *Tender Comrade* (1943), made up a remarkably small percentage of that output. This was no doubt for the same reason so little of the Depression had made it into film: "the public's resistance to paying for what they could see all around them."[17]

Through Depression and war, the movie world remained stable, traditional, and secure. On-screen American families seemed to have plenty of everything to eat rationing notwithstanding, enough gasoline to go wherever they wanted, nice wardrobes, comfortable homes, and the spare time and wherewithal to regularly attend restaurants and night clubs. In short, life seemed to go on much as it had before (or rather, as it had always been *pictured* before). The fact that the 1940s saw the birth of Rosie the Riveter as hundreds of thousands of women joined the labor force for the first time to work in war industries was never a major subject—or much of any kind of subject—in most wartime films.

Along with the wives, mothers, and girlfriends who waited anxiously for their men, and helped build the tanks and ships their men fought with, the tens of thousands of women who joined the various branches of the American military during the war were similarly relegated to second-tier status. There were occasional paeans to women in uniform, like *So Proudly We Hail!* (1943), which saluted the Army nurses who gutted out the fall of the Philippines, but the more typical role was as background as nurses and clerks.

For all these shortfalls, the studio system, when applied effectively (and it bears noting that it was *not* always applied effectively) could provide actresses with security and a support system they would never see again in Hollywood. Ideally, once a studio had contracted a fledgling talent, an actress would be put through classes to work on her performance abilities, then introduced to the public through carefully orchestrated publicity campaigns.[18] The studio would then roll out a string of films tailored to build up her popular image and box-office appeal.[19] An actress with an audience following would never be off the screen very long, a circumstance that, along with the support of the studio's publicity machinery, kept her name and image vital in her fans' psyche.

Yet the studio system had its flaws. It was not always a deft gauge of novice talent. Starlet Colleen Townsend, for example, got the full publicity buildup in the late 1940s but her career only lasted four films.[20] Nor were studio execs always particularly astute to how best use a demonstrated talent. Marion Davies, who had shown a flair for light comedy, was regularly miscast in heavier fare and her career suffered accordingly.[21] Studios could ruin an actress's box-office viability by putting her in too many inferior films, or vehicles that made a poor fit, and would punish uncooperative talents by suspending them, keeping them off the screen with the threat that an extended absence would cool the actress's box-office appeal. The history of any major studio contains a fair share of tales of battles between performers feeling misused and/or underappreciated and the moguls who held their contracts. Columbia star Rita Hayworth, in one case, considered her standing as the studio's top star, went to studio chief Harry Cohn complaining that she was underpaid, only to have Cohn punish her by replacing her in an upcoming project with rising star Kim Novak.[22]

But this insular, protective environment dissolved in just a few years, replaced by one that was infinitely more competitive, hostile, and economically volatile for women in the industry. The cause was a sea change in the motion picture factory style of business, and the subsequent ripple effects of that change. That first, inundating wave was an antitrust case against the studios that, in the 1950s, forced them to divest themselves of their theater chains.

The immediate impact was twofold. For one thing, studios now had to split the box-office take with exhibitors. Of more impact, however, was that studio pictures, without the mother company's guaranteed screens, had to vie against each other for theater space. Badly performing pictures could no longer be absorbed into the weekly change of fare at the local bijou; each film was now compelled to carry its own fiscal weight and the studio could suffer grievously with each failure.

A compounding negative factor was that for the first time in their history, the various players in the movie industry were competing for a rapidly evaporating audience.

In the summer of 1948, only 350,000 American households had the equipment to watch the first televised Republican and Democratic national presidential conventions.[23] By 1950, the number had grown to almost 4 million, in 1960 to over 45 million, and by 1970 almost 60 million, or 95 percent of American households, meaning virtually everyone who could afford a TV had at least one set in the house.[24] The impact of this proliferation on motion picture theater attendance was devastating. Movie attendance had peaked in 1940 at 85 million tickets sold *per week,* and attendance would hover around 80 million throughout the war years.[25] But after nearly twenty years of TV-generated attrition, weekly attendance reached as low as 15 million in 1967.[26]

The loss of their theater chains and a massive migration of ticket-buyers to home TV viewing were body blows to the studio's collective corpus. The fiscal stability of the closed-loop factory system collapsed in just a few years. Studios no longer had the financial resources to maintain vast on-hand resources of people and materiel. Many of the backlots would be sold off, props auctioned, and talent stables disbanded. Movies became an ad hoc affair, with cast and crews hired for individual projects.

This led to a rapid increase in production costs. Popular actors and actresses, no longer on salary, could bargain for substantial fees and even levy their box-office appeal against percentages of a film's revenue. Stars like Burt Lancaster, Kirk Douglas, and Steve Mc-Queen, among others, went as far as to set up their own production companies to give themselves both greater creative control over their vehicles, as well as increased financial participation. These elements set the stage for the modern day era of multimillion-dollar talent packages and profit participation. Whereas sixty years ago all of the revenue of a studio film was returned to the studio, the collapse of the studio system in the 1950s gave way to an era when profit shares would be siphoned off by exhibitors, distributors (for those studios that no longer had their own distribution apparatus), and profit participants. The division of spoils would become so tilted away from studios in cases of major talent that a film like *Lethal Weapon 4* (1998) could generate blockbuster revenues and there would still be a question as to whether or not it would return a worthwhile profit to the studio.[27]

Increased costs meant fewer films. From 1940 to 1958, the major studios had managed to produce an average of 275 feature films annually. But from 1970 to 1985, the per annum average was a comparatively paltry 113, and during several years the combined output of the majors was less than 100 titles, dropping to as low as 78 in 1977.[28]

Hollywood dabbled with a variety of strategies with the goal of drawing an audience by providing its members with attractions unavailable on TV. This led to technological innovations, some of which like wide-screen projection, stereophonic sound, and the regular use of color became staples.[29] Others, like Smell-O-Vision and 3-D, smacked of desperation and were short-lived.[30]

That same frantic quest for audience led the studios, despite diminishing revenues, to produce a series of lavish all-star spectacles to compete against the small screen with epic stories told on a grand scale such as *The Greatest Show On Earth* (1952), *Around the World In Eighty Days* (1956), *Ben-Hur, Spartacus* (1960), *The Longest Day* (1962), and *It's A Mad, Mad, Mad, Mad World* (1963). But more of them failed than succeeded both critically and at the box office. Some, like *Cleopatra* (1963) were such colossal financial disasters that they crippled studios already struggling financially. By the early 1960s, as an effective counter to TV, the binge of epics began to falter.[31]

There was, however, one thing movies could offer an audience that TV couldn't, and which didn't add to production costs the way wide-screen projection and full-scale recreations of the Roman forum did. This was in the area of material.

With the majors having lost their chokehold on exhibition, the way was now clear for a proliferation of independent production companies willing to explore more provocative fare than the traditionally escapist-leaning studios had developed during their heyday. The studios, in turn, responding to this challenge from the "indies," as well as to TV, began to show more backbone in tackling heretofore controversial subjects.

In these first years of the studio collapse, the movies finally and directly began to deal with such subjects as racism (*No Way Out* [1950], *Edge of the City* [1957]), anti-Semitism (*Crossfire* [1947], *Gentleman's Agreement* [1947]), rape (*Johnny Belinda* [1948], *Last Train From Gun Hill* [1959]), a deromanticized view of World War II combat (*Twelve O'Clock High* [1949], *Attack!* [1956]), the postwar rise of a dehumanizing corporate culture (*The Man in the Gray Flannel Suit* [1956], *Executive Suite* [1954]), media manipulation (*A Face In the Crowd* [1957]), juvenile delinquency (*Knock On Any Door* [1949], *The Blackboard Jungle* [1955], *Twelve Angry Men* [1957]), even the entertainment industry's own seamier side (*All About Eve* [1950], *In a Lonely Place* [1950], *The Sweet Smell of Success* [1957]). There were also slice-of-life movies, small-scale, highly intimate dramas that gave blue-collar life an attention the movies had previously rarely afforded it (*Marty* [1955]), and pictures willing to delve into unglamorous stories built around the new noirist concept of the "antihero" (*The Hustler* [1961], *Champion* [1949], *The Big Carnival* [1951]).

This evolution in cinema storytelling provided actresses with some of the choicest roles in the history of movies. Bette Davis's performance in *All About Eve* as an actress worried about being eclipsed by newcomer Anne Baxter is one of her acknowledged best; Baxter herself had been made a star two years earlier by her appearance in *Yellow Sky* (1948) as the Winchester-wielding guardian daughter of a gold miner in a Western transplanting of Shakespeare's *The Tempest;* in *A Face in the Crowd,* Patricia Neal carries more weight than colead Andy Griffith, and limns a successful media professional without sacrificing femininity or moral decency; and Doris Day would become one of the 1950s' major box-office draws in an admirable mix of light comedies (*Teacher's Pet* [1958]), musicals (*Calamity Jane* [1953]), and dramas (*Love Me or Leave Me* [1955]).

But such opportunities were outweighed by the negative fallout of the industry's fundamental changes. The collapsing studio system and cannibalizing effects of TV on movie attendance meant a large number of dispossessed, freelancing actresses competing for a smaller and smaller number of roles. Despite such choice parts as mentioned above, and the broadening diversity of material now finding its way to the screen, women generally still held a supporting role in the industry. Most of the films mentioned above, for example, are carried by male leads, and filled with predominantly male casts (some of them, like *Twelve Angry Men,* are *exclusively* male).

The Man in the Gray Flannel Suit, Executive Suite, and *Patterns* (1956) all deal with the 1950s social angst over corporate service and questionable suburban values. In all three films, the wives of the erstwhile heroes are all homemakers. Some are supportive (June Allyson in *Suite*), some are suburban nags pushing their husbands for more material gains (Jennifer Jones in *Gray Flannel Suit),* but none really participate in the male hero's resolution of his moral dilemma, and the roles (despite, in Jones's case, holding costarring status with lead Gregory Peck) are decidedly supporting in nature. Wives of major executives are portrayed as rarely seen figures, jealous over the attention their husbands give their businesses over their families. In the halls of the featured corporations, women are only seen as secretaries and receptionists.

While the industry has always had an unfillable maw for new, physically attractive talent, a generation of actresses once maintained by the studios now found themselves hobbled in this new cutthroat casting environment by their years.

If Hollywood has always been somewhat preferential toward men over women, it has been downright bigoted toward them in terms of ageism. The career duration of many lead actresses has been dictated by their age while male counterparts have kept playing leads into their senior years, sometimes in on-screen romances with women young enough to be their daughters. Cary Grant wooed the much younger Grace Kelly in *To Catch a Thief* (1955), even though he was closer in age to character actress Jessie Royce Landis, who played Kelly's mother; John Wayne, thick in the middle, could still charm Elizabeth Allen in *Donovan's Reef* (1963); fifty-nine-year-old Clark Gable, pot-bellied and craggy, was still "permitted" to capture the heart of Marilyn Monroe in *The Misfits* (1961).[32]

And when a male actor's years (or more specifically, looks) had grown to the point where even Hollywood couldn't abide him as a romantic lead, he could still be cast in vital starring roles. Far into his dotage, fat, double-chinned, and bedecked with an obvious toupee, a geriatric John Wayne could still outshoot villains (*Chisum* [1970], *Big Jake* [1971]) and outfight bad guys half his age (*The Cowboys* [1972]) as could a gray-topped James Stewart (*Firecreek* [1968]).

For women, the window of opportunity was never open as wide or as long. Men were accepted as living footloose, independent lives well into their senior years, but mature women in lead roles were either married or wound up getting married (i.e., the Tracy/Hepburn films). Single middle-aged women were usually either pitiable spinsters (think Agnes Moorehead in *The Magnificent Andersons* [1942]), or comic relief supporting parts played by the likes of high-flying Jessie Royce Landis, grittier Thelma Ritter, or tough-hided rural type Ellen Corby. The older woman able to manage her own, active life was a cinematic rarity (Lillian Gish in *Night of the Hunter* [1955]), and a romance between geriatric peers even more scarce (John Wayne and Katherine Hepburn in *Rooster Cogburn* [1975]).

As for the male/female age disparities in on-screen romances, there was no distaff equal. An older woman involved with a younger man could only be portrayed as grotesque, a vain attempt by a callow succubus to stave off age by latching on to a handsome young lad. As for the handsome young lad, his interest could only be mercenary (i.e., Gloria Swanson/William Holden in *Sunset Blvd.* [1950], Geraldine Page/Paul Newman in *Sweet Bird of Youth* [1962]).

One-time leading ladies now often found themselves channeled into supporting character roles playing wives, mothers, dignified old women (an Ethel Barrymore specialty), brassy comic relief (Landis and Ritter), or they moved into television, as Loretta Young and Ida Lupino did, where their names carried a prestige no longer theirs on the big screen. They could still pick up movie leads but often in sensationalistic, low-budget B-features, as Olivia de Havilland did in *Lady In a Cage* (1964), Joan Crawford in *Berserk* (1967) and *Trog* (1970), and Debbie Reynolds and Shelley Winters together in *What's the*

Matter With Helen? (1971). But their place in the mainstream limelight was in eclipse.

In a bitter irony, one of the few recurring types of lead roles still available to women throughout the failing studio era was that of the fading actress, usually *played* by a fading actress. While Gloria Swanson's turn as a past-it silent movie star in *Sunset Blvd.* may be the prototype, Bette Davis created a folio of such parts in *All About Eve,* the appropriately titled *The Star* (1952), and the macabre *Whatever Happened to Baby Jane?* (1962) (playing opposite another fading star playing a faded star, Joan Crawford).

All of Hollywood's efforts to regain the loyalty of its audience— provocative stories, big-scale epics, technological gimmicks— couldn't stem the erosion of ticket sales. The liberalization of "acceptable" content continued in a new direction. Not only were the studios becoming more brazen in the material they presented, but also in *how* it was presented.

Where years before the movie-going audience had gasped at Clark Gable's Rhett Butler telling Scarlett O'Hara at how he didn't "give a damn," in *Gone With the Wind,* twenty-seven years later it was sent reeling as Elizabeth Taylor, the sweet ingenue many audience members remembered from *National Velvet,* spewed four-letter invective at on-/off-screen husband Richard Burton in *Who's Afraid of Virginia Woolf?* (1966). Where on-screen killings had happened with a minimum of fuss and muss, with perhaps just a trickle of blood from the corner of a mouth, now audience members could see the impact of bullets and spurting blood, and linger on the sight of bodies writhing in slow motion (*Bonnie and Clyde, Butch Cassidy and the Sundance Kid* [1969]). Breasts were bared (*The Killing of Sister George* [1968]), and lovemaking now took place on screen rather than after a fade-to-black (*Don't Look Now* [1973]), and even taboos like male-male romancing were falling by the wayside (*Sunday, Bloody Sunday* [1971]).

Movies were now dealing with controversial subjects more graphically and with a new frankness which some considered refreshingly honest, others felt was rank sensationalism, and that sometimes was a bit of both. And these were not small, independent films, but mainstream releases from the major studios. There were films dealing with male and female homosexuality (*Reflections In a Golden Eye*

[1967] and *The Killing of Sister George* respectively), police brutality and urban vigilantes (*Dirty Harry* [1972], *Death Wish* [1974] respectively), sex (*Midnight Cowboy* [1969]), drugs (*The Panic In Needle Park* [1971]), ribald political humor (*The President's Analyst* [1967]), Holocaust horrors (*The Pawnbroker* [1965]), sex crimes (*The Boston Strangler* [1968], *The Detective* [1968]), and morbid black humor (*Where's Poppa?* [1970], *Harold and Maude* [1972]). Sex and violence were not only elements of storytelling, sometimes they were the subject (*A Clockwork Orange* [1971]).

As in the 1950s, this sudden broadening of filmable subjects provided some of the most memorable female roles in cinema: Elizabeth Taylor's bloated, boozy harridan in *Virginia Woolf;* Julie Christie's neurotic, straying wife in *Petulia* (1968) and her opium-smoking madam in *McCabe & Mrs. Miller* (1971); Faye Dunaway's sociopathic Bonnie Parker in *Bonnie & Clyde;* Anne Bancroft as the alcoholic Mrs. Robinson in *The Graduate* (1967) marking suburban ennui in a pointless sexual fling with college grad Dustin Hoffman.

But what stood out about such performances was not only the quality of the roles and the women who so expertly filled them, but also their rarity in a field giving still more ground to male actors and male-oriented stories.

Action films, even those without marquee draws and made on tight budgets, were becoming a valuable and exportable Hollywood commodity. Dramas and sophisticated comedies require a certain cultural savvy for an overseas audience to grasp an American story's imperatives and nuances. An urbane Woody Allen film like *Manhattan* (1979), for example, is practically a series of American inside jokes to, say, an Asian audience (for that matter, even Americans outside of Los Angeles and New York don't always get the humor). But gunfights, explosions, the formula of "manly men doing manly things" were, Hollywood was learning, something international audiences could respond to at a visceral level, particularly when stories were set against almost mythical, culturally neutral backdrops like battlefields, the Old West, or science fiction. Films like *The Dirty Dozen* and *The Good, the Bad, and the Ugly* and later *Star Wars* (1977) had an almost primal appeal to ticket-buyers around the globe.

Such films, by their nature, had little use or room for prominent female characters. They were often extraneous, usually in the vein of the proverbial "obligatory love interest." In films like *The Magnificent Seven* and *Butch Cassidy*, the women's parts could be cut with no appreciable impact on the main thrust of the story. More often, as in the Eastwood films, and war films like *The Great Escape* and *The Dirty Dozen*, even the mere presence of women was minimal if evident at all. As the international popularity of the action/adventure type of films grew, they evolved from moderately budgeted affairs with midrange stars to expensive, A-list projects like *Bullitt* (1968), *Patton* (1970), *The Longest Yard* (1974), *The Sand Pebbles* (1966), *Deliverance* (1972), and the James Bond films and their clones like *Our Man Flint* and the Matt Helm series. With each such success the number and quality of roles for women was pinched that much further.

Heating up the commercial dynamic of the male-oriented adventure tale still more was the 1975 film adaptation of Peter Benchley's best-selling novel *Jaws* (1975). The film had been a troubled project, what is described in the movie trade as a "runaway" production, one that seems to be spinning fiscally and logistically out of control.[33] *Jaws* had originally been scheduled for a 55-day shoot on a budget of $3.5 million.[34] By the time the film wrapped, it had nearly tripled both its shooting schedule and costs.[35] Despite its problems abirthing, the film was a phenomenal success both at home and around the world, rapidly shooting to the top of the all-time box-office champion list and making a directorial star of its young helmer, Steven Spielberg.

The summertime bonanza of *Jaws*—along with the similar success of all-star disaster films like *Airport*, *The Poseidon Adventure* (1972), *The Towering Inferno* (1974), and *Star Wars*—confirmed for Hollywood executives that exorbitant budgets and logistical headaches were worth the trouble on the chance (repeat; only on the *chance)* of harvesting the kind of box-office bumper crop these films reaped. Spielberg and Spielberg-like films were to become a summer staple.[36]

What this period in the history of moviemaking augured for women, however, was less spectacular. Rather, it was downright dismal. Indicative of an industry trend, in every one of the above-mentioned blockbusters—*Airport*, *The Poseidon Adventure*, *The Towering Inferno*, *Jaws*, and *Star Wars*—women were clearly relegated to secondary roles:

Airport—Jean Seberg and airport manager Burt Lancaster have warm feelings for each other while Dana Wynter, in her two short scenes as Lancaster's wife, is depicted as a bitch incarnate. Lancaster juggles a dozen different airport crises while Seberg extends her sympathy;

Jacqueline Bisset is the love interest for pilot Dean Martin whose innocuous wife Barbara Hale barely appears on screen. Martin saves his jetliner after a bomb explosion while Bisset, wounded by the same bomb, spends the climax of the film unconscious;

Maureen Stapleton is the brooding blue-collar wife of Van Heflin who is planning to kill himself for insurance money. Van Heflin blows himself up, Stapleton cries;

Helen Hayes has the "lovable old bitty" part as an airliner stowaway.

With the exception of Hayes's comic relief the women are all in the vein of we-also-serve-who-stand-and-wait characters. With each succeeding blockbuster, women fared even worse:

The Poseidon Adventure—Of the ten principals in this all-star disaster epic, only four are women.

Carol Lynley broods for her dead brother while Pamela Sue Martin has eyes for Gene Hackman, a fiery priest trying to lead a small party to safety in a capsized ocean liner. Neither has more than a handful of lines;

Stella Stevens is a cartoonish ex-hooker who spends most of the movie flashing her legs, the film's attempt at sex appeal in a picture dominated by yelling, sweaty men and special effects;

Shelley Winters is the lovable old bitty this time around, given an improbable rescue scene where she saves Hackman from drowning, her only real contribution to the plot.

Again, all the roles of decision are male: Hackman as the determined priest, Ernest Borgnine as his obstreperous opposition, Red Buttons as their referee, Roddy McDowall as their crewman/guide, Leslie Nielsen as captain of the doomed ship. Even prepubescent Eric Shea is of more substantive help to the party's survival than any of the female characters.

The Towering Inferno—Of the dozen principals only four are
women.
Headliner Faye Dunaway and Susan Flannery are obligatory love
interests for Paul Newman and Robert Wagner, respectively;
Susan Blakely barely appears as the long-suffering wife of Richard Chamberlain, shady contractor;
And the lovable old bitty role this time goes to Jennifer Jones.

Still again the action of the film is dominated by men: Newman
as the building's architect, Steve McQueen as a fire chief, William
Holden as the skyscraper's builder, Chamberlain as the party responsible for the threatening fire.

Jaws—The only female role of note is Lorraine Gary as police
chief Roy Scheider's supportive wife, a small role that disap-
pears completely when the story moves to the shark hunt,
which comprises the last third of the film, leaving the movie
solely to leads Scheider, Richard Dreyfuss, and Robert Shaw.
Star Wars—Even in a film supposedly boasting Mark Hamill,
Harrison Ford, and Carrie Fisher as coleads, the bulk of the
saving-the-universe actions falls to Hamill and Ford. In this
film and its two sequels, *The Empire Strikes Back* (1980) and
Return of the Jedi (1983), Fisher, playing Princess Leia, though
supposedly the head of the Rebel Alliance, is more often the
stock "woman in jep," regularly being bailed out of one pre-
dicament after another by Hamill and/or Ford.

One sign of how the pool of quality roles for women was drying
up was the frantic search through much of the 1970s for enough performances to fill out the annual Oscar nominations for Best Actress
and Best Supporting Actress. Louise Fletcher won Best Actress for the
1975 adaptation of Ken Kesey's novel, *One Flew Over the Cuckoo's
Nest,* but the size and weight of the performance would have dis-
counted the part to supporting role status a decade or so earlier. The
following year saw Beatrice Straight win the Supporting Actress statu-
ette for her work in *Network,* a part consisting of little more than one
scene of a few minutes. It was the mark of how little opportunity
women could find to display their expertise that roles too small to

have shown up on Oscar's radar years earlier were now contenders—
the *only* contenders—for awards.

★   ★   ★

This lengthy, digressive discourse does have a relevant application to
the subject at hand. When one overlays the career Sam Peckinpah—
which we will look at in the next chapter—on these trends, one sees
that the elements of sex and violence in the director's work, and the
weak presence women have in most of his films, were neither singular
nor unprecedented. Though his graphic depictions may have ratch-
eted up both the portrayal and debate over cinema sex and violence a
few notches, he was neither a groundbreaker nor the last word. His
work was very much part of an already-established trend. This raises
the question as to why he and his films came to be singled out by
feminist critics.

Peckinpah's career did not begin to break wide until the 1969
release of *The Wild Bunch*. As we saw in the first section of this chapter, that release coincided with a period of assertive feminism, a social
explosion of women making their claim on equal opportunities and
declaiming mistreatment professionally, socially, and culturally. But
while it makes prima facie sense to say that the rising social consciousness of activist women would bridle at the psychological and physical
injuries Peckinpah's women characters suffered, that still doesn't
completely explain his stature in the pantheon of feminism's villains.

Consider that within a few years of the release of *Bunch,* and after
just a handful of films, Peckinpah was a favorite target in Molly Haskell's *From Reverence to Rape* alongside other filmmakers with much
more substantial filmographies who were also perceived to have an
antifemale sensibility (i.e., John Ford, Alfred Hitchcock, and others).
Though Peckinpah's work may have only been a point on the line
of escalating sex and violence in movies, he seemed to draw special
attention. Faye Dunaway's orgasmic death scene in a slow motion hail
of machine gun bullets during the finale of *Bonnie and Clyde* has never
become the touchstone of feminist criticism that, say, the infamous
rape scene in Peckinpah's *Straw Dogs* (1972) became.

Considering the trends we've seen already at work in the industry at the time, that special regard is something of a left-handed com-

pliment, a tribute to the power of Peckinpah's filmmaking ability. Critics—feminist and otherwise—could shrug off a piece of sensationalism like *Death Wish,* complete with its brutal opening rape scene, because it registered as little more than an exploitative confection by trade hack Michael Winner. But even a Peckinpah flop like *Bring Me the Head of Alfredo Garcia* sparked raised voices over its scene of attempted rape. Feminists felt compelled to reckon with Peckinpah's work because they felt he and his work compelled reckoning with.

Another factor to this special attention, as we shall see later, was Peckinpah's own fault. Often paranoid and insecure about criticism, he was not a filmmaker to simply roll with a negative opinion. He could be disproportionately combative. Worse, there were times when he seemed to take a childish delight in antagonizing his critics. In an environment where women were actively pushing an agenda of equality, and showing open dismay at the abuse and second-class status they suffered in the media, Peckinpah had the annoying tic of going into such a combustible situation and spouting off igniting remarks.

But there is another contextual factor as well that had very little to do with the American women's movement, or Hollywood trends, or Peckinpah's temperament. It was the fault, if you will, that lay in scrivenings made the decade before from a then little-known movie critic an ocean away brainstorming a new way of looking at movies.

AUTHOR OF *AUTEUR*

Though he would later go on to international acclaim as one of the leading film directors in France's *nouvelle vogue* renaissance of the 1950s and 1960s, in the early 1950s François Truffaut was only one of a small group of little-known French critics that launched the film journal *Cahiers du Cinéma.* It was Truffaut who first proposed what he called *la politique des auteurs,* the policy of authors. Today, most students of film refer to this simply as the *auteur* (French for "author") theory.[37]

Truffaut's proposition granted the best film directors with the creative status of an author. He felt that all other collaborators on a film put their talents at the service of the director so that the director could execute his personal vision on the screen. For example, Truffaut considered a screenplay a "neutral" component of a film, given only weight by the director's turning the page into moments of filmed action.

Truffaut did not think personalized auteur filmmaking styles were restricted to European "art house" fare, such as his own auto-biographical *The Four Hundred Blows* (1959) or *Cahiers* mate Jean-Luc Godard's surreal *Weekend* (1967). He and other auteurists believed that unique, idiosyncratic styles could even be detected in the work of Hollywood studio directors working on assigned pictures coming off the Dream Factory's assembly line. Recurring visual and thematic motifs, even when "snuck" into a film by a studio director, formed the basis for *Cahiers*-nurtured director's cults for the likes of Alfred Hitchcock, Samuel Fuller, John Ford, Howard Hawks, William Wellman, and others.[38]

Auteurism was not wholly accepted by the Hollywood creative community for obvious reasons. Many creative contributors—producers, writers, actors, editors, cinematgraphers, and so on—felt (and still do) that it negates their contributions to a cooperative effort. Not even all directors have subscribed to auteur.

Alfred Hitchcock, ironically one of the *Cahiers* cult idols, always disclaimed auteur status.[39] Writer/director David Mamet demystified the position in a series of lectures at Columbia University describing film directing as a learnable trade.[40]

Alexander Mackendrick, in a 1994 interview, gave a particularly succinct judgment on the problems with auteur. Mackendrick had been one of the house directors at the British Ealing Studios during their string of brilliant comedies in the 1950s and showed his versatility by helming the wonderfully acrid urban drama *Sweet Smell of Success* for Burt Lancaster's production company:

> *Q: For a while your own contribution to* Sweet Smell of Success *was often not mentioned nor played up as much as the other elements.*
> Mackendrick: It should not be mentioned.
> *Q: But in fact you did direct this movie, it did turn out the way it did . . .*
> Mackendrick: The diagram that I draw for the kids up at CalArts (Mackendrick was founding dean of the Film and Video School at

the California Institute of the Arts), of the function of the director, is a huge spider web of people. And students always think, Oh yes, he has power over all these people. The opposite is true: they all have power over *him* . . . I am a dedicated enemy of the cult of the director and auteurism and all that. The slogans I keep repeating are "Trust the tale, not the teller" and . . . "The author should be everywhere implicit but nowhere in evidence." The great directors managed to dissolve and disppear into the work. They make other people look good.[41]

Yet, for all the objections and objectors, there was an appealing simplicity to auteur theory. Rather than parse a film into component parts, critics and film theoreticians boiled down the cooperative effort of filmmaking to a single, responsible party analogous to a concert composer; the music might not be the composer's, and the composer certainly didn't play every instrument, but the performance was credited, good or bad, to the gentleman on the podium with the baton. The view quickly gained popularity among the critical community and by the late 1960s, auteur theory had been assimilated into most serious film discussion.[42]

Auteur theory had been an oversimplification of the filmmaking process intended to redress the lack of deserved recognition for directors who, while constrained by a studio's "house style" and factory production process, were nonetheless able to infuse a degree of personal storytelling into their films. That within the commercial confines of Hollywood these directors might be, as Sam Peckinpah once described himself, whores trying "to slip in a few comments on the side" didn't make them any less cinema artistes. But, following the Law of Unintended Consequences, that same oversimplification actually did a disservice to those same worthy cinema maestros.

To be fair, this was less as a result of the inherent flaws in auteur theory than it was a rather freewheeling application of auteurism. Like a finely balanced wheel, over time the theory began to wobble and wander. It disseminated across the breadth of film discourse, from the academic to the popular, showing up obviously and tacitly in everything from *Sight and Sound* to *Entertainment Weekly* and *People*. Director came to equal auteur and any moviemaker with good negotiating skills could get himself or herself a proprietary credit ("A Film By So-

and-So"; "A So-and-So Film") by contractual condition regardless of how much or how little they were involved in the total production.

Truffaut and the *Cahiers* critics had never intended auteurism as a blanket application. The theory had only ever been meant to be applied to a select group of filmmakers that the *Cahiers* crowd subjectively viewed as having distinctive, identifiable styles, filmmakers who seemed to have something to say—some feeling or sensibility they wanted to convey—to an audience that went beyond the plot unfolding on the screen.[43] Auteur purists would always maintain that not all films were auteurist films, and not every director was an auteur. Auteurism was the exception, not the rule.[44]

A downside of this indiscriminate view of all directors as auteurs was to put directors on an equal footing they didn't all warrant. A hack like Mark L. Lester, responsible for such insipid box-office fodder as *Firestarter* (1984) and *Roller Boogie* (1979), would now stand next to a solid (if unexceptional) craftsman like Richard Donner. And Donner, whose four *Lethal Weapon* films carry as much the imprimatur of his editors, special effects crews, and stunt teams as any directorial vision, would stand next to Stanley Kubrick, one of those directors who was a virtual auteur archetype taking a hand in every aspect of his films from development, through production, and even into the distribution and marketing of his works.[45]

Of more direct relevance to this discussion, however, is a flaw in auteur theory evident even in its scrupulous application by auteurist purists. Auteur-based criticism views a director and his or her work as if it occurs in a vacuum. It does not take into account the corporate dynamic in which virtually all mainstream moviemaking takes place, an environment in which a director's self-determination and creative choices can be extremely limited.

Throughout the course of Hollywood history, there have been producers who have been as much auteurist creators as directors; producers like David O. Selznick in the heyday of Old Hollywood, impresario Richard Todd, and today's Jerry Bruckheimer, who wield direct creative influence over a production. *Around the World in Eighty Days* is often referred to not as director Michael Anderson's *Around the World,* but as Richard Todd's *Around the World.*

After the collapse of the studio system, the box-office clout of so-called superstars gave actors the chance to override the artistic judgment of directors, writers, and even producers. Star Steve Mc-Queen, for example, would have the original music score for Peckinpah's *The Getaway* replaced by one from Quincy Jones, and because of his status as one of the top box-office draws in the world at that time, nobody involved with the project could veto him.[46]

But even when not in combat for their creative vision with other powers-that-be on a particular production, few directors have, over the course of their careers, been able to do the films they wanted to do and do them the *way* they wanted to do them. Under the old studio system, contract directors generally did the pictures assigned to them. After the collapse of the system, the gun-for-hire status of directors did not improve their overall lot appreciably. Filmmakers found they had only as much latitude in their choices as their success could earn them. A director who turned in a successful action picture might find himself being offered only more action pictures. Directors have been as subject to typecasting as performers.

Over the course of American moviemaking, only a handful of filmmakers have been able to establish near-total autonomy from outside influences. Orson Welles managed it on a number of his films by self-financing them. Alfred Hitchcock, Stanley Kubrick, and Woody Allen called for it in their contracts, while directorial superstars like Steven Spielberg, George Lucas, and Ron Howard went the ultimate step of creating their own production companies (Amblin and later Dreamworks for Spielberg; Lucasfilms for Lucas; and Imagine for Ron Howard) to provide a sheltering, creatively autonomous environment for their work.

This skewed auteurist vision not only compensated directors for their previous creative anonymity. Auteurist writings automatically credited—and debited—filmmakers for elements of their films and their careers not wholly their own. If, in the process, their reputations benefited from others' creative input, there were those who found themselves being called to account for sins sinned by others.

Sam Peckinpah, as we shall see, was a director constantly at odds with Hollywood, who—often through his own missteps—found himself directed down a narrow channel of options. The only time Peckinpah was capable of initiating his own project, on *The Ballad of Cable Hogue,* it turned out to be one of his warmest, most heartfelt, most un–Peckinpahesque films. It was also a film barely noticed in its time.

★   ★   ★

It was at the nexus of these currents that Sam Peckinpah stepped to the fore:

> A time when disarray in the motion picture industry opened the moviemaking field to controversial topics and increasingly graphic displays of sex and violence;
> The same trends were pushing women further from the commercial core of the movie industry;
> This second-class status of women on screen was occurring at a time when American women were finding their voice to declaim demeaning treatment in the media as well as in society as a whole;
> And that voice, when found in feminist film criticism, absorbed the widely accepted concept of auteurism and considered a director wholly culpable for the perceived antiwomen films he made and the elements that comprised them.

This is not to say that Peckinpah was simply a victim of circumstance. But what we see when we examine the direction of his career is that in this volatile mix, his combative temper, unrestrained vitriol, whimsical critic-baiting, and other personal foibles made Sam Peckinpah his own worst defender.

NOTES

1. Henry James, *The Bostonians* (New York: Vintage Press, 1991), 224.
2. "A Time of Tumult," *Life: 50th Anniversary Collector's Edition 1936–1986* (Fall 1986): 187–95.
3. Clark Dougan and Stephen Weiss, *Nineteen Sixty-Eight. The Vietnam Experience* (Boston, Mass.: Boston Publishing, 1983), 91.
4. Gloria Steinem, "I'm Not the Women In My Mind," *Parade* (January 12, 1992): 11.

5. "1936–1986: Year by Year," *Life: 50th Anniversary Collector's Edition 1936–1986* (Fall 1986): 38.

6. "Year," 39.

7. John Baxter, *Sixty Years of Hollywood* (Cranbury, N.J.: A.S. Barnes, 1973), 101.

8. Joel W. Finler, *The Hollywood Story* (New York: Crown, 1988), 280.

9. Finler, *Hollywood*, 276–78.

10. Jeanine Basinger, "Ann Sothern," *Film Comment* (November/December 1999): 24.

11. Jeanine Basinger, "Ladies Matinee," *Film Comment* (November/December 1999): 27–28.

12. James Robert Parish, ed., *The Great Movie Series* (Cranbury, N.J.: A.S. Barnes, 1971), 243.

13. Basinger, "Sothern," 24.

14. Joel W. Finler, *The Movie Director's Story* (New York: Crescent, 1985), 101.

15. Michael Webb, ed., *Hollywood: Legend and Reality* (Boston, Mass.: Little, Brown, 1986), 36.

16. Ken D. Jones and Arthur F. McClure, *Hollywood at War: The American Motion Picture and World War II* (Cranbury, N.J.: A.S. Barnes, 1973), 16.

17. Webb, *Hollywood*, 36.

18. David E. Scherman, ed., *Life Goes to the Movies*. 2nd printing (New York: T/L Books, 1975), 86.

19. Gary Carey, *All the Stars In Heaven—Louis B. Mayer's MGM* (New York: Dutton, 1981), 95.

20. Scherman, *Life,* 98–99.

21. Gary Carey, *All the Stars In Heaven—Louis B. Mayer's MGM* (New York: Dutton, 1981), 115.

22. Gary Jennings, *The Movie Book* (New York: Dial, 1963), 57.

23. Roger Simon, "Philadelphia Story," *U.S. News & World Report* (August 7, 2000): 32.

24. Finler, *Hollywood*, 289.

25. Baxter, *Sixty Years of Hollywood*, 127.

26. Baxter, *Sixty Years of Hollywood*, 233.

27. Peter Bart, *The Gross: The Hits, the Flops—The Summer That Ate Hollywood* (New York: St. Martins, 1999), 161.

28. Finler, *Hollywood*, 280.

29. Jennings, *Movie Book,* 40–41.

30. Jennings, *Movie Book*, 42.

31. Baxter, *Sixty Years of Hollywood,* 207.

32. Jennings, *Movie Book*, 53.

33. Steven Bach, *Final Cut: Dreams and Disaster in the Making of* Heaven's Gate (New York: Plume, 1985), 262.

34. Carl Gottlieb, *The Jaws Log* (New York: Dell, 1975), 62.

35. Gottlieb, *The Jaws Log*, 202.

36. Bart, *The Gross*, 120.

37. Louis D. Gianetti, *Understanding Movies*, 2nd ed. (Englewood Cliffs, N.J.: Prentice, 1976), 437.

38. Gianetti, *Understanding Movies*, 439.

39. Charles Higham and Joel Greenberg, *The Celluloid Muse: The Directors Speak* (New York: Signet, 1972), 13.

40. Higham and Greenberg, *Celluloid Muse*, 105).

41. Kate Buford, "Do Make Waves: Sandy—Alexander Mackendrick," *Film Comment* (May/June 1994): 43.

42. Gianetti, *Understanding Movies*, 439.

43. Higham and Greenberg, *Celluloid Muse*, 13.

44. Ernest Lindgren, *The Art of the Film*, 2nd printing, Collier ed. (New York: Collier, 1972), 7.

45. Finler, *Director's,* 210.

46. Marshall Terrill, *Steve McQueen: Portrait of an American Rebel* (New York: Donald Fine, 1993), 244.

· 3 ·

Life and Career: Siege Mentalities

He doesn't think life is very delightful, in the nature of things.

—*Henry James,* The Bostonians (1885)[1]

The great strengths Sam Peckinpah brought to his Westerns derived from his upbringing. The stories and surroundings of his youth gave Peckinpah a sensibility about the West and Westerners that distinguished his work. Yet, that same source gave Peckinpah his personal weaknesses: combativeness, a nearly arbitrary resistance to authority, a bent toward brawling and whoring, and a drinking habit that would eventually lead to drug abuse.[2] Peckinpah's relationship with his mother set the stage for a line of disastrous relationships with women, including several wives and lovers, and even with his daughters; relationships worsened by physical and emotional abuse exacerbated by his alcohol and drug problems. In considering the personal and professional battles that checkered his life and career, more than one Peckinpah acquaintance would declare the filmmaker to be his own worst enemy.[3]

★   ★   ★

By right of birth and family history, David Samuel Peckinpah felt that he "came by (making Westerns) naturally."[4] He was born in the mining area of Fresno, California, in 1925.[5] His paternal grandparents had emigrated from Illinois in the 1850s.[6] On his maternal side, his grandfather—Denver Church—was California-born and his grandmother had come from Carson City, Nevada in the late 1800s, marrying

Church in 1889.[7] All of Peckinpah's grandparents were alive during his years as a boy, and he was often treated to stories of their sundry ventures in lumber, ranching, hauling borax, and wagon-making during those years when the California hinterlands were still very much part of the Wild West.[8]

Peckinpah often spent time as a boy at the Church ranch in the Sierras, accompanying his father and Grandfather Church on hunting trips. Although Peckinpah was raised in the town of Fresno, it was the time on the ranch that made the deepest impression on him. "In later years, [he] liked to give the impression that those days at the Church ranch told the whole story of his childhood and upbringing."[9]

Interviewed in the 1970s, Peckinpah reflected on his rustic upbringing: "My brother Denny and I were in on the last of it. A lot of the old-timers dated back to when the place had been the domain of hunters and trappers, Indians, gold miners—all the drifters and hustlers."[10] Until the 1970s, Peckinpah would maintain an annual ritual trek into the mountains around Fresno for a hunting trip with friends and relatives. In the mountains, Peckinpah "was able to just relax, kick back, sit by the fire, and swap lies," according to his nephew, David Peckinpah.[11]

Peckinpah's mother, Fern, also shared his affinity for the outdoors. She had her own rifle and Peckinpah used it to shoot his first deer.[12] The mother and son shared little else. Marshall Fine's 1991 biography *Bloody Sam: The Life and Films of Sam Peckinpah* offered the first complete accounting of Peckinpah's upbringing. According to the author, Fern Peckinpah thought so little of the rustic background of her husband's family, and maintained an inflated sense of importance about her own family, that she kept her four children as isolated from their paternal grandparents as possible.

She had an odd maternal sense. Inexplicably, she ignored two of her children while doting on the others, including young Sam. "Sam was my mother's pride and joy," according to Peckinpah's brother Denny. "He could do no wrong in her eyes. No matter what he did, it was forgivable."[13]

Fern Peckinpah was a manipulative individual.[14] When her husband, Dave, was invited to run for Congress, Fern, concerned that her husband's accomplishments might eclipse those of her father whom she adored, threatened to leave him if he accepted. Years later, when Dave Peckinpah wanted to accept an offer to sit on the California Superior Court in Madera County, Fern again opposed him, trying to scare him with talk about his bad heart. When he accepted the position, "there was almost a divorce."[15] Eventually, Fern "banished" Dave to a cabin on the Peckinpah property, far from the main house where she continued to live.[16] Watching "the most important man in his life being emasculated by the most important woman," Sam Peckinpah grew estranged from his mother.[17] Fern would spend her last years in a nursing home a diagnosed schizophrenic.[18]

Years later, one of Peckinpah's women companions would say that "all his love/hate feelings for women were based on his mother."[19] "Love/hate feelings" is the label that best covers Peckinpah's erratic behavior toward women. Mariette Hartley, who had the female lead in *Ride the High Country,* found him supportive and affectionate. "From the day I walked into his office, I felt blessed," she remembered.[20] Such was not the case for Stella Stevens who costarred with Jason Robards in *The Ballad of Cable Hogue.* Stevens reported that the director "had a cruel streak that delighted him. Instead of encouraging me to do my best, he battered and belittled me. Anything he could do to throw you off, he would."[21] Yet, on the same production, after the management of the hotel housing the cast and crew "fired two coffee-shop waitresses for hustling on the side, an indignant Peckinpah hired them as production secretaries to keep them in the community (he later sent them to secretarial school)."[22] On *The Getaway,* Peckinpah hired his eldest daughter, Sharon, to work on the project, then crossed swords with her during her tenure on the film. "He'd take your ego, throw it on the ground and stomp on it," Sharon recalled. "He fired me three times in the same night."[23] On the same film, after female lead Ali MacGraw was universally panned by the critics, Peckinpah—who had had MacGraw thrust on him by the film's producer Robert Evans and star Steve McQueen—wrote her in support saying, "I thought you were damn good. . . . You're a much better actress than anyone else gives you credit for, including yourself. I think you are a natural."[24]

The domestic violence that marked Peckinpah's private life also had antecedents in his childhood. "My father was a gentle man," according to brother Denny, "but he tended to be violent when he was disciplining us kids."[25] Peckinpah himself cited his stunted height—he grew to only five-foot-nine in a family of six-footers—as another contributing factor to his developing combativeness.[26] It was, perhaps, this "runt" mentality that caused him to constantly test his relationships, even those with his male acquaintances.

David Warner, who made three films with Peckinpah, said the director was "sometimes impossible" in the way he treated cast and crew members of either sex.[27] Another male acquaintance once said, "He was my friend, and Sam loved to fuck his friends." From lifelong pal Joe Bernhard: "He torpedoed everybody who ever did anything with him. Why do you fuck with loyalty? He always did it." Actor L.Q. Jones, who appeared in all of Peckinpah's period Westerns, summed it up saying, "Sam had a death wish for his friends."[28]

With the circumstances of Peckinpah's home life in mind, it seems unsurprising that Peckinpah's first marriage disintegrated in physical and emotional abuse, as did his relationship with his second wife whom he married twice.[29, 30] Alcohol and violence destroyed his third marriage in six months, and his fourth in less than a month.[31, 32] Even in his comparatively sedate relationships, Peckinpah seemed to require at least some element of volatility. According to Carol O'Connor, a woman with whom he was living in a clean and sober state after *The Osterman Weekend*, Peckinpah would tell her, "I don't believe you love me unless you fight with me. . . . [That] was how he worked things out emotionally."[33]

His Fresno upbringing explains other facets of Peckinpah's life and storytelling. Northern California was a redoubt of Wild West mentality well into the twentieth century. Not far from Fresno is the town of Jackson, which "entered the second half of the twentieth century with most of its virtues and all of its vices intact." Jackson did not close the last of its bordellos until 1956, after more than forty years in which the City Council had gone without receiving a single whorehouse-related complaint.[34] The Fresno of Peckinpah's youth shared more than geography with Jackson. It "was a wide-open town, with $3 whorehouses, dozens of them. There was dice gambling. In the Plantation Club across the street from the police station, there was always heavy gambling."[35]

The contributors to Marshall Fine's Peckinpah biography often relate stories of Peckinpah cavorting with prostitutes. Peckinpah himself was not shy about discussing his relationships with prostitutes, claiming he had enjoyed the company of whores of all stripes: "American, Chinese, English, Mexican, any nationality."[36] When, in 1963, Peckinpah was asked "[who] the most instrumental [people were] in helping you become the character you are?" Peckinpah replied, "My father, my grandfather, my brother, my ex–wife and a 75-year-old Nevada prostitute who told me the story of her first love for $3.00 and a four-bit bottle of beer. The story became 'Jeff,' the first [episode of] 'Westerner' [the TV series Peckinpah produced] on the air."[37]

Growing up with an attitude of tolerance toward prostitutes, while having a dismal domestic record, Peckinpah tended to wax romantic about prostitutes. "Of all the whores I've been with," he said in a 1972 interview, "I've failed to end up with some kind of warm relationship with only ten percent. I've *lived* with some good whores. They've taken me home and I've taken them home. We've been human beings together." When asked if his relationships with prostitutes indicated "some need on your part to remain either superior or emotionally uninvolved?" he responded, "Possibly, but I believe it signifies mostly that I like an honest woman, a woman who's honest with herself and the people she cares about. Not infrequently, in one way or another, she turns out to be a prostitute." As for other women, "most married women fuck for the money that's in it."[38]

For all his proclaimed affection for prostitutes, Peckinpah was not above treating them as badly as he did his other female acquaintances. In the late 1970s, during one of several periods he spent in Mexico, "occasionally, Peckinpah would find a whore who pleased him, only to end up mistreating her before the evening was through."[39] Said Paul Peterson, an ex–brother-in-law of Peckinpah's who spent some time living with the director in Mexico, "I think Sam had a contempt for whores at the same time that he really believed they were as honest as women could be. . . . He was a misogynist. He believed he'd been screwed over by women. He didn't have to worry that a whore would do that. . . . He'd hassle the whores, though. He didn't want to pay them."[40]

★   ★   ★

Growing up in the raucous environs of Fresno, Peckinpah developed a "contempt for rules, regulations and anything else that interfered with his quest for a good time." Demerits for poor conduct kept him off the cum laude list at San Rafael Military Academy where he finished his final year of high school. The next year, 1943, after joining the Marines, Peckinpah's conduct again undercut his talents and he was cut from his Officer Candidate's School Class and ended up serving as an enlisted man.[41]

After mustering out in 1946, he registered at California State University at Fresno where he became interested in theater and married his first wife. Later, he and his wife moved to the Los Angeles area. Peckinpah directed local theater productions and did odd jobs at a local television station both before and after completing his master's degree in theater from the University of Southern California.

Eventually, Peckinpah wound up working for director Don Siegel as a "gofer" on several films, most notable *Invasion of the Body Snatchers* (1956) in which he worked as a bit actor and dialogue coach.[42] Siegel was impressed with Peckinpah's ability, enough so that when he declined an offer to produce TV's "Gunsmoke" he suggested his young protégé for a writing position on the new Western series.[43]

Television in the 1950s was a training ground for directors who would often go onto acclaim and success in films. Among the more renowned TV alumni are the likes of Franklin J. Schaffner (*Planet of the Apes* [1968], *Patton* [1970]), Sidney Lumet (*Twelve Angry Men, Network),* and John Frankenheimer (*The Manchurian Candidate* [1962], *Seven Days In May* [1964]). Peckinpah, too, would come to stand among that front rank, "arguably [being] the most important of all American directors to have graduated from TV."[44] Along with "Gunsmoke," he wrote for several other series including "Zane Grey Theatre" and "The Dick Powell Theater," most of his work being Westerns. Peckinpah was able to parlay his growing stature in television into the positions of producer and director. He created "The Rifleman," and directed four episodes from the series' first season.[45] Although the series was a hit and would run for five years, Peckinpah left after the first season over creative differences with the series' producers. "I walked from ['The Rifleman'] because [the producer] . . . had taken over my initial concept and perverted it into pap."[46] It was the first time that Peckinpah's problems with authority figured in his career, signaling the beginning of a self-defeating pattern.

Despite his leaving the show, the hit status of "The Rifleman" earned Peckinpah the Hollywood currency to develop a series in which he could maintain a larger measure of creative control. Peckinpah created "The Westerner," starring Brian Keith. The series was a critical favorite, playing as "both homage to the Old West of legend and an exploration of the reality behind that legend."[47] Despite the critical plaudits, few viewers tuned in and the show was cancelled after thirteen episodes. Though short-lived, "The Westerner" would launch Peckinpah on his feature film career.

★   ★   ★

Peckinpah had sold one feature film screenplay as early as 1957. Once out of his hands, however, "The Authentic Death of Hendry Jones," an adaptation of a 1956 novel by Charles Neider, spent four years winding through the Hollywood development maze. In 1961, it emerged virtually unrecognizable as the quirky *One-Eyed Jacks,* Marlon Brando's sole directorial effort.[48] Peckinpah's true feature film break came when "The Westerner" star Brian Keith was signed for the lead in *The Deadly Companions.*

Keith played Yellowleg, a former Union Army sergeant hunting Turk (Chill Wills), a Confederate deserter who had tried to scalp him during the Civil War. Yellowleg locates Turk and persuades him to join him in a bank robbery in Gila City along with Turk's sidekick, gun-happy Billy (Steve Cochran). The three get into a shoot-out with members of another outlaw band who have come to Gila City for the same purpose. The nineteen-year-old son of dance hall queen Kit Tilden (Maureen O'Hara) is caught in the crossfire and accidentally killed by Yellowleg. Penitent, Yellowleg forces Turk and Billy to help Kit escort her son's body across Apache territory to bury him next to her husband's grave. On the journey, Billy is driven out after attempting to rape Kit and Turk deserts. In the ghost town where Kit's husband is buried, Yellowleg again meets up with Turk and Billy. There is another shoot-out, Billy is killed, and Turk and Yellowleg are wounded. A posse from Gila City arrives and apprehends

Turk. Yellowleg and Kit, who have come to love one another over the course of their trek, ride off together.[49]

The film was produced by an independent production company formed by A. S. Fleischman, who had also written the screenplay; Maureen O'Hara; and O'Hara's brother, Charles FitzSimons, who took on the responsibility of line producer for the project. FitzSimons had hired Keith hoping to capitalize on the expected success of an upcoming Disney film also starring Keith and O'Hara.

While Peckinpah would always have trouble relating to studio brass, he would, throughout his career, manage to maintain strong ties to cast members, and the backgrounds of his films usually boast a number of the same faces; a stock company of sorts not dissimilar to that of John Ford. Peckinpah and Keith had developed a tie over the short span of "The Westerner," and Keith had been impressed enough with Peckinpah's work on the series to recommend him for the director's position on *Companions*. But once hired, Peckinpah and FitzSimons were almost immediately at odds with each other.[50]

"The trouble started with the script, which Peckinpah declared unmanageable." The director's offer of a rewrite was refused by Fitz-Simons.[51] FitzSimons had invested time and money in the script and felt an obligation to his partner Fleischman to keep it intact.[52] Additionally, FitzSimons was financing the film partly with money put up by Pathe-America, a distribution chain, on the condition that there would be no changes made in the script shown them. Still, Peckinpah and Keith "working nights, between takes, on breaks, and generally on the sly, managed to rewrite about a fifth of the dialogue, primarily Keith's."[53]

FitzSimons and Peckinpah fought over the tight budget and schedule, and "FitzSimons resisted various images that Peckinpah felt were necessary to achieve the grittiness [Peckinpah] hoped would disguise the script's problems."[54] Relations between the two grew so strained that FitzSimons eventually forbade Peckinpah to speak with his sister, O'Hara.[55] O'Hara's consequent performance as a woman "frozen in a posture of righteousness" may have less to do with Peckinpah's skill—or lack of same—and the script, than with the ban on his directing her.[56] "That Kit . . . is seen less clearly than other main characters is probably more a result of the constraints under which the director was working. . . . He could do little more than treat her according to the standard western euphemism allowed for prostitutes—a barroom or dance hall girl."[57]

Peckinpah left the picture after delivering his first cut of the film.[58] FitzSimons then recut the film "and got into such a mess that he had to return to [Peckinpah's] original pattern," although FitzSimons installed his version of the ending.[59]

The Deadly Companions was a little-noticed release. There were, however, compliments among the few reviews. *Variety*, for example, reported that despite the film's "lapses and weaknesses," it was a "fairly engrossing Western . . . an interesting and sufficiently novel slice of frontier fiction . . . an auspicious debut as a director by Sam Peckinpah, a fine TV helmsman."[60]

Peckinpah returned to TV for spot work, most of it in Westerns, but it was the quality of his work on "The Westerner" that still tickled the interest of film producers. Even more than his film debut on *Companions,* it was the stature of his short-lived series that brought Peckinpah his next feature job.[61] On this, only his second feature directing assignment, Peckinpah created one of the acknowledged classics of Western cinema: MGM's *Ride the High Country* (aka *Guns in the Afternoon).*[62]

One-time legendary lawman Steve Judd (Joel McCrea) is contracted to escort a gold shipment from the mountain mining town of Coarsegold to a bank on the more settled lowlands. Judd enlists old riding partner Gil Westrum (Randolph Scott) and Westrum's young friend Heck Longtree (Ron Starr) to help him. Gil, aging and as down on his luck as Steve, actually plans to rob the shipment along with Heck. On their way up the mountain, they stay with Joshua Knudsen (R. G. Armstrong), a religious fanatic, and his daughter Elsa (Mariette Hartley). Elsa leaves with the party, running away from her father to marry her miner boyfriend Billy Hammond (James Drury). At the mining camp, Elsa is married in a drunken saloon bacchanal, and learns that Billy intends to share her with his barbaric brothers. Elsa runs off with Steve, Gill, and Heck as they head back down the mountain with the gold. Gil and Heck unsuccessfully try to steal the gold, and are taken prisoner by Steve. Gil later escapes after the Hammonds try to ambush the party. Gil returns when Steve is ambushed again at the Knudsen farm. Side by side, Steve and Gil face the Hammonds killing them all. Steve, however, is fatally wounded. As he is dying, Gil promises him the safe return of the gold.[63]

Again, Peckinpah was a director-for-hire on a completed script. Soon after being hired Peckinpah expressed dissatisfaction with the screenplay, calling for a rewrite. "By the estimate of [producer Richard E.] Lyons and McCrea, [Peckinpah] re-wrote about 'eighty percent of the dialogue'; he reconciled the two old westerners and their friendship in terms of greater richness, depth, and complexity."[64]

Unlike FitzSimons, there is no record that Lyons had any problems with the rewrite. The project actually ran more or less smoothly up through Peckinpah's delivery of the first cut of the film. Some of the junior MGM executives, concerned over the length of time Peckinpah had spent cutting the film "feared he would take as long with the dubbing and scoring and ordered him barred from the lot."[65]

The film was released in the form that Peckinpah had wanted, and the stellar reviews justified his directorial vision:

- "Superior Western. . . . It is a resourceful young director's attempt to create something original."[66]
- "A downright pleasure to watch. . . . Mr. Peckinpah and [screenwriter] Mr. [N. B.] Stone (Jr.) certainly have what it takes."[67]
- "It is Sam Peckinpah's direction . . . that gives the film its greatest artistry. . . . He gives N. B. Stone, Jr.'s script a measure beyond its adequacy."[68]
- "This story could have been sheer slumgullion, but under Sam Peckinpah's tasteful direction it is a minor *chef-d'oeuvre* among Westerns."[69]

In Europe, *Ride the High Country* was one of MGM's highest grossing films that year.[70] In the United States, however, it was a box-office failure, but not because the film had no appeal for the domestic audience. In fact, the reaction of audiences at previews of the film was "sensational."[71] The problem was the general audience was given little chance to see the film as, *Newsweek* reported, it was "dumped carelessly as the bottom half of neighborhood double bills."[72] That decision is traced to Joseph Vogel, head of Loews, Inc., which was MGM's parent company at the time. When Peckinpah's cut was screened, the MGM execs overseeing the film were pleased, but Vogel loathed what he saw and refused to support the film.[73]

Peckinpah again returned to television. He moved with some regularity from project to project working for, among others, Four Star Theatre, and Walt Disney. He returned to feature films hired by Columbia Pictures producer Jerry Bresler for a Civil War–era Western entitled *Major Dundee*.

Charlton Heston played the title character, a Union officer in the closing months of the Civil War, relegated to the post of warden over several hundred Confederate prisoners at an isolated fort in the New Mexico territory. Dundee enlists prisoner Captain Tyreen (Richard Harris), a one-time West Point colleague, and several of Tyreen's men, along with a hodgepodge of civilians and Union troopers, in pursuit of Sierra Charriba (Michael Pate), an Apache raider. Dundee illegally leads his unit across the Mexican border after the Apache chief, and they camp at a small, impoverished village they free from occupying French soldiers. The relationship between Dundee and Tyreen becomes increasingly strained by an enmity that stems back to their West Point days, aggravated by their torn loyalties to North and South, and then by Dundee's distraction by Teresa Santiago (Senta Berger), a widow whose husband was hanged by the French. After leaving the village, Dundee's unit is ambushed by the Apaches after which Dundee returns to the village. On a tryst outside the village with Teresa, Dundee is wounded by an Apache sniper. Smuggled to a doctor in a nearby city, Dundee indulges in a wandering, self-pitying drunk after his leg heals. He is saved from discovery by his men, returns to command his unit, and leads his own ambush against the Apaches, destroying them. Their objective completed, Dundee and Tyreen look to settle their personal differences, but put them aside to lead their men against the French troops blocking their escape across the border. In the battle, Tyreen is killed and Dundee leads the few survivors home.

The film, conceived as a sprawling, big-budget Western epic with a top-ranked cast, promised to be the fledgling director's "break-out" film. Unfortunately, the project was suffering serious problems months before production began. There were weaknesses in the original script and after five and a half months of Peckinpah's rewriting, they were still unsolved.[74]

One of the screenplay's main flaws was the part of Teresa. Three months before production began, Heston wrote in his journal, "I'm convinced the woman's role is a major flaw. She's artificial and contrived."[75] On the eve of shooting, Peckinpah still hadn't resolved the problem: "The main thing wrong," wrote Heston, "is the girl's part, which is very sloppily written."[76]

The situation worsened with the casting of Senta Berger. Critics would later bear out suspicions by Heston and even Peckinpah himself that Berger simply did not have the talent required to bring off the part (admittedly, a badly written part) in acceptable fashion. "I should have fought her casting from the start," Peckinpah later said. "The end result, all too prominently on display in the film, is some of the silliest scenes [Peckinpah] has ever laid his name on."[77]

To complicate matters still further, two days before shooting began, Bresler informed Peckinpah that fifteen days had been cut from the shooting schedule, and the budget had been reduced by one third.[78] Throughout the production, Bresler incessantly harped on Peckinpah about speeding up production and keeping costs down.[79] Columbia Pictures began to send executives to the Mexican locations to reinforce Bresler's stand. Peckinpah's response to pressure from above was habitual. "The more Columbia tried to twist Peckinpah's arm, the more he went his own way."[80]

Not all of Peckinpah's production problems stemmed from his conflicts with the higher-ups. With only two, small-scale features behind him, Peckinpah may very well have overreached himself on a major project like *Dundee*. Jim Silke, one of Peckinpah's regular collaborators, thought as much. "*Dundee* was a mess," Silke said. "Peckinpah was lost on *Dundee*."[81] At one point, the production had fallen two weeks behind schedule and as much as $1 million over budget. Afraid the film was becoming a "runaway," Columbia considered firing Peckinpah and finishing the film with another director. Heston backed Peckinpah, and the director was allowed to finish the shoot.[82]

Peckinpah called his two-hour, forty-four-minute cut of *Major Dundee* "possibly the best picture I've made in my life."[83] Columbia did not agree. Despite Peckinpah's pleas to put the film in front of a test audience, Columbia and Bresler released the director from the project and recut the film.[84] "In all, fifty-five minutes of material that Peckinpah considered essential were removed or never included in the first place."[85] The film stands as "a dramatic composite and compression of several things that either did happen or might have happened."[86] When Peckinpah saw the release print, he "requested that his name be removed from the credits, claiming it was not 'the picture I made.' "[87]

Film historian John Baxter wrote that of Peckinpah's films of the 1960s, *Major Dundee* "most impressively balances poetry and realism, unmarred even by producer Jerry Bresler."[88] This was a decidedly minority view. Reactions to the film were generally negative and many specifically targeted the weakness of Senta Berger's role:

- "The script begins traditionally and therefore well. . . . Later when the authors feel that romance is overdue, the story gets wobbly and slow. . . . The producer's wish to include Miss Berger is very understandable; but credibility is not a component of her role."[89]
- "*Major Dundee* . . . left me with the impression that I had seen a movie of no distinction whatsoever—crude . . . its plot meandering over a florid landscape of clichés. . . . What's this beautiful girl doing there with all those starving Mexicans? She's for Major Dundee, during certain interludes in the chasing and fighting."[90]
- "The intrusion of an alien love interest plays havoc with the realistic context."[91]

"For Peckinpah . . . the experience sharpened his distaste for producers," which had been snowballing since his first film, "and refined his rebellion toward any type of authority."[92] "Already paranoid, he was even more convinced that producers were not a necessary evil—they were just plain evil . . . his attitudes and behavior were forever affected by *Major Dundee*."[93] Certainly Peckinpah's next project did little to discourage either his view of producers or his growing reputation as an uncontrollable maverick.

Producer Martin Ransohoff next hired him to direct his Depression-era tale of high-stakes poker players, *The Cincinnati Kid* (1965). As Ransohoff viewed the film as "a gunfight with a deck of cards," the film—Peckinpah's first non-Western, would provide an appropriate genre transition for the director.[94] Ransohoff and Peckinpah ran afoul of each other almost immediately. Peckinpah wanted to shoot the film in black-and-white and didn't want to cast Sharon Tate (Ransohoff's protégée at the time) in the role later won by Tuesday Weld.[95]

In the first few days of shooting, Peckinpah filmed "a damn good riot scene, then another long scene between Rip Torn and a Negro prostitute in bed, and that was it."[96] Learning of a nude scene shot with an unknown black actress that Ransohoff felt needless, the producer declared that Peckinpah was making "a dirty movie."[97] This time, a producer would not wait for Peckinpah to finish shooting; four days into *Kid*, Peckinpah was fired.

★   ★   ★

"For the better part of the next two years, Peckinpah would find it virtually impossible to obtain work within the film industry."[98] It would be even longer before he was offered the opportunity to direct a feature. Phone calls to producers considering him warned that Peckinpah was "difficult."[99] "By his own reckoning he was bankrupt, his [second] marriage in ruins, and he was writing under five different pseudonyms, sometimes new material, other times peddling old scripts."[100] Of these projects, only *The Glory Guys* (1965), a routine cavalry-versus-Indians tale, and *Villa Rides!* (1968), a pedestrian Mexican Revolution adventure rewritten by Robert Towne, made it to the screen.[101]

He was, however, able to secure directing work in television. The most important of these jobs occurred in 1966 when producer Daniel Melnick went to Peckinpah with the offer of an adaptation of Katherine Anne Porter's novella, "Noon Wine." Peckinpah said, "Don't you know that no one will hire me?" Melnick replied, "Yes, that's one of the things which makes you attractive."[102]

The announcement in the trade papers promoting the production and Peckinpah's role as writer/director sparked a round of warning phone calls. "Melnick got calls from people who not only had never worked with me," said Peckinpah, "but who didn't even know me. They all tried to warn him off me."[103] Melnick stuck with his choice. With Peckinpah's adaptation "enthusiastically" endorsed by Ms. Porter herself, Peckinpah fashioned "one of the most highly acclaimed hours of television in the medium's [then] short history."[104, 105] Melnick considered the finished work "a wonderful job."[106]

Both *The Hollywood Reporter* and *Variety* touted the program, with *Reporter*'s John Mahoney writing:

> [They] could have found no director so committed to an under-
> standing of the period. . . . Peckinpah's realization emerged as one
> of the finest hours of many a season, something of a milestone in
> location color videotape production, and one of the few TV mo-
> ments which might be termed poetic. . . . While Peckinpah was
> faithful to the original text, he amplified it . . . and devised connec-
> tive tissue and additional scenes which might well have been dic-
> tated by Miss Porter herself.[107]

Peckinpah's peers agreed. He was nominated by the Writer's Guild for Best Television Screenplay Adaptation and also by the Director's Guild for Best Television Directing.

On the basis of his work on "Noon Wine," Peckinpah was again asked to direct a feature film. The invitation came from Kenneth Hyman, new president of Warner Bros.-Seven Arts.[108] Peckinpah's executive producer on his first Warners project was Philip Feldman. The film was *The Wild Bunch*.

Pike Bishop (William Holden) leads a band of outlaws—Dutch (Ernest Borgnine), Lyle and Tector Gorch (Warren Oates, Ben Johnson), sometime Mexican revolutionary Angel (Jaime Sanchez), and old-timer Sykes (Edmond O'Brien)—through the American Southwest c. 1910. The Bunch flees to Mexico after an attempted robbery goes wrong when they are ambushed by a posse of bounty hunters led by Deke Thornton (Robert Ryan). Thornton had ridden with Pike years before and is leading the posse to secure a parole from prison. At the Mexican village of Aqua Verde, the Bunch meet up with Mapache (Emilio Fernandez), a self-styled "general" fighting for Juerta during the Mexican Revolution. Mapache, in turn, is being "managed" by two German agents working to foment discontent against America in Mexico. Mapache hires the Bunch to hijack a rail shipment of U.S. Army rifles. Angel at first resists. He has already killed his fiancé for running off with Mapache, but agrees to participate in the theft when the Bunch promise him some of the rifles for his rebel associates. Thornton has anticipated the raid on the train but is unsuccessful at stopping it. In fact, Army guards mistakenly think that Thornton and his bounty hunters are part of the hijack. When the Bunch go to trade the rifles for their payment, Mapache takes Angel prisoner for taking his share of the rifles, his dead fiancé's mother having informed on him. Thornton's bounty hunters ambush Sykes. Pike, looking for safe haven, leads the Bunch back to Aqua Verde where the town is raucously celebrating Mapache's new rifles. Part of the celebration is the torturing of Angel. Pike offers his gold to Mapache for Angel's return, but Mapache refuses. Pike and the Gorch brothers retreat to a bordello while Dutch sulks outside. Rising from his self-pity, Pike leads the Bunch against Mapache in a suicidal bid to take back Angel. When the shooting is done and the Bunch are dead, Thornton leads his posse into the village where they pack up the bodies for bounty. Thornton refuses to return home with them. The bounty hunters are ambushed by Mexican rebels led by the escaped Sykes. Thornton rides off with Sykes to join the rebels.

The Wild Bunch is indelibly stamped on the collective cineaste conscience as one of two definitive Peckinpah's films (the other being *Ride the High Country*). Yet, like that earlier film, Peckinpah came onto the project as a hired gun. He was given a script by Walon Green, although he would do enough rewriting to earn a coscreen-writer credit. Still, while Peckinpah made "a number of noteworthy changes," the script remained substantially Green's.[109] The film would be Peckinpah's long-awaited feature career breakthrough. A substantial commercial successes, *Bunch* earned $12 million in its first year alone, producing enough revenue to keep "the studio in operation for a year."[110]

The film was also a stylistic landmark for Peckinpah. Stunt choreographer, and later film director, Buddy Van Horn, who had worked with Peckinpah on earlier films, noted how the director had rethought filming action sequences. "[When] he first started out, [Peckinpah] had to rely on a lot of people to help him out," said Van Horn. "[On] his earlier films . . . he would photograph the action eight miles away, and it never had any impact. But he learned. . . . *The Wild Bunch* is a classic."[111] His use of slow motion during scenes of violence, while not new to films, was handled in an exceptionally deft manner. "[He] used it better," said critic Andrew Sarris. "The combination of frenzied cutting and the slow motion and the blood and balletic grace of people dying carried it to the ultimate level."[112]

Film historian William K. Everson took the opposite view. Repulsed by the extreme violence of the film, he described the ultimate effect as "revulsion and nausea."[113] But this time, the negatives—like Everson's—were in the minority:

- "A brilliantly made, thought-provoking movie. . . . It seems inappropriate to talk of *The Wild Bunch* as a beautiful film. But, in fact, is beautifully made . . . [Peckinpah] makes movies which are real movies, which ripple with power and crackle with energy."[114]
- "One of the few American films of recent memory that doesn't seem to have been concocted by a market research computer. . . . Peckinpah is wildly original and individualistic."[115]
- "The promise of *Ride the High Country* has been fulfilled in what may someday emerge as one of the most important records of the mood of our times and one of the most important films of the era."[116]

In relating the film to the turbulence of the late 1960s, critic Richard Shickel touched on a point that cropped up in a number of reviews. Many writers turned their pieces into position papers on the issue of film violence and its effect on American culture. Over the years, as the shock of Peckinpah's slow-motion gun battle "ballets" wore off, the aesthetic estimation of the film seemed to rise still further. Books and articles would cite the film as a milestone in Peckinpah's development as a director, in the Western genre, and as one of the more significant films of the time, describing it as, "Extremely original, exciting"[117]; "magnificently moving"[118]; a "masterpiece"[119]; and "a masterwork of directorial craft and vision."[120]

Beginning the project, Peckinpah held the studio execs who had rescued him from a de facto blacklist in the highest esteem. "I find them to be very creative, tough, stimulating and damn fine people," he said in an interview before the completion of *Bunch*.[121] However, during the postproduction period the relationship soured.

Peckinpah wanted to trim down episodes of violence more than

Warners.[122] Warners went on to make additional cuts although it is difficult to ascertain how much was taken out of the film. One source reported that the film was previewed in Kansas City at 190 minutes in length; 148 minutes in Los Angeles; 140 minutes in Manhattan; 135 minutes in Washington, D.C.[123] Another source puts the Kansas City preview at 150 minutes.[124]

Even revival prints of the film differed substantially. Since the film's initial 1969 release, at least three different prints circulated, not including the severely edited print prepared for network television. One missing sequence concerns a flashback romance between Pike Bishop and a married woman. Both are caught in her bedroom by the woman's husband. She is killed and Bishop wounded by the husband.[125] "This flashback also served to contravene a general objection often lodged against *The Wild Bunch* to the effect that all the women characters are unsympathetic."[126] The first opportunity an audience had to see the intact, uncut film since its first previews was the twenty-fifth anniversary rerelease of *The Wild Bunch*.

The fallout from Peckinpah's arguments with Warners over the reediting had an unfortunate impact on his next film, also made for Warners: *The Ballad of Cable Hogue.*

Prospector Cable Hogue (Jason Robards) is abandoned in the desert by his two partners, Taggert and Bowen (Strother Martin, L. Q. Jones). Hogue wanders through the desert, praying aloud to God, and finally stumbles across a well on the stage route between two towns. Hogue talks one of the local bankers into financing his claim. Hogue also becomes enamored of Hildy (Stella Stevens), the town prostitute. Hogue prospers at the well, selling food and water to passing stagecoaches. Hildy moves in with him but leaves when Hogue refuses to marry her and take her away from the desert. Hogue wants to stay, sure that eventually his two betrayers will appear. When they do, Hogue kills Bowen but spares Taggert, no longer feeling the need for vengeance. Hildy returns, now a wealthy widow from San Francisco. Hogue bequeaths the well to Taggert and prepares to leave with Hildy. Before they can leave, Hildy's automobile accidentally runs over Hogue. He is buried on the grounds of his stage station in his beloved desert.

The Ballad of Cable Hogue, Peckinpah's sole romantic film (romantic comedy, actually), is the only film the director initiated in his career and would be viewed as "Peckinpah's most personal and lyrical tribute to the West," a "neglected . . . masterpiece," and, by critic Vincent Canby, one of the ten best films of 1970.[127, 128, 129] Yet this, the first film that could have broadened Peckinpah's reputation far beyond the action genre, disappeared from theaters in two weeks when released in March 1970.[130]

Warners' tolerance for Peckinpah had worn thin in the fighting over the reediting of *The Wild Bunch*. When *Hogue* ran over schedule and over budget—mainly because of weather problems—the relationship between the director and the studio eroded further still.[131] Warners previewed an unfinished cut of the film to distributors. The print shown was a half-hour longer than Peckinpah had intended the finished film to be and did not include a finished soundtrack or score. Distributors came out of the screening convinced the film would do little business.[132] Warners used their reaction to justify their handling of the film's release. They "dumped [the film] on the market [with a] promotion campaign [that] seemed designed to keep filmgoers away."[133]

The box-office death of *Cable Hogue* would become another part of the Peckinpah legend, yet another instance of an artist's mishandling by studio proles. But while Warners' decision to "dump" *Cable Hogue* may have been an easy one to make in light of their now-eroded relationship with the director, to give the devil its due, the studio's reservations about the film may not have been totally unwarranted. As we saw in chapter 2, the more profitable trend for the major studios had been away from small, personal, sweet-natured films like *Cable Hogue* in favor of films like—ironically—*The Wild Bunch*.

Even under better circumstances, the film would have been a difficult title to market. Here was a genre—the Western—that appealed to men, wrapped around a story—a sweet and funny romance—that generally drew women. And even as a romance it provided the not-necessarily-audience-pleasing twist of a title character who dies, rather than the romantic leads winding up together. Additionally, neither the name of Jason Robards nor Stella Stevens carried much weight at the box office. It is also worth bearing in mind that this was the same studio that just three years earlier had nearly fumbled the release of *Bonnie and Clyde,* completely miscalculating the film's ability to draw an audience.[134]

A film like *Cable Hogue,* if it were to find an audience, would be through a carefully nurtured limited release, with the studio babying the film through the art house circuit in the hopes of garnering positive press and good word of mouth to drive business. But the distribution apparatus of a major studio is like an overpowered racecar that only runs well when it is running all out. Major studios know how to distribute major films, but for them, a small picture like *Cable Hogue* requires more effort than it's worth. It would not be until the 1990s when several of the majors would set up specialty divisions like Columbia/Tri-Star's Sony Classics and 20th Century Fox's Fox Classics to take advantage of the small-scale successes managed by the growing number of successful small production/distribution companies like Miramax. *Cable Hogue* was the wrong picture at the wrong time. Two years later, despite the presence of one of the world's most popular stars, many of these same debits would cripple another nonviolent Peckinpah film at the box office—*Junior Bonner.*

The critical praise for his last two films and the commercial success of *The Wild Bunch* had made Peckinpah a "hot" director, but had damned him at the same time as a director of Westerns and/or action films. Author Joan Didion and her husband, writer John Gregory Dunne, wanted Peckinpah to turn her novel of Hollywood—*Play It As It Lays*—into a film. Unfortunately, "No one else could see 'Bloody Sam' behind the camera on a neurasthenic film about Hollywood."[135] Peckinpah was well on the way to being typed as an action director.

Daniel Melnick, looking to produce his first feature, asked his "Noon Wine" colleague to direct what would be Peckinpah's first modern-day film, a screen story based on Gordon William's novel *The Siege of Trencher's Farm.* In its final form, as *Straw Dogs,* the project would be the most controversial of Peckinpah's career. The film was a contemporary "worm turns" story of an astral mathematician (Dustin Hoffman) who retreats to the hometown of his English wife (Susan George) in the Cornwall countryside to avoid the social upheaval going on in the United States at the time. Eventually, the mathematician is forced to defend his home against a band of vigilantes after a child molester and ends up killing them all.

What provoked a storm of criticism and debate was a rape scene in which Susan George, after being slapped into submission by an ex-boyfriend, is sexually assaulted while her husband has been left stranded on the moors on a "snipe hunt" arranged by the ex and his thuggish mates. But what begins as an attack evolves into an act that George seems to enjoy. However, once completed, a second man brutally forces himself on the woman.

Despite being told to cast Susan George against his wishes, and having to cut five minutes from the film to avoid an MPAA X-rating, Melnick and Peckinpah managed to maintain the productive collaboration that had produced "Noon Wine."[136, 137] After the production wrapped, Peckinpah went to Melnick and told him, "you're the only good producer I've ever had. You're the only creative producer I've ever worked with. You're the only producer I'd ever trust with my film."[138]

Straw Dogs went on to make more money than *The Wild Bunch,* but Peckinpah had lost some of the critical support he had gained with the earlier film. A *Filmfacts* canvass showed the major critics almost evenly split on the film, in contrast to the overwhelming support *Bunch* had received.[139]

Released in 1972, the film—along with such other controversial works as *Dirty Harry* and *A Clockwork Orange*—"touched the newly sensitive nerve of violence toward women, sexual and otherwise."[140] In the eyes of Peckinpah's critics, the film epitomized the macho "obsession behind most of [his] other films."[141] "It gets at the roots of the fantasies that men carry from earliest childhood," wrote Pauline Kael. "It confirms their secret fears and prejudices that women respect only brutes; it confirms the male insanity that there is no such thing as rape. The movie taps a sexual fascism—that is what machismo is— that is so much a part of folklore that it's on the underside of many an educated consciousness and is rampant among the uneducated."[142] Molly Haskell described the film as typical of those movies negatively responding to the women's liberation movement, and referred to the film's treatment of women as "violent abuse and brutalization."[143]

★   ★   ★

It would be ingenuous to say that Peckinpah's major problem was that he made the wrong movie at the wrong time with *Straw Dogs,*

but the film did fall into an unfortunate confluence of hostile circumstances that would color his career thereafter. With *Cable Hogue* having been a nonevent because of Warners' handling, a great deal of
critical attention was drawn to *Straw Dogs* to see if Peckinpah was, or
was not, in show business vernacular, a "one-hit wonder." In a year
boasting Woody Allen's farce *Everything You Always Wanted To Know
About Sex But Were Afraid To Ask,* the elegiac Western *Jeremiah Johnson,* Peter Bogdanovich's homage to screwball comedy with *What's
Up Doc?,* the all-star disaster melodrama *The Poseidon Adventure,* and
the screen adaptation of Anthony Shaffer's drawing room "who-
dunit" play *Sleuth,* Peckinpah's strident film was sure to stand out.

At the same time, Peckinpah's work was to get, for him, an unprecedented amount of attention, as the feminist movement was in
a phase of great polarization.[144] The rising feminist sensibility would
inevitably cross paths with Peckinpah's film. "Ultimately, the impact
and image of *Straw Dogs* grew out of proportion to anything Peckinpah ever intended. He was making a statement about violence in man
. . . but people saw it as much more."[145]

For Peckinpah, the negative feminist viewpoint was yet another
authority imposing restrictions. His response was typical. He wrote a
letter to Kael threatening to contact his lawyer over her use of the
term "fascist."[146] He responded to the feminist stand with such comments as, "I can't see why they have to make such assholes of themselves over the issue."[147] Certainly the filmmaker's personal conduct—his drinking, brawling, womanizing, hunting, and endless
combinations of same—did little to dilute the image of a macho heel.

The director also had an unfortunate tendency toward posturing
during interviews.[148] He was an unredeemable provocateur "doing
something frightening or infuriating just to get a rise out of people,
to see how they would respond."[149] Friend and critic John Bryson
said that, "He loved to stir things up and see what happened."[150] It
then becomes difficult to say how earnest Peckinpah was in tossing
off interview responses like, "There are two kinds of women. There
are women and then there's pussy. One of the advantages of being a
celebrity is that a lot of attractive pussy that wasn't available to you
before suddenly become available"[151]; or, "Somebody asked if I hit
women and I said, 'Of course I do. I believe in equal rights for

women' "[152]; and there was this exchange during an interview following the release of *Bring Me the Head of Alfredo Garcia:*

> Q: The female lead in your new movie
> belongs to a whole Peckinpah line of
> women who enjoy rape.
> Peckinpah: Well, most women do.
> Q: You'll get differences of opinion on that.
> Peckinpah: Not from women.[153]

Heartfelt or not, his "kidding-on-the-square and posing undercut the impact of the sober-minded words he had to say about his work and his vision. Which were you supposed to take seriously: the thoughtful philosophizing or the seemingly stewed self-parody?"[154]

In his later years, Peckinpah's contentiousness grew worse as his public and private image blurred together. Viewed as an icon of machismo, of being a brawling and profane individual, or looking for a fight or an argument wherever he could find one, he *became* that person. According to his nephew David Peckinpah, "after a while, he wasn't able to stop playing the part of Sam Peckinpah."[155]

★   ★   ★

Given a choice, Hollywood will take a badly reviewed movie that makes money over one that earns plaudits but few dollars. The debate over *Straw Dogs* did not offset a profitable balance sheet and Peckinpah was soon at work again with another contemporary piece, though one set in the modern-day West: *Junior Bonner* (1972). A pastoral version of *The Wild Bunch, Bonner* replaced the earlier film's gunfighters looking for one last score with a fading rodeo star searching for a last triumph. It was considered an atypical film for Peckinpah, having, in the words of producer Joe Wizan, "no action, no shooting, no guns."[156] Sexual content was restricted, as critic Roger Ebert wrote, to co-stars "[Robert] Preston and [Ida] Lupino [as Bonner's divorced parents] engaging in some nostalgic and yet suspicious memories, and then finally (in one of the most tender love scenes I can remember) going upstairs to one of the rooms over the saloon to make love (offscreen) for the first time in years."[157]

Unfortunately, the theater circuit at the time was glutted with rodeo films: *J. W. Coop, The Honkers,* and *When Legends Die.* In fact, *Bonner* was the third rodeo film released inside of a month. It may be that, considering the major box-office trends of the time, none may have done well under better circumstances. Be that as it may, all failed at the box office.[158]

Still, *Bonner* star Steve McQueen and Peckinpah had gotten along well enough for the star to pick the director to helm his next project, *The Getaway.* Another contemporary piece set out West, it was the story of a couple-on-the-run, with McQueen and Ali MacGraw playing a husband and wife bank robbery team heading for Mexico ahead of the police, their betraying mobster bosses, and other greedy members of their heist team.

Although the typical critical response was that the film was "disinterested, mechanical," the film would be the only one of similar stories released that year—*Sugarland Express, Badlands,* and *Thieves Like Us* were the others—to hit it big at the box office.[159, 160] In fact, grossing $20 million, *The Getaway* would be the biggest commercial hit of Peckinpah's career.[161] Screenwriter Walter Hill gave a fair share of the credit for the film's success to Peckinpah, saying, "[Anything] that happens to be good in *The Getaway* has a lot more to do with Sam [Peckinpah] than it does with me."[162]

Though the shoot went relatively smoothly, the relationship between Peckinpah and McQueen—whose company was producing the film at Paramount—deteriorated. "According to reports, McQueen not only re-edited Peckinpah's final cut but discarded the original score composed by Jerry Fielding [who had scored *The Wild Bunch* and earned an Oscar nomination for *Straw Dogs*] and commissioned Quincy Jones to write a new one. Consequently, Peckinpah repudiated the release print and went as far as demanding his name be removed from the credits."[163]

The period 1969–1972 would, in good ways and bad, define Peckinpah for the moviemaking trade. Of the five films he directed in that period, the three box-office hits—each making more money than the one before—had been films of action and violence. The critical standing of *Hogue* and *Bonner* did not offset their box-office failure. They may have removed doubt that Peckinpah was capable of making a good film without resorting to graphic violence and sex, but the worth of that opinion was established by the box office: zero. Following *The Getaway,* Peckinpah would never again be given the chance to say something on screen without an exchange of gunfire.

MGM producer Gordon Carroll approached Peckinpah to direct what would be the filmmaker's first period Western since *Cable Hogue* three years earlier. *Pat Garrett and Billy the Kid* was a screenplay by Rudolph Wurlitzer, "a young novelist who had written *Two-Lane Blacktop,* a film Peckinpah admired."[164] The story would give Peckinpah a chance to revisit the Pat Garrett/William Bonney source material that had been behind his first script, "The Authentic Death of Hendry Jones." Even though the film would be for old nemesis MGM, Louis Vogel—the Loews chief who had seen to the premature box-office death of *Ride the Hide Country*—was gone. Auspiciously, the head of production for MGM was Daniel Melnick.

James Coburn played Sheriff Pat Garrett who, now concerned about his security as he grows older in a settling West, has been co-opted by the business and political powers in 1881 New Mexico to hunt down his old friend Billy the Kid (Kris Kristofferson) whom they consider a threat to the business future of the state. When The Kid ignores Garrett's warning to leave the territory, Garrett captures him and holds him in jail to await trial. The Kid escapes, killing two deputies. Garrett begins a pursuit that takes him through his haunts from his days riding with The Kid, and leaves one after another of their old gang dead. Eventually, Garrett finds The Kid at a ranch near Fort Sumner. Garrett waits on the porch swing in the night until Billy finishes making love with his girlfriend Maria (Rita Coolidge). When Billy steps outside for some fresh air, Garrett kills him. His mission finished, Garrett rides off.[165]

Despite all the promising components that went into the production, the film would send Peckinpah "into a tailspin, both personally and professionally, from which his career never recovered."[166] The film was one that, in the words of editor Roger Spottiswoode, "was destroyed by circumstances and a studio."[167] But while the popular myth among Peckinpah fans is that *Pat Garrett* was ruined by the studio, Peckinpah's hands were not completely clean.

Peckinpah's work style was more improvisatory than other directors. He did not storyboard his films or diagram shots. In fact, he rarely seemed to be sure how a scene was to be shot until he was on the set.[168] Sometimes this produced cinema gold. One of the most notable scenes from *The Wild Bunch* is when the Bunch leaves Angel's village on their way to their destiny at Aqua Verde. According to first assistant director Cliff Coleman, it was a scene "Peckinpah created on his feet . . . [the scene] developed by stages; [Peckinpah] had no idea in the beginning that he was going to . . . stage this farewell."[169]

But this methodology could also put a script in a constant state of flux. Peckinpah demanded rewrites from Wurlitzer continually during shooting. "[As] the demands for more and more changes mounted, Wurlitzer became less and less pleased, and once complained to a reporter, 'There's *no* script left.' "[170] By the end of shooting, Peckinpah was asking for script changes almost daily.[171]

Peckinpah's problems with producer Carroll echoed those with Jerry Bresler ten years earlier on *Major Dundee*. Producer and director never settled on a shooting schedule, even after production commenced. MGM continued to insist on a schedule short of what Peckinpah felt was the minimum required.[172]

Peckinpah's battles with Carroll would pale next to those with James Aubrey, then head of MGM. Aubrey had come to MGM in 1969 and rapidly instituted strict cost cutting to try to turn the debt-ridden studio around. His conduct of MGM's cinematic affairs had earned him a reputation as a "philistine" among directors even before his dealings with Peckinpah.[173] Aubrey and Peckinpah immediately clashed over the director's concept of the film. Peckinpah wanted an introspective work; MGM "wanted a Sam Peckinpah picture awash with action."[174]

"On one side was Peckinpah, demanding to be supported and left alone to make his movie his way; on the other side were Aubrey and MGM, pressuring Carroll to rein the director in, to cut corners wherever possible." Peckinpah reacted predictably. The more that Carroll "tried to control him, the more Peckinpah went in the opposite direction." According to *Pat Garrett* stuntman Gary Combs, "Nobody was going to tell Sam what to do. The minute he fell behind, the producer would want him to speed up. . . . The more they would push, the slower Sam would go."[175]

The film finished shooting three weeks over schedule. Almost immediately MGM informed the director that he would have less than two months—a fairly short time for a major film—to complete the editing that had already begun during production.[176] Peckinpah delivered a 121-minute cut and called it, "the best film I ever made." The studio disagreed and recut the film. When Peckinpah saw the result, he claimed that MGM had removed "the heart of the film."[177] Peckinpah went as far as to sue the studio on several counts. "Among other things, the suit demanded either that the cuts be restored or that his name be removed from above the title . . . as he did not . . . consider the released version his own."[178]

Among the missing scenes was one between Garrett and his wife depicting their marriage as an emotionally dead union; Garrett has married because it is expected of him, not out of love.[179] Other cuts concerned the relationship between The Kid and Maria. In describing how the courtship scenes between the two characters had been cut down, Coolidge said, "She thought all that was left of her role was 'like a groupie.' "[180] This would account for misperceptions by some critics that Maria was another of Peckinpah's movie whores.[181] That Maria, a role with no dialogue and only a few minutes of screen time in which she exchanges shy glances with The Kid, would be considered a prostitute says something about the predisposition of Peckinpah's critics.

But again, as during the *Pat Garrett* shoot, and hearkening back to his own failings on *Major Dundee,* Peckinpah was not guiltless here. Spottiswoode said of Peckinpah's first cut of the film that, "There was no narrative thrust," that the film was "bloated and incohesive," which would seem a natural consequence of the endless meddling with the script. At a private screening of Peckinpah's cut attended by several critics and Martin Scorsese, Scorsese took the minority view that the film was "brilliant," while critic Pauline Kael spoke for the majority saying she thought it "unfinished, very rough. . . . There were long scenes that sort of drifted around." At a preview of Peckinpah's cut, "the film still didn't work; the audience was restless." It was at that point that Aubrey took the film away from Peckinpah.[182] Upon its theatrical release, the film, now disowned by Peckinpah, was a commercial and critical failure.[183]

Peckinpah followed with the macabre *Bring Me the Head of Alfredo Garcia.* Set in contemporary Mexico, *Alfredo Garcia* is the story of Bennie (Warren Oates), an expatriate American piano bar player who, with his prostitute girlfriend Elita (Isela Vega), is on a quest for the aforementioned head for which a $10,000 bounty has been offered by a South American *jefe* whose daughter was impregnated by Garcia.

The film's "most infamous" scene resurrected the issues of *Straw Dogs.* Bennie and Elita, camping by the road one night, are set upon by two bikers. Elita walks off with one of the bikers (Kris Kristofferson). Without a word from the biker, she kneels in front of him and begins to disrobe. Before things progress any further, Bennie escapes from the other biker and kills both invaders. Critics Kathleen Murphy and Richard T. Jameson described Elita's submissions as "a peculiar sense of complicity between rapist and victim—that, stated in those terms merely, would appear to justify the most outraged charges against the director as a male chauvinist pig."[184]

The film did not last long enough to sustain the controversy. Received with nearly unanimous hostility,[185] Peckinpah's name helped the offbeat film bring in "a hefty $578,596 by the end of its fourth week [in release], and rose to number nineteen before sinking into . . . oblivion."[186]

★   ★   ★

Peckinpah's career now began to pay the price for his accumulated professional transgressions, industry ill will, and the icing of the back-to-back failures of *Pat Garrett* and *Alfredo Garcia.* If Peckinpah had not been fired from *The Cincinnati Kid* and had, instead, turned out a film as popular as the Norman Jewison version . . . Or, if *Play It As It Lays* had come to a profitable fruition . . . Or if *The Ballad of Cable Hogue* and/or *Junior Bonner* had been even moderate successes . . . Any one of these alternative fates might have given the filmmaking community reason to consider Sam Peckinpah something other than an action director.

The typecasting was not insurmountable. A film like *The Wild Bunch* that wedded the elements of Western action with fine filmmaking could, possibly, refire his career as had happened in 1969, but Peckinpah could find no such project nor did he have the creative ability to draft one on his own that could attract backing (he could be an effective cowriter, as he'd shown on *The Wild Bunch* and *Straw Dogs,* but never in his career did he direct an original feature screenplay). Peckinpah also lacked the commercial clout or financial resources to initiate an independent project.

Fine's biography tells of Peckinpah repeatedly pitching projects, including Westerns, for the remainder of his career without success. As a genre, the Western had passed out of vogue. Only a handful of commercially important period Westerns would appear between Clint Eastwood's *The Outlaw Josey Wales* (1976) and his Oscar-winning *Unforgiven* (1992): 1985's *Pale Rider* and *Silverado,* both only moderate successes, and *Young Guns* (1988) and its sequel, *Young Guns II* (1990).

Peckinpah's professional difficulties stemmed from more than changing tastes. Of the eleven directorial assignments (including *The Cincinnati Kid)* he'd had since 1974, the director had clashed with the producers and/or studios behind eight of them. Fewer producers were willing to deal with a director so volatile and intractable, with a reputation for going over schedule and over budget, and with only a checkered box-office record. With all of these factors working against him, Peckinpah was pushed outside the Hollywood mainstream to find work.

In 1975 there was *The Killer Elite,* a contemporary espionage thriller done for the producers of *Alfredo Garcia* and Arthur Lewis, a newcomer to film producing.[187] "There was a great deal of tension between Peckinpah and his producers, resulting in a film that is uneven."[188] Costar Burt Young would later say that the script by the normally capable Stirling Silliphant was not what it should have been. "I rewrote half the script," Young said. "It was that faulty that they would take a baloney like me and listen to him."[189]

His next project came from German producer Wolf Hartwig: the World War II Eastern Front combat drama *Cross of Iron.* The film was Hartwig's first attempt at a major production. Hartwig never secured sufficient financing and Peckinpah spent the production battling ever-tightening budget restrictions.[190]

The film was picked up for distribution by Sir Lew Grade who, at that time, was best known for bringing "The Muppet Show" to American TV. *Cross* was to be part of an ambitious slate of feature films Grade was compiling as an entrée into American film distribution. Grade's priorities did not mesh with Peckinpah's. "He doesn't want to talk about the artistic aspects of the movies," said Stuart Rosenberg, director of another Grade release, *Voyage of the Damned* (1976), "and he doesn't want to hear you talk about it." Sir "Low Grade," as he'd been dubbed, was hardly one to argue. "I'm not trying to teach morals or philosophy to people, just entertain them."[191]

The film fell afoul of the MPAA and had to be cut by eleven minutes to avoid an X-rating.[192] Overseas, *Cross of Iron* did well enough to warrant a sequel (*Breakthrough* [1978]) not directed by Peckinpah and not receiving a theatrical release in the United States. The domestic return for *Cross*, however, was dismal.

EMI was another British company looking to enter the U.S. film market. They had planned a range of large-scale films including Michael Cimino's *The Deer Hunter* (1978). EMI, which had put up completion money for *Cross of Iron,* hired Peckinpah to direct *Convoy*. A modern-day tale of rebel truckers set in the American Southwest, the film was inspired by a 1975 hit song by C. W. McCall.[193] Although *Convoy* did moderate business, the film put Peckinpah's artistic standing at it lowest ebb.[194]

The filmmaker did not work again for four years. When he again stepped behind a camera, the years of hard living, drinking, drug abuse, tumultuous personal entanglements, and a faulty heart (he had worn a pacemaker since the 1970s) had taken their roll. "[He] looked shockingly frail . . . his skull barely papered over by fine-drawn skin. Suddenly very small, he seemed to be holding himself together by sheer will."[195] Having already suffered one severe heart attack, Peckinpah approached what would be his final film "obviously husbanding his strength" and looking older than his fifty-six years.[196]

There were signs he'd begun to rein in his more destructive habits. He had stopped his cocaine use and was controlling his alcohol intake.[197] His attitudes were mellowing. "Agents and executives like to be creators and filmmakers—and they're not," he said in an interview, but uncharacteristically gave them the benefit of the doubt saying, "But sometimes the damnedest things happens: they're *right.*"[198]

Peckinpah supporters at first had high hopes when he went to work again on a major production: the screen adaptation of best-selling author Robert Ludlum's thriller *The Osterman Weekend*. On closer examination the omens were less auspicious. Again, Peckinpah was working for producers attempting their first major film.[199] "Neither he nor his admirers have any illusions about *The Osterman*

Weekend. . . . The book, as [Peckinpah] himself politely put it, 'is not among Ludlum's best' . . . the project is not one Peckinpah originated, or would have chosen to. It was, however, the least despicable option available."[200] Peckinpah's own dissatisfaction with the project was evidenced when he refused his right to a proprietary credit.[201] The film was a critical and box-office failure.

Though *Osterman* was his last film, there was a touching coda to his career when he was hired to direct a pair of music videos in conjunction with the release of Julian Lennon's hit debut *Valotte* album.[202] One of the songs was "Too Late For Goodbyes," which, in Peckinpah's hands, became a bittersweet farewell to Julian's Beatle father, John. The concerned parties were so pleased with the work that there was even discussion between Lennon's management and Peckinpah about a possible "rockumentary" about Julian, but the project never came to pass.[203] In filming the video for "Too Late For Goodbyes," Peckinpah had unwittingly filmed his own swan song. In December 1984, two months short of his sixtieth birthday, David Samuel Peckinpah died of heart failure.

★   ★   ★

Raised in the rustic California north country, Sam Peckinpah envisioned himself at one with the Western pioneer spirit. That sensibility distinguished his work and eventually brought him to the forefront of American film by the late 1960s. At the same time, the dynamics of his dysfunctional upbringing left him with a hair-trigger hostility toward discipline and criticism. His compulsion to posture and antagonize blurred the lines, in the eyes of his critics, between the less savory aspects of Peckinpah's personal character and elements of his work, even when that work did not originate with him. As a result, through the latter part of his career he stood branded as an indulgent promulgator of macho myth-making, including machismo's incorporated sexist view of women. It was a view held so strongly by some critics that—as we shall see in the next chapter—they approached the filmmaker and his work already negatively predisposed, sometimes to the point where they interpreted his films in arguable fashion, and even saw things on screen that weren't there.

After a certain point in his career, there was no way for Peckinpah to reconstruct his reputation and commercial viability. By the late 1970s, his abrasive conduct, his being typed as an action director, and the dwindling popularity of the genre that best displayed his strengths—the Western—had pushed him away from the opportunities that could offer him professional and artistic redemption.

NOTES

1. Henry James, *The Bostonians* (New York: Vintage Press, 1991), 350.
2. Marshall Fine, *Bloody Sam: The Life and Films of Sam Peckinpah* (New York: Donald I. Fine, 1991), 237.
3. Paul Seydor, *Peckinpah: The Western Films* (Urbana: Univ. of Illinois Press, 1980), 71.
4. William Murray, "Interview: Sam Peckinpah," *Playboy* (August 1972): 72.
5. Rita Parks, *The Western Hero in Film and Television: Mass Media Mythology*. Studies in Cinema. (Ann Arbor, Mich.: UMI Research Press, 1982), 115.
6. Seydor, *The Western Films*, 252.
7. Fine, *Bloody Sam*, 13.
8. Fine, *Bloody Sam*, 12–13.
9. Fine, *Bloody Sam*, 16.
10. Murray, "Interview," 72.
11. Quoted in Fine, *Bloody Sam,* 239.
12. Seydor, *The Western Films*, 253.
13. Fine, *Bloody Sam,* 15.
14. Fine, *Bloody Sam*, 14.
15. Fine, *Bloody Sam*, 18–19.
16. Fine, *Bloody Sam*, 58.
17. Fine, *Bloody Sam*, 19.
18. Fine, *Bloody Sam*, 362.
19. Quoted in Fine, *Bloody Sam,* 19.
20. Fine, *Bloody Sam*, 73–74.
21. Quoted in Fine, *Bloody Sam*, 175–76.
22. John Bryson, "Sam Peckinpah," *American Film* (April 1985): 22.
23. Quoted in Fine, *Bloody Sam*, 228.
24. Fine, *Bloody Sam*, 232.
25. Fine, *Bloody Sam,* 19.
26. Fine, *Bloody Sam,* 19.

27. Fine, *Bloody Sam,* 176.

28. Fine, *Bloody Sam,* 328–29.

29. Fine, *Bloody Sam,* 57.

30. Fine, *Bloody Sam,* 110.

31. Fine, *Bloody Sam,* 225.

32. Fine, *Bloody Sam,* 338–39.

33. Fine, *Bloody Sam,* 365.

34. Curt Gentry, *The Last Days of the Late, Great State of California* (New York: Putnam, 1968), 60–61.

35. Fine, *Bloody Sam,* 17.

36. Murray, "Interview," 69.

37. Quoted in Christopher Wicking and Tise Vahimagi, *The American Vein: Directors and Directions in Television* (New York: Dutton, 1979), 102.

38. Murray, "Interview," 69.

39. Fine, *Bloody Sam*, 324.

40. Quoted in Fine, *Bloody Sam,* 325.

41. Fine, *Bloody Sam,* 22–23.

42. Fine, *Bloody Sam,* 35–36.

43. Seydor, *The Western Films,* 4.

44. Wicking and Vahimagi, *The American Vein,* 103.

45. Garner Simmons, "Sam Peckinpah's Television Work," *Film Heritage* (Winter 1974–1975): 3.

46. Simmons, "Television Work," 4.

47. Wicking and Vahimagi, *The American Vein,* 104.

48. Seydor, *The Western Films,* 183.

49. *"The Deadly Companions,"* *Filmfacts* (January 1962): 331.

50. Fine, *Bloody Sam*, 59.

51. Seydor, *The Western Films,* 16.

52. Fine, *Bloody Sam*, 60.

53. Seydor, *The Western Films,* 18.

54. Fine, *Bloody Sam*, 61.

55. Seydor, *The Western Films,* 19.

56. Jim Kitsis, *Horizons West.* Cinema One (Bloomington: Indiana University Press, 1969), 153.

57. Seydor, *The Western Films,* 20.

58. Kitsis, *Horizons West*, 151.

59. Fine, *Bloody Sam*, 63.

60. *"Deadly Companions,"* *Filmfacts*, 331.

61. Simmons, "Television Work," 8.

62. William K. Everson, *A Pictorial History of the Western Film* (Secaucus, N.J.: Citadel Press, 1969), 225.

63. "*Deadly Companions,*" *Filmfacts,* 137.

64. Seydor, *The Western Films,* 24.

65. Seydor, *The Western Films,* 27.

66. Joseph Morgenstern, *The New York Herald Tribune,* quoted in "*Deadly Companions,*" *Filmfacts,* 138.

67. Howard Thompson, *The New York Times,* quoted in "*Ride the High Country,*" *Filmfacts* V (July 6, 1962): 138.

68. Dale, *Variety,* quoted in "*Ride the High Country,*" *Filmfacts,* 138.

69. *Time,* quoted in "*Ride the High Country,*" *Filmfacts,* 138.

70. Seydor, *The Western Films,* 44.

71. William Goldman, *Adventures in the Screen Trade: A Personal View of Hollywood and Screenwriting* (New York: Warner, 1983), 70.

72. Fine, *Bloody Sam,* 75.

73. Fine, *Bloody Sam,* 74.

74. Charlton Heston, *Charlton Heston: The Actor's Life—Journals 1956–1976* (New York: Pocket, 1979), 247.

75. Heston, *Journals,* 237.

76. Heston, *Journals,* 249.

77. Seydor, *The Western Films,* 49.

78. Seydor, *The Western Films,* 49.

79. Fine, *Bloody Sam,* 88.

80. Fine, *Bloody Sam,* 91.

81. Quoted in Fine, *Bloody Sam,* 91.

82. Fine, *Bloody Sam,* 92.

83. Quoted in Fine, *Bloody Sam,* 96.

84. Fine, *Bloody Sam,* 97.

85. Seydor, *The Western Films,* 52.

86. Seydor, *The Western Films,* 56.

87. "*Major Dundee,*" *Filmfacts* VIII (July 1965): 105.

88. John Baxter, *Sixty Years of Hollywood* (Cranbury, N.J.: A.S. Barnes, 1973), 228.

89. Stanley Kaufmann, *The New Republic,* quoted in "*Major Dundee,*" *Filmfacts* VIII, 106.

90. Hollis Alpert, *The Saturday Review,* quoted in "*Major Dundee,*" *Filmfacts* VIII, 106.

91. Eugene Archer, *The New York Times,* quoted in "*Major Dundee,*" *Filmfacts* VIII, 107.

92. Fine, *Bloody Sam,* 100.

93. Fine, *Bloody Sam,* 100.

94. Marshall Terrill, *Steve McQueen: Portrait of an American Rebel* (New York: Donald Fine, 1993), 112.

95. Terrill, *Steve McQueen*, 113.

96. Seydor, *The Western Films*, 70.

97. Seydor, *The Western Films*, 113.

98. Simmons, "Television Work," 11.

99. John Bryson, "Sam Peckinpah," *American Film* (April 1985), 22.

100. Seydor, *The Western Films*, 72.

101. Seydor, *The Western Films*, xiii.

102. "Daniel Melnick," *American Film* (March 1982): 18.

103. Seydor, *The Western Films*, 73.

104. Simmons, "Television Work," 12.

105. Seydor, *The Western Films*, 73.

106. "Daniel Melnick," *American Film*, 18.

107. Simmons, "Television Work," 12.

108. Joel W. Finler, *The Movie Director's Story* (New York: Crescent, 1985), 225.

109. Fine, *Bloody Sam*, 127.

110. Seydor, *The Western Films*, 142.

111. S. Gaydos, "After the Falls," *Hollywood Reporter* (February 10, 1992): S-22.

112. Quoted in Fine, *Bloody Sam*, 145.

113. Everson, *A Pictorial History*, 237.

114. Charles Champlin, *The Los Angeles Times,* quoted in "*The Wild Bunch*," *Filmfacts* XII (June 1969): 220.

115. Andrew Sarris, *The Village Voice,* quoted in "*The Wild Bunch*," *Filmfacts* XII, 220.

116. Richard Shickel, *Time,* quoted in Fine, *Bloody Sam*, 151.

117. Finler, *Director's,* 225.

118. Michael Parkinson and Clyde Jeavons, *A Pictorial History of Westerns* (London: Hamlyn Publishing, 1973), 89.

119. Jack Nachbar, *Focus on the Western*. Film Focus. (Englewood Cliffs, N.J.: Prentice, 1974), 119.

120. Ron Shelton, "*The Wild Bunch*," *American Film* (April 1989): 18.

121. Stephen Farber, "Peckinpah's Return," *Film Quarterly* (Fall 1960): 6.

122. Fine, *Bloody Sam*, 144.

123. *"The Wild Bunch,"* *Filmfacts* XII, 217.

124. Fine, *Bloody Sam*, 146–57.

125. Seydor, *The Western Films*, 89.

126. Seydor, *The Western Films*, 90.

127. Murray, "Interview," 66.

128. Finler, *Director's*, 225.

129. Nachbar, *Focus*, 119.

130. Fine, *Bloody Sam*, 184.

131. Fine, *Bloody Sam*, 182.

132. Fine, *Bloody Sam*, 182.

133. Seydor, *The Western Films*, xiv.

134. Matt Zoller Seitz, "All TV—Love and Bullets," *The Star-Ledger* (August 10, 2000): p. 59.

135. Fine, *Bloody Sam*, 187–88.

136. Pat Berman, "A Strange Fascination for Violence," *Columbia Record* [Columbia, S.C.] (February 1, 1975, Sunday ed.): p. 1-B.

137. *"Straw Dogs," Filmfacts* XV (February 1972): 1.

138. "Daniel Melnick," *American Film*, 18.

139. *"Straw Dogs," Filmfacts* XV (February 1972): 3.

140. Fine, *Bloody Sam*, 208.

141. *"Straw Dogs," Filmfacts* XV, 3.

142. Quoted in *"Straw Dogs," Filmfacts* XV, 3.

143. Molly Haskell, *From Reverence to Rape: The Treatment of Women in the Movies* (New York: Holt, 1974), 361, 323.

144. Charles U. Larson, *Persuasion: Reception and Responsibility*, 5th ed. (Belmont, Calif.: Wadsworth Publishing, 1989), 271.

145. Fine, *Bloody Sam*, 213.

146. Fine, *Bloody Sam*, 208.

147. Murray, "Interview," 69.

148. Murray, "Interview," 66.

149. Fine, *Bloody Sam*, 186.

150. Quoted in Fine, *Bloody Sam*, 186.

151. Murray, "Interview," 68.

152. Quoted in Fine, *Bloody Sam*, 275.

153. Quoted in Fine, *Bloody Sam*, 275.

154. Fine, *Bloody Sam*, 212.

155. Quoted in Fine, *Bloody Sam*, 239.

156. Quoted in Fine, *Bloody Sam*, 222.

157. *"Junior Bonner," Filmfacts* XV (September 1972): 412.

158. Fine, *Bloody Sam*, 221.

159. Fine, *Bloody Sam*, 232.

160. Carl Gottlieb, *The Jaws Log* (New York: Dell, 1975), 52.

161. Fine, *Bloody Sam*, 232.

162. Mike Greco, "Hard Riding," *Film Comment* (May/June 1980): 16.

163. *"The Getaway," Filmfacts* XV (December 1972): 627.

164. Seydor, *The Western Films*, 184.

165. *"Pat Garrett and Billy the Kid," Filmfacts* XVI (February 1973): 86–87.

166. Fine, *Bloody Sam*, 240.

167. "Peckinpah's Cut of *Pat Garrett* Finally Emerges for a Screening," *Variety* (May 7, 1986): 110.

168. David Weddle, "The Making of *The Wild Bunch*," *Film Comment* (May/June 1994): 50.

169. Quoted in Weddle, "Making," 51.

170. Seydor, *The Western Films*, 190.

171. Seydor, *The Western Films*, 193.

172. Seydor, *The Western Films*, 184.

173. Fine, *Bloody Sam*, 243.

174. Fine, *Bloody Sam*, 241.

175. Fine, *Bloody Sam*, 250.

176. Fine, *Bloody Sam*, 254.

177. "*Pat Garrett*," *Filmfacts* XVI, 87.

178. Seydor, *The Western Films*, 198

179. Seydor, *The Western Films*, 212.

180. Anthony F. Macklin, "Pat Garrett and Billy the Kid," *Film Heritage* (Winter 1974–1975): 35.

181. Seydor, *The Western Films*, 199.

182. Fine, *Bloody Sam*, 256–57.

183. "Peckinpah's Cut," *Variety*, 110.

184. Kathleen Murphy and Richard T. Jameson, "*Bring Me the Head of Alfredo Garcia*," *Film Comment* (January/February 1981): 46.

185. Fine, *Bloody Sam*, 276.

186. Harry Medved with Randy Dreyfuss, *The 50 Worst Films of All Time (and How They Got That Way)* (New York: Warner, 1984), 55.

187. Fine, *Bloody Sam*, 281.

188. Garner Simmons, "The Peckinpah Tapes," *American Film* (May 1985): 61.

189. Peter Lester, "Actor–Writer Burt Young Has an Ex-Pug's Mug. But He Can Knock Out Scripts in Three Weeks," *People* (July 17, 1978): 74.

190. Fine, *Bloody Sam*, 297.

191. "Art Is Out," *American Film* (February 1979): 80.

192. "*Cross of Iron*," *Filmfacts* XXII (August 1977): 203.

193. Stuart Byron, "Something Wicker This Way Comes," *Film Comment* (November/December 1977): 30.

194. Fine, *Bloody Sam*, 320.

195. Kathleen Murphy, "Sam Peckinpah: No Bleeding Heart," *Film Comment* (April 1985): 75.

196. Richard T. Jameson, "Lost Weekend," *Film Comment* (April 1984): 28.

197. Fine, *Bloody Sam*, 357.

198. Quoted in "The Wild Hunch," *American Film* (June 1979): 80.
199. Fine, *Bloody Sam*, 347.
200. Jameson, "Weekend," 28.
201. Jameson, "Weekend," 30.
202. Fine, *Bloody Sam*, 367.
203. Fine, *Bloody Sam*, 372.

· *4* ·

Women in the Period Westerns
of Sam Peckinpah

I shall remember you as an example of what women are capable of.

—*Henry James,* The Bostonians (1885)[1]

To better comprehend the character of the women in Sam Peckinpah's period Westerns, we have to understand that they are a synthesis
created by the interaction of several elements, a number of which we
have already examined. It is necessary to examine how the various
elements came together to see what it was Peckinpah alone brought
to them, what it was the director himself had to say, a voice often lost
in the chorus of competing, sometimes conflicting voices that com-
prised the finished film.

We can then take a closer look at Peckinpah's women, and, in
the process, see that the criticism against them—and against the acts
sometimes visited upon them—did not always square with the content. A skewed interpretation may have been a product of the heated
discourse of the times, but with the remove of thirty years it is easier
to see that the movie some critics perceived and the movie that was
being screened were not always the same thing.

THAT WAS THE WEST THAT WAS

Perhaps the factor that makes Peckinpah's period Westerns his most
personal films was that here was subject matter with which he could

draw a personal connection. Informed by the environment of his upbringing, by the family tales of his ancestors, and by the lore of a part
of California still carrying the last, fading echoes of the Wild West,
Peckinpah was able to bring to his Westerns a heart and honesty few
filmmakers could attain. It is that color in his storytelling that supported his high critical standing from his TV days through his feature
film peak.

It is interesting to compare the work of Peckinpah and other directors of Westerns who shared his historical grounding with purvey-
ors of the Western who didn't. John Ford, the acknowledged leader
of the Western herd, was born in Maine of Irish immigrant parents.[2, 3]
His rendering of the Old West was based on "how it should have
been rather than how it was."[4] In contrast, even Peckinpah's earliest
feature work is free of the romantic idealism and sentimentality that
bathes even a dark Ford work like *The Man Who Shot Liberty Valence*
(1962).

Nor do Peckinpah's Westerners share the flinty, tight-lipped re-
serve of John Sturges's characters (*The Magnificent Seven, Escape From
Fort Bravo* [1953]), or the cool-headed professionalism of Howard
Hawks's gunmen (*Rio Bravo* [1959]), both representing a more brutal,
contemporary brand of Western romanticism but a quality as legendary as that of Ford nonetheless.

Peckinpah's Westerners find their compatriots in the works of
Delmer Daves (*The Hanging Tree* [1959], *Cowboy* [1958], *3:10 to Yuma*
[1957]); not tough, but toughened, self-possessed but not icy. It is no
coincidence that Daves's family had a pioneer background not dissimilar to Peckinpah's.[5] One also finds a connection to the wonderfully
compact Westerns Budd Boetticher made with Randolph Scott, such
as *Ride Lonesome* (1959) and *The Tall T* (1957), the director evidently
picking up a Peckinpah/Daves-like affinity for the hard-baked yet
full-blooded Western character in years spent in Mexico.[6]

The point here being that history infuses Peckinpah's period
Westerns. Consequently, one gains an insight into Peckinpah's
women when one begins to have a better grasp on our traditional
ideas of women in the historical West and their mythic derivatives.
That historical picture may be unsettling from a feminist point of
view, but it is one thing to criticize content as the product of a story-

teller's indulgence or perpetuation of macho myths and fantasies, but another to chafe over an uncomfortable truth.

The harsh conditions and generally second-class status of women in the historical Old West belies the popular image of the pioneer wife as partner in the Western adventure, toiling by her husband's side and enthusiastically extending the reach of Eastern civilization. Here, one might think of the fresh-scrubbed Jean Arthur in *Shane* (1953), or the stoic, stolid women in any number of John Ford Westerns.

The historical record is less rosy. The pioneer wife did work in the fields but more out of necessity than shared enthusiasm, and she also tended to the endless, backbreaking labor of maintaining a household under brutally primitive conditions. For all her effort, she was still never a true equal partner in the development of the West.

The expansion of the United States west of the Mississippi was male-originated, male-controlled, and male-dominated. The male agenda of the times demanded women who were "meek and passive, modest and silent," and "expected to submit to the wills of their husbands. Piety, purity, and submissiveness became the ideal."[7] In moving West, women were relegated—and even forced—into a secondary position. "[The] archetypal Pioneer Wife and Mother . . . was often a reluctant traveler, heading west at her husband's decree."[8]

The settlement of the West, marked by a scarcity of women and isolation, only strengthened the male-dominant status quo. "In the primitive conditions of the frontier the woman's traditional role of mother, cook, and keeper of the hearth was usually reinforced. . . . The frontier would be a retrogressive force, one that strongly reinforced the traditional roles of the sexes."[9]

The second-class status of women was not restricted to the wives of pioneers, but extended throughout the society of the West. Along with frontier farms, ranches stood as isolated outposts in the vast expanse of the plains.[10] The world of cattle with its ranches, cattle drives, and cow towns was "a masculine world, and out of it came a cult of masculine virtues. Women . . . were largely irrelevant to the cattle world."[11] On the riverboats that trucked gamblers up and down the river highways, women, by accepted custom, left the gaming tables exclusively to the males and slept in segregated quarters.[12]

Despite the West's adaptation and confirmation of the institutionalized sexism of Eastern society, the vast, underpopulated, under-governed West stood in great enough social flux to present the adventurous, entrepreneurial, iconoclastic nineteenth century woman with unprecedented opportunity. It was a place where women willing to run counter to the accepted status quo could seek "fulfillment of long-suppressed aspirations."[13] The lack of manpower in the thinly populated West presented women with the chance to "[surge] into business and [elbow] their way into professions that were traditionally a man's province. . . . They became . . . doctors, dentists, lawyers and journalists. By 1890 the West was, comparatively speaking, a fount of opportunity for women."[14]

However invigorating the independence of the West was for women, it was considered by nearly all males—and even the majority of females—only a temporary product of the unsettled environment. The "Wild West" eventually evolved into a series of settled communities where Eastern-style conventions reigned, and in which women were expected to return to their "proper place" and "proper work": "home . . . caring for her husband and children."[15] Under these more domestic conditions, those women, who either out of necessity or desire, had sought paying work now found their opportunities limited. A compilation of 533 jobs available to women compiled in 1861 "effectively documented . . . what every woman who needed to earn a living already knew. Jobs for women offered painfully little of anything but the barest sustenance."[16]

With all these circumstances in mind, one can posit the rise of prostitution in the West as inevitable. It matched a largely unskilled female population and the poor financial prospects of "legitimate" work with the outstanding scarcity of women in the region. Harriet Frances Behrins, who settled a mile from a California mining camp in 1851, wrote, "During the two years that followed my establishing in this wild spot I did not, with one exception, see a white woman."[17] Ms. Luzena Stanley Wilson told of seeing only two other women in her six months in Sacramento during the days of the Gold Rush.[18] The first California census in 1850—the year after prospectors began to flood California following the news of the discovery of gold at Sutter's Mill—showed that *less than 10 percent* of the white population consisted of women.[19] An 1860 federal census in Colorado showed 32,654 males to only *1,577 white females!*[20]

So valued was even the *sight* of females that gambling houses hired women "not necessarily prostitutes" to serve coffee and cakes and to work the gaming tables. "Their mere presence, in . . . [San Francisco] where men outnumbered women by as much as ten to one, pulled in customers who were happy simply to gawk at the rare sight."[21] In mining country, "women were so scarce . . . that any female was treated with a respect that sometimes verged on idolatry."[22] In the small, isolated communities of the West, "Any female from eight to eighty could count on a full dance program."[23] Wrote Luzena Wilson, "Any woman who had a womanly heart, who spoke a kindly sympathetic word to the lonely, homesick men, was a queen, and lacked no honor which a subject could bestow. Women were scarce in those days."[24]

The demand for female company was so pressing that Native American and African American women were forcibly enlisted into prostitution on the frontier.[25] In most cases, however, economic opportunity/necessity provided sufficient impetus for women to enter the trade. In a letter to a friend, turn-of-the-century prostitute Maimie Pinzer explained her choice of profession thusly: "I don't propose to get up at 6:30 to be at work at 8 and work in a close, stuffy room with people I despise, until dark, for $6.00 or $7.00 a week! When I could . . . spend an afternoon with some congenial person and in the end have more than a week's work could pay me."[26] "As new communities arose in the West, prostitutes followed the gold trail in search of a secure income."[27] The towns that sprang up among the mines, along cattle trails, and at rail heads were invariably accompanied by a row of saloons that became "the core of the community. [Saloons] rapidly developed solid creature comforts for drinking and gambling men, including one irresistible attraction—women, sometimes the only women in town."[28] Prostitution was not only an open trade but also often a welcome one. Said one Idaho mayor, "I always encouraged parlor houses [bordellos]. What else are you going to do in a frontier community with twenty men to every woman?"[29]

The profession could be harsh. The light-hearted, healthy, and unfailingly attractive nymphs that populate bordellos in movies about the Old West like *The Cheyenne Social Club* (1970) and *Butch Cassidy and the Sundance Kid* have few real life counterparts. "Most [prostitutes] . . . were ignorant, raucous women who died early. Crude abortions, alcoholism and other diseases took an appalling toll. Suicide

. . . was commonplace.''[30] There was drug addiction, with the expected resultant cases of overdose, and assault by customers. Whether by choice, or good or bad fortune, the girls, often young, rarely continued on in the trade into their thirties. Only a few managed some sort of success and a number found husbands.[31]

Some prostitutes became renowned madams and their houses well-known for the comfort and opulence not found in the private homes of the frontier.[32] Those more accomplished in the trade took an unapologetic, unashamed view of their lives, as did Denver's Mattie Silks. "I went into the sporting life [prostitution] for business reasons and for no other," she once recalled. "It was a way in those days for a woman to make money and I made it. I considered myself then and do now—as a business woman.''[33]

"Whether driven to prostitution by economic desperation or forced to prostitution by unscrupulous hustlers, prostitutes were a significant social group."[34] The acceptance of prostitution into the culture of the West became so ingrained that, even after the West became less wild and began to "emulate Eastern respectability . . . the oldest profession continued to prosper."[35] "City councils may have enacted laws against prostitution and gambling, but officials usually considered these ordinances more as a source of revenue (through fines and bribes) than as extensions of morality. With a clear conscience, business continued as usual."[36] In some cases, as we saw in the chapter on Peckinpah's upbringing, it was a mind-set that continued well into the twentieth century.

*   *   *

When the facts of the Old West got into the hands of literary myth-makers, the substance of the roles of the Western true-life drama began to change. As myth magnifies some desired element of reality, so did the American myths that arose out of the Old West, nurtured by dime novelists like Ned Buntline and "Wild West" showmen like William "Buffalo Bill" Cody, romantically skew historical fact. Buntline, Cody, and others exaggerated both the importance and contrapuntal unimportance of certain truths. "Myth . . . refers here to a metaphoric depiction of human experience. That depiction's historical accuracy is of much less import than its ability to convey the human conditions as it is perceived at a specific point in time."[37]

Those first mythmakers of the American West cultivated elements that we now consider "traditional": "the lawmen, the outlaws, the honorable and the tarnished ladies, the railroad, the town."[38] The West was tamed by men who were "upright, clean-living, sharp-shooting." The proverbial Man of the West was "a white Anglo-Saxon Protestant who [respected] the law, the flag, women and children."[39] The West became "a virgin world suspended out of time and history, awaiting the inevitable intrusion of civilization."[40]

When myth met truth, truth usually lost. From relations of Anglo Saxon pioneers with the Native American populations they displaced to the way Westerners dealt with each other, history was subsumed by dime novel fiction.

Take Wyatt Earp, for example. Within his own lifetime, dime novels had portrayed Earp and his brothers as bastions of law and order, a legend that carried forward into the cinema age in films like John Ford's *My Darling Clementine* (1946) or John Sturges's Fordian *Gunfight at the O.K. Corral* (1957). When Sturges revisited the Earp legend with the darker *Hour of the Gun* (1967), the Tombstone lawman was portrayed as sometimes excessive but still generally in the right. The legend persisted even later in *Tombstone* (1993) and *Wyatt Earp* (1994). While the famed marshal's character showed a few more streaks of tarnish, in the main he remained a force for good. The historical record, however, shows a more amoral character, working both sides of the law as both marshal and saloon owner/gambling maven. The infamous gunfight at the O.K. Corral was not the act of lawmen cleaning up a town, but rather a power play between two competing factions vying for supremacy in Tombstone.[41]

Similarly, Jesse and Frank James, whose bank robbing image had, during their lifetimes, benefited from the spin doctoring efforts of their mother, became popularly imagined as Robin Hood–like cavaliers, an image confirmed in films like *Jesse James* (1939). It was an image that did not include such troubling truths as Jesse's out-of-hand killing of a bank cashier simply because he reminded the outlaw of a Yankee Army officer he recalled from the Civil War.[42]

William Bonnie aka Billy the Kid, in tale after tale and movie after movie, usually came off as a good boy turned bad by circumstance and/or the devious actions of others; a youth more misguided than immoral. In *Billy the Kid* (1930 & 1941), *The Left-Handed Gun* (1958), *Chisum,* and Peckinpah's own *Pat Garrett and Billy the Kid,* Bonnie is repeatedly portrayed as being simpatico with the common man, the enemy of greedy land barons and business interests. His movie image is hardly that of the smiling sociopath who'd been a life-long fugitive from the age of fifteen.[43]

Colorful Western women were not exempt from the legend treatment either. Doris Day played the title role in *Calamity Jane* (1953) as a rough-housing tomboy of good heart, but the real Calamity Jane was a "brawling alcoholic," inveterate liar, and occasional whore.[44]

★   ★   ★

Owen Wister codified the traditional elements of the Western when he elevated Western fiction from the dime novel of the late nineteenth century into his "serious novels" of the early twentieth century. Wister heroes like The Virginian and Lin McLean, in novels of the same names, were the author's representatives of the free-living West. "The initiative, the energy, and the aggressive action were all masculine."[45] As the West eventually stabilized and generally assumed Eastern values, so do Wister's archetypal Western heroes through the device of marriage. "Wister's West [is] populated by Huckleberry Finns who lit out from Miss Watson for new territory, and perhaps marriage still signifies at the end of his novels, not so much entrance into a new strength and maturity as a return to being 'civilized.' "[46]

In Western fiction—first literary, then in film and television— Western myth quickly and easily assimilated the more universal myths of European-based Western culture, including those concerning women. "It is . . . an unfortunate fact that . . . Western culture has always been dominated by men. As a result, many of the myths and literary works produced in our society are filled with specifically male fantasies."[47] Consequently, the mythical Old West was a place " 'where men are men'; in Western movies, [and] men have the deeper wisdom and the women are children."[48]

In Western fiction, "good" women assumed the cultural archetypes of "ministering angel, captive princess . . . and—one of the most powerful mythic figures of all—the Mother."[49] The fantasy good woman of Westerns was frequently from the East, bringing with her the virtues of same. "In the American mind, refinement, virtue, civilization, Christianity itself, are seen as feminine, and therefore women are often portrayed as possessing some kind of deeper wisdom, while the men, for all their apparent self-assurance, are fundamentally childish."[50]

The fantasy "bad" woman found her place in the character of the dance hall girl, a restrained euphemistic image for the frontier whore. "One of the most powerful and prevalent male fantasies is that of the lovely but lethal woman who bewitches men."[51] The dance hall girl could entice the hero, but she ultimately had to lose him to the virtuous woman who was his true love.[52] The film Western, evolving from the "tradition of Wild West literature that had dominated the mass taste of nineteenth-century America," incorporated the same archetypes.[53] Fred Zinneman's *High Noon* (1952), featuring pacifistic Grace Kelly, angelic right down to her halo-like golden hair, winning Gary Cooper's affections over saloon owner-cum-madam Katy Jurado, can trace its thematic roots directly to Wister's pre–World War I novel, *The Virginian*.

While the true-life status of the Western prostitute was as victim of the puritan New England ethic that traveled West with the pioneers, Western "types" were a reflection of those typical of Victorian melodrama.[54] So repressive were Victorian standards that the prostitutes who proliferated in the West could not even be labeled as such in print. "Many areas were not openly explored in writing at that time, and this applies in particular to the relationships between [a] man and a woman."[55] "Veiled allusions to danger-fraught 'whited sepulchers' were as much as the cast-iron moralists of the time would tolerate." Not until Stephen Crane's story, "Maggie: A Girl of the Streets," would American literature be able to look into the eyes of the prostitute without flinching, and even then, Crane reserved the conventional punishing climax for his ostensibly sympathetic heroine.[56]

By the 1950s, the picture began to change albeit slowly. "This reflects both a relaxation in censorship and the changing status of women in society. . . . Just as one cannot any longer tell the good guys from the bad guys, one cannot with quite the same ease distinguish between the good girls and the bad girls."[57] Consequently, "These changes . . . have occasionally led to the depiction of more mature relations between the sexes."[58] In a film like Anthony Mann's *Man of the West* (1958), for example, ex-saloon girl Julie London is portrayed with earnest sympathy, although she still cannot end up with hero Gary Cooper. John Sturges's biting *Last Train From Gun Hill* offers up another dance hall girl—Carolyn Jones this time—who helps sheriff Kirk Douglas bring in the men who raped and murdered his Native American wife, but—as the Bad Girl—she must still lose the hero's heart to the Good Girl, even if the Good Girl exists only as a widower's memory.

Even into the 1960s, the woman of the Western remained, by and large, both idealized and weak. She sat "on a pedestal, distant and untouchable," with the hero's own reverence "not [allowing] them to step down from their elevation. . . . She is seldom if ever a Scarlet O'Hara or a Becky Sharp—that is, a strong woman who knows far better than men what is really going on."[59]

CAUGHT IN THE CURRENT

It was not just Western history that infused Peckinpah's films. The trends of the industry and the dynamics of the director's career were just as great—and sometimes a greater—an influence on his work than auteurists and Peckinpah critics might be willing to admit.

Peckinpah's directorial career rather neatly circumscribed the changing direction of the motion picture industry in the early 1960s into the 1970s, and the changing status of the movie Western. Those industry trends, to a large degree, explain the films Peckinpah made, or, in a more appropriate sense, one should say was *allowed* to make.

From the time of Edwin S. Porter's ten-minute opus *The Great Train Robbery* (1903), into the 1970s, Westerns had been a Hollywood staple. Their appeal to male audiences, their reliance on physical action to resolve dramatic situations, and their male-dominated casts made them particularly viable in the post-studio period as studios found international profitability in action-oriented films from the 1960s on. Peckinpah did not choose to make Western features; rather, the industry chose Peckinpah—because of the expertise he had demonstrated in TV Westerns—to direct features that fit into a developing trend.

Peckinpah's work on the TV series "The Westerner" was the direct inspiration for his being hired to helm *The Deadly Companions* and *Ride the High Country*. The accolades from his TV work combined with the critical acclaim for *High Country* led to *Major Dundee*. Though it's usually reported that Peckinpah's highly lauded turn behind the camera on the TV production of "Noon Wine" led to his directing *The Wild Bunch*, it's just as likely that Warners and the film's producers had in mind Peckinpah's track record on big- and small-screen Westerns. One is hard put to see how the introspective "Noon Wine" directly connects to the sprawling, kinetic, and brutal *Bunch*. Even the flawed *Major Dundee* evidenced more than "Noon Wine" the possibility of Peckinpah pulling off a large-scale, big-screen Western with heavy doses of action.

The point here is that Peckinpah's first four features—including *The Wild Bunch,* which made him both a Hollywood commodity and a figure of controversy—sought him out. All four films were projects he did not initiate, based on scripts that he did not originate. While he did contribute to the material, those contributions, as we shall see later in this chapter, may have been important but, in ways relevant to this discussion, limited.

The Wild Bunch through *The Getaway* were the years of Peckinpah's greatest commercial viability. While his critics focused on the violently themed films of that period (which included *Straw Dogs)* as confirmation of his bent toward machismo and mayhem, the commercial failures of *The Ballad of Cable Hogue* and *Junior Bonner* within that same time frame have never been given their due weight in what they demonstrated about Peckinpah's eagerness to work outside action genres, and the quickly developing commercial constraints against his doing so.

It was a simple equation with an obvious conclusion that any nonindustry layman could reach: *The Wild Bunch, Straw Dogs,* and *The Getaway* were highly profitable pictures, each succeeding one more so than its predecessor; whatever their artistic merits, *The Ballad of Cable Hogue* and *Junior Bonner* were flat out box-office failures. End of story.

Normally, a string of box-office successes can buy a director (or actor, screenwriter, and so on) the clout to indulge his or her creative juices. *Predator* (1987) and *Die Hard* (1988) bought John McTiernan the opportunity to make *Medicine Man* (1992), whose underperformance no doubt was at least partly responsible for the director's return to the action genre with *Last Action Hero* (1993) and *Die Hard With a Vengeance* (1995). Steve McQueen's success in action and adventure pics like *The Magnificent Seven, The Great Escape, The Sand Pebbles* (1966), *Bullitt, Papillon* (1973), *The Getaway,* and *The Towering Inferno* made him one of the most popular actors in the world, consequently allowing him the indulgence of the bucolic *The Reivers* (1969) and extremely-against-character Ibsen adaptation *The Enemy of the People* (1979). The money that went into Warner Bros. coffers courtesy of Mel Gibson vehicles like the *Lethal Weapon* films and *Maverick* (1994) underwrote the studio's productions of Gibson's Shakespearean turn in *Hamlet* (1990) and his directorial debut, *The Man Without a Face* (1993). James Cameron's box-office bonanzas *The Terminator* (1984) and *Terminator 2: Judgement Day* (1991), *Aliens* (1986), and *True Lies* (1994) gave him license to do an abrupt about-face and make a grand, syrupy romance: *Titanic* (1997).

But Peckinpah never established a comparable record of consistent major box-office success; the proverbial "hot streak" eluded him. The commercial steam of *The Wild Bunch* was not allowed to build into that of *Straw Dogs,* but was somewhat vented off by the immediately following failure of *The Ballad of Cable Hogue,* the only film he had the opportunity to produce; the heat from *Straw Dogs* was undercut by another immediate succeeding failure, this time of *Junior Bonner;* the smashing success of *The Getaway* was completely lost on the back-to-back failures of *Pat Garrett and Billy the Kid* and *Bring Me the Head of Alfredo Garcia.*

Thereafter, Peckinpah's career was permanently hobbled, but not solely because of *Pat Garrett* and *Alfredo Garcia.* Having fought with production execs on most of his films, the major studios were reluctant to have much further to do with him, which resulted in him being pushed further and further away from the circuit of major films made by major producers. Typed by his successes with action films, minor producers funneled their action-oriented projects—another growing industry trend—Peckinpah's way. He ended his career selecting projects that, as film critic and Peckinpah fan Richard T. Jameson wrote, were the least objectionable a narrowing field offered.

The hope among fans had always been that Peckinpah would somehow find that one, golden project that could turn his waning career around, as *The Wild Bunch* had done after the de facto blacklist following *Major Dundee* and his firing from *The Cincinnati Kid.* More than one assumed that, as had also happened with *Bunch,* if such a turnaround were to happen it would be with the kind of film he seemed to do best: a Western. And, indeed, after *Convoy,* Peckinpah tried to develop or was attached to a number of Western-themed projects, but these were not the gun-filled epics that might have found root in the business at that time. They were projects like the contemporary Western "The Texans," about a retiring oil exec living out the fantasy of a cattle drive, and the self-explanatory "Songwriter," which would have starred Willie Nelson.[60] But even a Peckinpah "shoot 'em up" kind of Western might not have been able to find a studio home.

The commercial viability of the Western had ironically faded almost in parallel with Peckinpah's own commercial value. The sizable box-office success in the late 1960s and early 1970s of films like *The Professionals* (1966), *Butch Cassidy and the Sundance Kid, Little Big Man* (1970), *The Wild Bunch,* and the Italian-produced "spaghetti Westerns" kicked off a wave of Western movies in the early 1970s the industry has not seen before or since.[61] Period and modern-day, big- and small-budgeted, action-oriented and meditative, traditional and revisionist, comic and tragic, good and bad, they came in every size and stripe from John Wayne traditionals like *Chisum* and *Big Jake* to the rock musical/gunfighter opus *Zachariah* (1971) and Robert Downey Sr.'s surreal biblical allegory *Greaser's Palace* (1972).

The following partial list gives some idea of the size and breadth of that surge:

A Man Called Horse (1970)
Return of a Man Called Horse (1976)
Soldier Blue (1970)
Dirty Dingus Magee (1970)
There Was a Crooked Man (1970)
Hannie Caulder (1971)

One More Train to Rob (1971)
The Deserter (1971)
The Train Robbers (1973)
A Gunfight (1971)
Doc (1971)
McCabe & Mrs. Miller (1971)
Chisum (1970)
The Honkers (1972)
Posse (1975)
Joe Kidd (1972)
The Revengers (1972)
The Wild Rovers
Ulzana's Raid (1972)
Lawman (1971)
Chato's Land (1972)
The Hired Hand (1971)
The Cowboys (1972)
The Great Northfield Minnesota Raid (1972)
J.W. Coop
Monte Walsh (1970)
Big Jake (1971)
Pocket Money (1972)
Bite the Bullet (1975)
Valdez Is Coming (1971)
Duck You Sucker aka *A Fistful of Dynamite* (1972)
High Plains Drifter (1973)
Chino (1973)

But coinciding with the failure of *Pat Garrett and Billy the Kid,* as the 1970s wore on, the great wave of Westerns boasted more box-office misfires than hits. Perhaps the market had simply been oversaturated and audiences numbed to the Western's appeal. Or, possibly, many directors looking to put a new spin on an old genre had become so immersed in Western revisionism that they lost—if they ever had—their ability to mix nouveaux cinema sensibilities with the traditional charms of the Western, as Peckinpah had in *The Wild Bunch.* Or perhaps a new generation of filmgoer could find no connection to the Western myth, instead finding the genre's touchstone elements in more contemporary venues. These included science fiction a la the *Star Wars* and *Alien* films, over-the-top cop stories like the *Die Hard* and *Beverly Hills Cop* movies, nonstop adventures like the *Indiana Jones* and *Batman* series and the increasingly gargantuan James Bond pictures, and the outsized, overdriven actioners such as produced by Joel Silver (who was behind the *Lethal Weapon* franchise) and the team of Jerry Bruckheimer and Don Simpson (later Bruckheimer alone after Simpson's death), for example *Top Gun* (1986), *Days of Thunder* (1990), *The Rock* (1996), and *Armageddon* (1998). In any case, the sliding box-office performance of the genre, capped with such high-profile disasters as *Pat Garrett* and Michael Cimino's elephantine *Heaven's Gate* (1980; so costly a failure it broke the fiscal back of United Artists), put a toxic air around the movie Western as far as production execs were concerned.

While the genre did not die out completely, hits like the Clint Eastwood's *Shane* homage *Pale Rider* (1985), the pastiche *Silverado,* and the teen-oriented *Young Guns* films were few and moderate. Eastwood's *Unforgiven* (1992) would be the first major Western hit since the early 1970s. (Eastwood's ability to periodically return to the genre was based in large part on his warm relationship with Warner Bros., and *Silverado* came from director/cowriter Lawrence Kasdan at a particularly hot time in his career—assets Peckinpah never accrued.)

What this meant for Peckinpah's career was obvious. Even if he had managed to maintain some sort of amenable relationship with the major Hollywood players, the climate of the industry would not have permitted him to set up shop at a studio with a Western, particularly one sans the prerequisite volume of bloodshed. The financial risk, by the mid-1970s, was too great to cast with a director whose commercial performance was as checkered as Peckinpah's.

★   ★   ★

If Peckinpah was rarely the master of his own fate, neither was he ever in complete control over most of the projects he did helm. This is an important point to keep in mind because, glancing over the body of his work, it's an easy assumption to make that here was a director uncomfortable giving much weight to strong female characters as well as strong actresses.

Of his fourteen directorial efforts, only half feature a woman in something more than a secondary supporting role (here speaking in terms of the size and importance of the part rather than billing). Worse, some of the substantial women's parts that do exist in his films are of questionable value. The Ali MacGraw role in *Convoy* is so meaningless (unsurprising in a film both confused and witless) that it seems more a marketing device to shoehorn a female draw on to the marquee rather than an integrated part of the drama (such as it is). Senta Berger's part in *Major Dundee* was roundly criticized for being similarly valueless, though unlike *Convoy* (and more to the film's detriment) the story vainly tries to incorporate her as a major dramatic peg.

Poor casting further weakened the distaff side of the ledger. Peckinpah's authority to command casting decisions fluctuated with the highs and lows of his career as well as the willingness of other parties (say, McQueen on *The Getaway*) to exercise their greater power.

To turn again to Ms. Berger in *Dundee,* the appearance of the curvy European actress in a setting of extreme privation seemed to emphasize the sense that not only was the role there to provide gratuitous romance, but equally irrelevant décolleté.

Ali MacGraw's casting in *The Getaway* was similarly inane but for different reasons. Though the actress *cum* model was considered a hot property due to her appearance in a pair of big-screen successes (*Goodbye Columbus* [1969], *Love Story* [1970]), her patrician air and willowy bearing has to make one wonder what it was that made anyone think she would fit in a rough-and-tumble Peckinpah adventure playing the wife and active partner of a professional bank robber. Certainly, when one compares MacGraw to Peckinpah women cast by the director (the earthier Stella Stevens in *Cable Hogue,* and Isela Vega in *Alfredo Garcia* as examples), the actress seems an almost bizarre choice. But as Marshall Fine explains in his biography of Peckinpah, the choice had more to do with her being the girlfriend of Paramount production chief Robert Evans (*The Getaway* would be distributed under the Paramount label) and the object of star Steve McQueen's romantic attentions.[62] Indeed, on screen, though MacGraw's role is very much a costarring one, she can't hold the screen against McQueen. It seems a lopsided pairing, he easily the dominant, tougher, more in command—a presentation that again contributes to the image of a director who can't treat male/female partners as equals.

★   ★   ★

By one meaning of auteurism, Peckinpah was an auteur. His films have an obvious visual style and recurrent, personal themes. Yet both assets are insinuated around an established framework not of his devising.

Even at the peak of his career, Sam Peckinpah was a gun-for-hire director, working on properties that had already gone through some phase of development and were set up—or being set up—by people with authority over him. Of his fourteen directorial efforts, Peckinpah only carries a producing credit on one of them *(Cable Hogue)* and even that was a project he did not originate but had been brought to him by actors L. Q. Jones and Warren Oates who had appeared in a number of Peckinpah films. And while Peckinpah had begun his career as a prolific TV writer, he held a writing credit—and a cowriting credit at that, his work contribution coming in rewrites of initial drafts—on only four of his directorial efforts: *Major Dundee, The Wild Bunch, Straw Dogs,* and *Alfredo Garcia.* Though Writer's Guild guidelines on the award of credits have changed over the years, the rule of thumb is that a particular writer has to contribute a third or better to a screenplay to deserve an on-screen credit. However much Peckinpah's writing contributions to his films affected the flavor of the finished product, on a quantitative basis those contributions were limited.

In both his successes and failures, there was a recurring pattern in Peckinpah's writing methodology. For whatever reason, once he got into the feature film arena it became harder and harder for him to write original material without some kind of assistance. In the latter part of his career particularly he regularly cast about for a "string of accomplices . . . talked into writing with him—anything to avoid doing a first draft himself."[63]

How this plays out in his films is that one sees the same Peckinpah themes arise in a bizarre variety of venues as he tried to graft his feelings onto material already in development. Those sentiments so beautifully articulated in *Ride the High Country* and *The Wild Bunch*— the passing of The Old Guard and their brand of loyalty, professionalism, code of honor, and so on—are beautifully translated into contemporary terms in *Junior Bonner,* but make *Pat Garrett* feel like a botched rehash of *Bunch.* In an extreme reach they are touched on in the espionage thriller *The Killer Elite* and the World War II tale *Cross of Iron,* but look plain ridiculous sewn onto the silliness of *Convoy.*

So, in another sense, and by his own admission, Peckinpah was not an auteur. He infused, but rarely created. Like a lamprey, his dramatic vitality was wholly dependent on the health of the host property he latched on to. He had told one acquaintance, "I'm only as good as the people who work for me."[64] Or, as he put it another way, he was just a "whore" trying to "slip in a few comments on the side."

THE INDICTMENT

The foundation of the claim of misogyny against Peckinpah may be bolstered by elements that appear in most of his films, but it rests primarily on *Straw Dogs* and, to a somewhat lesser extent, *Bring Me the Head of Alfredo Garcia.* Before answering the charge with a close examination of his period women, it's worth looking at the matches that started the fire.

★   ★   ★

Straw Dogs is one of the very few Peckinpah films to feature a female colead. The character of Amy, played by Susan George, is an integral part of the story from beginning to end. For much of the film, the dramatic importance of Amy is the equal of her husband David, played by Dustin Hoffman, and they share the screen equally through most of the 118-minute running time.

For feminists of the time, Amy was an extremely problematic character. Involved in a complicated duel of domestic politics with her husband, feminist critics perceived her as a typical production of male mythology: a bitch, a tease, a woman who invites—and ultimately enjoys—rape. The film brought Peckinpah an unprecedented amount of attention, touching as it did on a number of feminist hot buttons the like of which mark the early militancy of any ideological movement.[65] "Ultimately, the impact and image of *Straw Dogs* grew out of proportion to anything Peckinpah ever intended. He was making a statement about violence in man . . . but people saw it as much more."[66] David, a "celestial mathematician," is something of an intellectual bully. He condescends to his wife and encases himself in an anesthetizing bubble of intelligence.[67] Amy, on the other hand, an expatriate of the small Cornwall village where she and David have come to live, is visceral, carnal. If David is the mind, Amy is the heart and gut.

Over the course of the film, the relationship between husband and wife grows increasingly strained. Workmen hired to roof their garage, including Charlie Venner with whom Amy had had some sort of intimate relationship in their younger days, consider David a tweedy sort not up to their provincial standards of masculinity. They display their contempt by openly leering at Amy, stealing into the couple's bedroom during their absence to take a pair of Amy's underpants, and eventually killing the couple's cat and hanging it in the bedroom closet. The more open their disrespect, the more cowardly David looks for ways to avoid a confrontation. Amy's attempt to step above her small-town station by marrying David becomes a step down: His humiliation is also hers.

Critics consider Amy a tease because of the coquettish way she treats Venner. She invites rape, goes the charge, when she exposes her breasts to the workmen after a disagreeable exchange with her husband. And then there is the rape itself, which she at first resists, then seems to enjoy.

To Molly Haskell, Amy was emblematic of male-held stereotypes. "The provocative, sex-obsessed bitch is one of the great male-chauvinist . . . fantasies, along with the fantasy that she is constantly fantasizing rape," she wrote.[68] This is right in line with Pauline Kael's pejorative assessment that Amy is "asking for it, she's begging for it . . . her every no means yes."[69]

But these readings of the key incidents that are the foundations of these charges are, on closer examination, superficial and selective.

The breast-flashing, for instance, provocative as it is, is clearly a protest against her husband. *If my husband won't protect me against their ogling,* Amy declares with the act, *then the hell with him. He wants to let you look? Then look!*

The more important incident, obviously, is the rape. David is lured off by the workmen on a "snipe hunt." Leaving David stranded on the moors, Charlie Venner (Del Hunney) sneaks back to the farmhouse. He tries to force himself on Amy, and when she resists he slaps her hard enough to knock her down. At the threat of a second slap, she tearfully acquiesces. As the sexual engagement proceeds, Amy becomes less reluctant and becomes a more willing partner. After the act is completed, Venner looks up to sees one of the other workmen standing over them. Scott (Ken Hutchison) pushes Venner away at the point of a shotgun, then brutally takes a painful turn at Amy.

It is that point of acquiescence that is the ignition point for the feminists; the fulfillment of the male fantasy of a rape victim enjoying rape. But that is a read that ignores the full breadth of the story to that point.

Venner and Amy have a romantic history. Their dialogue at points indicates that the relation did not so much conclude as was interrupted by Amy's leaving the village. But she did not leave for love. As we witness her and David together, there is sex and some playful teasing, but there is very little loving, tenderness, or romance between them. David is not a love but a tool for self-betterment, perhaps even a trophy (as no doubt Amy is for David).

Amy surrenders to Venner after the first blow clearly to avoid another blow (a not atypical behavior for rape victims). The encounter becomes more mutual as Amy's feelings, tumultuously mixed at the start, begin to sort themselves out. What began as self-preserving surrender evolves into the continuance of a hang-fire relationship. Though a feminist would no doubt argue the point for understandable reasons, it is clear that Peckinpah is not—at least in his view— dealing with a true rape at this point.

But there *is* an assault that by even Peckinpah's arguable standard is clearly a rape and that is the second attack by Scott. It is a brutal offense, primal and animalistic. Amy, in no way, is a willing accomplice here and even Venner only seems to allow it because of the shotgun threat from Scott. The trauma of the event haunts Amy in flashback later in the film as she evinces the same kind of psychological scars suffered by real-life rape victims; hardly a depiction indicating rape fantasy fulfillment. If anything, Peckinpah's handling of Amy's post-traumatic affect is entirely sympathetic.

Still agitated over *Straw Dogs,* with the possibly mitigating *Junior*

Bonner quickly disappearing from sight and *The Getaway* maintaining Peckinpah's reputation as a master of mayhem, feminist ire was stoked higher by yet another controversial scene of sexual assault in *Bring Me the Head of Alfredo Garcia*.

That sequence has Bennie (Warren Oates) and his prostitute girl-friend Elita (Isela Vega) camping by the road one night and set upon by two bikers. Elita knows what the men want. In her dialogue, she implies that this is not her first encounter with extortive sex, and quietly walks off with one of the men. Without a word from the biker, she kneels in front of him and begins to disrobe. Before there is any sexual consummation, Bennie manages to kill both bikers.

It does not require that much of a second look to see that this is neither willingness nor complicity. On reviewing the film it is clear that Elita's participation is a surrender. To resist promises only harm and probably death for both her and Bennie. Resistance will not change the outcome; only worsen it. Elita's act is one of resigned sacrifice and as such is no less a rape than the one perpetrated on *Straw Dogs*'s Amy by Scott.

The impact of *Alfredo Garcia* was disproportionate considering how swiftly the film disappeared from theaters, but its impact was amplified by coming just two years after *Straw Dogs* and, equally contributory, a number of deliberately feminist-antagonizing comments from Peckinpah.

Irredeemable provocateur that he was, there's no telling how earnest Peckinpah was tossing off remarks like "most women" enjoy rape. Feminist critics focused on specific elements of both films ignored the more explanatory context. The phrase "whole Peckinpah line of women who enjoy rape" indicates a growing mind-set among feminist critics regarding his work, since looking at the films Peckinpah had made to that point hardly evidences such a lineage. Even granting feminists their misperception of *Straw Dogs*'s Amy, the nine films preceding *Alfredo Garcia* show two other sexual attacks, both incomplete, both portrayed in highly negative terms. The argument over women in Peckinpah's work was becoming less about substance than two perceptions in conflict: the one developing among feminist critics and the one being fostered by the self-destructive director. If critics harbored any doubts about their interpretations of films like

Straw Dogs and *Alfredo Garcia,* the glib comments of the director himself only seemed to confirm them.

MEET THE LADIES

The six period Westerns of Sam Peckinpah fall neatly into two groups:

The Deadly Companions, Ride the High Country, and *Major Dundee* show a director whose style as well as thematic touchstones are still developing, still—even in the much heralded *High Country*—in flux, sitting somewhere between the traditional Hollywood Western and something newer and darker.

The Wild Bunch, The Ballad of Cable Hogue, and *Pat Garrett and Billy the Kid,* on the other hand, are films that even at a glance are easily recognizable as Peckinpah films. His stamp is in the visuals, the characterizations, the distinctive, disjointed, editing style and kinetic pace, and the full realization of the themes and motifs that, in the early part of the director's career, are only partially developed *(The Deadly Companions),* delivered with a touch of old Hollywood romanticism *(High Country),* or mishandled *(Major Dundee).*

Nevertheless, there is a consistent—if developing—attitude about women running through the films that stands contrary to the misogyny so often misperceived in his work.

The Deadly Companions

To recap the circumstances of the production, the film came to Peckinpah on a referral from star Brian Keith who had worked on Peckinpah's series "The Westerner." The production took place with a number of creative curtailments placed on the director that make *Companions* the most characterless work in the director's feature canon.

A. S. Fleischman's script was already "set" when Peckinpah was brought into the project. In his eagerness to graduate to features from television, Peckinpah expressed none of his reservations about the screenplay before signing, tacitly agreeing to the general form and content of Fleischman's story.[70] Producer Charles FitzSimons, committed to the script, forbade Peckinpah from touching the material. Peckinpah and Keith covertly reworked some of the dialogue and the director managed to include a number of images he desired, but generally the film adheres to Fleischman's script.[71] Restricting Peckinpah's input still further, the friction that developed between he and FitzSimons provoked the producer to ban Peckinpah from speaking directly with the film's costar, Maureen O'Hara.

The film is atypical of Peckinpah in many ways: small-scale, slow-moving, a dramatic miniature. In many ways, with its small cast and minor production values, it seems an amplified made-for-TV movie, something that might have been done in Peckinpah's days on "Dick Powell Theater." The film is also unusual in offering one of few female leads in the director's filmography, and the largest female part in any of his period Westerns, making it all the more unfortunate that he was not allowed to work more closely with Ms. O'Hara.

Despite the restrictions on Peckinpah, the film does present a picture of womanhood that is consistent with his other Westerns. Though it is rough-hewn here, it will clarify and become more detailed and declarative with each succeeding Peckinpah film.

The character of dance hall queen Kit is historically on point: She is an unskilled widow in a male-dominant society. The story of a woman turning to prostitution to support herself and child may be trite but—particularly in the Old West context—nevertheless true. Peckinpah views her situation in an accepting, nonjudgmental manner, while, on the other hand, he plainly holds little empathy for the townspeople and their reproving attitude toward Kit.

As in most Peckinpah films, there is a grand difference between what a character is labeled and the higher moral plain he or she actually holds. It is normally those figures of the high conventional social orders in a Peckinpah film (i.e., townspeople, law enforcement officials, businessmen) for whom the director displays his greatest disdain, depicting them in almost knee-jerk fashion as hypocritical and valueless. On this score *Companions* is no exception. More often than not, it is a woman—in this case Kit—who sits at Peckinpah's story's moral apex. Of all the characters in the film—respected town folk, repentant gunman Yellowleg and his unrepentant compadres—it is Kit the whore who morally stands above all.

But restricted in his storytelling as he was on *Companions,* Peckinpah is left to say the most about women through what he says about men. As the script remained essentially Fleischman's throughout, it is not possible to know how much of the presented image of men was Peckinpah's and how much was the screenwriter's and later adapted as a favored theme of Peckinpah, or was a Fleischman creation with which Peckinpah was in matched step, or was a synthesis of the two. What is obvious to anyone who's seen any number of Peckinpah films is that there are themes and ideas in *The Deadly Companions* that by his very next film—*Ride the High Country*—would become Peckinpah trademarks.

Bluntly stated, to Peckinpah men are children. But in Peckinpah's universe, to be childlike is not necessarily to be innocent and/ or pure. Peckinpah's children are guileless, but rarely innocent. Children are uncultivated ids, their senses of empathy and compassion, of long-term constructive and productive living (to Peckinpah, all signs of adulthood, i.e., maturity) still undeveloped. Children in Peckinpah films are often as not senselessly cruel, but it is not a true and a self-aware cruelty. It is the same blithe callousness that has children frying ants with a magnifying glass on a hot summer sidewalk (or, as in *The Wild Bunch,* siccing an army of ants on a pair of scorpions, then covering them all with burning grass).

Untempered, left growing wild in the untamed West, that childish id in Peckinpah's universe becomes a full-grown sociopath; callousness *does* evolve into sadistic cruelty. While Peckinpah's boys and girls may be equally horrific as youngsters, his heroines are females who have grown into emotional maturity, while his heroes (actually, *anti*heroes more often than not) are cases of arrested development. The difference between Peckinpah's antiheroes and his obvious villains (in this case, Yellowleg versus Turk [Chill Wills] and Billy [Steve Cochran]) is not a difference in childish character, but a difference of degree. Peckinpah's heroes are measured by smaller negatives than his villains. This is a dynamic and a measurement apparent even in a work like *Companions* to which he was allowed to overtly contribute so little.

Consider: Kit is the only major character in the film to have attempted to make something approximating a normal life for herself. She married, began a family. With her husband dead, she turned to whoring because her priority was providing for her son; something worth sacrificing her virtuous image for. And with her son dead, she again tries to maintain a sense of family fidelity by undertaking an arduous trek to see him buried alongside his father. These devotions are all the actions of the iconographic Mother; selfless, protective, maintaining the spiritual hearth even after the earthly one has gone cold.

As for the men in *The Deadly Companions?* There is Yellowleg, not driven by love of—or mourning for—family, or anything else comparably positive, but revenge, a motive so selfish and narrow-visioned that he will put innocents at risk in a bank robbery for the sole purpose of using it to avenge himself against Turk who tried to scalp him during the Civil War. This robbery is the act that results in the death of Kit's son, which, in turn, involves Yellowleg in Kit's journey "home"—her husband's graveside—as an act of penance.

Then there are the loathsome Turk and Billy, vultures prowling the postwar West, not looking to build but for easy money. Turk's attempt to scalp Yellowleg is cruelty unwarranted even within the context of war; it is the sign of his baseness.

If Kit seems less sympathetic than Yellowleg, or more colorless than even lowlifes like Turk and Billy, this does not necessarily indicate a discomfort or inability on Peckinpah's part to render full-blooded on-screen women. It is not a hard case to make that Kit's aloof—and sometimes grating—righteousness is more squarely the result of the shackles FitzSimons put on Peckinpah.

Appropriately enough, this first film by a director notorious in feminist critical circles for mistreatment of women features an attempted rape. It is worth noting that the rape was Fleischman's invention; not Peckinpah's, but, again, one will see echoes of the encounter in subsequent works.

It is Billy who attempts to force himself on Kit. Peckinpah shows nothing manly about it. Billy (together with Turk) are pillagers (the almost scalping of Yellowleg during the war, the bank robbery, the attempted rape form a consistent pattern of violation—all are forms of rape). To Peckinpah, sexual assault is the act not of a man but a brute and here and in his following films, sexual violators will be presented as base, animalistic creatures (which explains the difference in *Straw Dogs* between Amy's first "assailant," rekindling a not-quite extinguished connection to his old girlfriend, and the—literally—hairier second attacker, Peckinpah taking the animal allusion as far as depicting this second attack as a painful rear entry). Billy is the first in a line of Peckinpah sexual Neanderthals who mistakenly think that what they can take they should have.

Billy's attack presages another Peckinpah trope that, in common parlance, "What goes around comes around." Peckinpah reserves an Old Testament wrath for sexual assailants. His characters may steal, kill, commit crimes for hire, break their word, and be general practitioners of the Seven Deadly Sins and regular violators of most of the Ten Commandments, but there is only one transgression *guaranteed* to bring its perpetrator to a bad end and that is rape. In every Peckinpah film beginning with *Companions* where there is a sexual attack, or even an *attempted* attack, the transgressor is, sooner or later, punished with death. Sometimes—as in the World War II tale *Cross of Iron*—the punishment is exceptionally horrible.

Peckinpah's depictions of the attack on Kit, of her assailant, and of the revenge that follows hardly seem to fit any interpretation of rape as an act of macho fantasy fulfillment. If that message comes off as only half-realized in a film of such limited accomplishments like *The Deadly Companions,* it was presented with crystal clarity in his next film.

Ride the High Country

The Peckinpah oeuvre properly begins here. Although this was another project offered to Peckinpah as a prepared script, Peckinpah was permitted to rewrite. While accounts indicate that Peckinpah did not alter the structure of N. B. Stone Jr.'s original script, he substantially overhauled Stone's dialogue, relationships between characters, and the climactic gunfight.

A bittersweet etude on aging and dying, honor and friendship, *High Country* doesn't cut across the grain of the traditional Western as *The Wild Bunch* would seven years later. Rather, it *evolves* the mythic Western, taking it to a naturally extrapolated vision of its twilight. For that reason, despite its melancholic undertones, *High Country* is closer to the romantic style of traditional John Ford–type Westerns than to the mordant tenor of Peckinpah's later works. Its sense of homage to the Old West of the movies is present in the film's unhurried pace, the quiet dignity of its lead characters, even in the casting of its leads, two hero icons of an earlier film age: Joel McCrea and Randolph Scott.[72] It is also there in some of the plot elements of the film, which, while well integrated, are stock elements of the traditional Western tale. This is particularly relevant to the issue of the female lead Elsa (Mariette Hartley), which we will consider further on.

For his contributions, Peckinpah drew on the people and events of his own life. Ex-lawman Steve Judd (Randolph Scott) became a vessel for Peckinpah's admiration of his father, while into Joshua Knudsen (R. G. Armstrong) he poured his ambivalence about the same man.[73]

The film is also infused with a sense of Western history. "Those mining sequences and the brothel sequences . . . took a great deal of research, but it paid off," he would say later.[74] The historical record of the mining camps of the turn of the century finds the film's renderings on point. The mining town of Coarsegold seems a textbook example of those slapdash frontier communities: muddy, rowdy, lawless, and overwhelmingly male. The one permanent structure—the community's center, one island of creature comfort, and sole source of female companionship—is Coarsegold's saloon/brothel.

With *High Country* Peckinpah began to schematize his films in a way bespeaking his theatrical training. In the classic tradition, each character, or group of characters, stands for an ideological concept. With the exception of *The Ballad of Cable Hogue,* which is practically a desert-set chamber piece, the conflicting cultures of both Peckinpah's men and women are illustrated through this approach in *High Country* and each of his succeeding period Westerns (and in most of his other films as well). It is Peckinpah's storytelling skill—his ability to create full-blooded characters to people his schematic—that, for the most part, prevents the film from being one of battling symbols.

It is evident here in how Peckinpah literally stratifies the West of *High Country.* The "New West" sits at the bottom of the gold-laced mountains. This is the sedate, domesticated, turn-of-the-century West where fast-draw artists and fancy horsemen are show pieces and curiosities. The West has become civilized and businesslike, a junior version of the thoroughly restrained East, its primal nature displayed only in Wild West shows.

Coarsegold, on the other hand, sits atop the mountain (symbolically and literally above the reach of domestication), an isolated aerie-like preserve of the old "Wild West." The aptly named town and its environs is a place of brutish, toughened men, living in a makeshift town of tents and mud (think of H. G. Wells's *The Time Machine* turned upside down with the thuggish Morlocks in the high ground and the soft, meek Eloi below). Here, all of the Old West icons still thrive: the drunken judge, the bawdy dance hall girls, and the law of the gun.

Stranded between the two worlds is the Knudsen farm, a place of self-imposed isolation mandated by Joshua Knudsen. It is a place neither fish nor fowl: isolated, but not insulated, tethered to the society below by the religious nostrums and paranoia of its master (a warped version of the societal restraints of the lowlanders), and equally connected to the attitude of Coarsegold, it being a place where a man—in this case, Joshua Knudsen—makes his own law.

The character of Elsa is, no doubt, the root of Molly Haskell's complaint that Peckinpah treated his early women characters with a "benign neglect." This is feminist criticism's way of acknowledging that these characters don't commit offensive acts, nor have offensive acts perpetrated against them.

If Elsa does not offend the feminist view it is not because Peckinpah is benign or neglectful in her presentation, but because Elsa (and her *Deadly Companions* and *Major Dundee* sisters) is so *un*-Peckinpah-like. Elsa tends to be more of a device than a character, and this is a flaw that goes to N. B. Stone's original story.

The script means to excuse her naifishness through her father's closeting of her from most outside contacts. The script's intent is that stranded between two worlds, she is of neither, thus a being only half-formed, a child/woman. While a dramatically valid proposition, in practice Elsa presents as too good to be true.

Part of the problem is the casting of Mariette Hartley. Fresh-faced and girl-next-door pretty, she looks shockingly untouched by the rustic life the Knudsen's obviously live. Hartley's clean-cut demeanor coupled with the dialogue given her make her seem not so much a half-formed wild child as a designed icon of innocence. The most compromising element of her character's reality is her betrothal to Billy Hammond (James Drury). While the film makes clear the understandability of Elsa jumping at a chance to get out from under her father's oppressive reign, it's hard to comprehend what—even in her desperation—she could possibly have seen in the loud, offensive, ham-handed behavior of the boorish miner. If anything, it would seem to make more dramatic sense that Billy Hammond's conduct—unless radically different in previous meetings not depicted in the film—would only confirm for Elsa the horror stories of sin and temptation with which her father badgers her.

Elsa's impact on the main thrust of *High Country* illustrates just how much of a plot device she is. She is not an organic part of the story. To delete her from the story line does not change the main thrust of *Ride the High Country*. The betrayal at the heart of the story between lead characters Gil Westrum (McCrea) and Steve Judd (Scott) (Judd signs on to help his old friend escort a gold shipment from Coarsegold to the town with the intent of coaxing Westrum into joining him in stealing the gold) is only tangentially effected by Elsa's story arc.

Elsa falls for Scott's sidekick, young aspiring fast-gun Heck (Ron Starr). In a plot contrivance as old as Owen Wister, the love of a good woman turns a bad man good and Heck bows out of the plot to steal the gold. This has a minimal effect on the main story, and has the feel of an Old Hollywood obligatory love interest between secondary characters: "something for the youngsters." Judd still betrays his friend, and, when the chips are down, returns to take his friend's side. That Judd and Westrum have to fend off the Hammonds coming to reclaim Elsa rather than outlaws trying to steal the gold is somewhat irrelevant to the dynamics of the main plot line and between the major characters. The Hammonds could just as well have been outlaws, and the Westrum/Judd plot line would change only minimally and in no way substantively.

More fully realized than Elsa are the Coarsegold prostitutes. Despite the oft-held opinion that Peckinpah showed some on-screen favoritism to whores, he neither sanctifies nor condemns the madam, Kate (Jenie Jackson) and her wards. More than Elsa, the Coarsegold whores seem an obvious product of their environment: bawdy, earthy, yet toughened, a match for the high country louts they must contend with.

Kate is a grotesque cherub, the kind of sexual cartoon that could only entice women-starved men such as the miners are. Despite

Peckinpah having waxed sentimental about whores in interviews, and the perception of him as a someone with a sexist fixation on the whore-with-a-heart-of-gold myth, neither Kate nor her minions are played sentimentally or sympathetically, at least in comparison to Elsa. The mockery of a wedding Kate "chaperones" is depicted as a disturbing debauch. Kate and her cadre are horribly insensitive to the fact that Elsa does not (in fact, *cannot*) share their sensibility and enthusiasms. Peckinpah does not declare the whores immoral in any way for what they do, but neither does he give them the moral high ground over a Pollyanna like Elsa. It is obvious, however, that the film indicts them for their inability to recognize, in Elsa, a woman for whom sex has a more precious meaning.

Yet, it is a mild indictment. The whores and their values are the obvious product of their circumstances. Throughout the brothel scenes the most egregious moral offenders are not the whores, but the Hammond clan. Despite the formality of a marriage, it is the intent of the brothers to force Elsa into the role of their own, privately held— and shared—whore.

Peckinpah does not condemn the whore for choosing whoredom, but *forcing* a woman into the role . . . this is a violation— another form of rape—that rates the greatest of punishments. For their collective attempted sin, all of the Hammonds are slain in the climactic gun battle.

Consistently, throughout all of his films, Peckinpah will find a moral tolerance for murder, robbery, and nearly every other act of moral transgression. But the director who tweaked critics by claiming that most women enjoyed rape, and who was roundly and repeatedly criticized for perpetuating the male fantasy of rape, regularly visited upon on-screen perpetrators of rape the most extreme punishments whether they succeeded in the act or not. Even in *Straw Dogs,* both Scott *and* Venner are killed horribly. It is a dynamic so traditional, didactic, and adamantine as to be considered (to use a horribly un-Peckinpah adjective) *romantic.*

However seriously flawed *Major Dundee* emerged, both Peckinpah's thematic scheme and his little acknowledged romantic strain would declare themselves even stronger.

Major Dundee

In *Ride the High Country,* Peckinpah's scheme posited two kinds of women: the innocent (Elsa) and the amoral whore (Kate et al.). In *Dundee,* he would offer a third. But there is a stumbling block in parsing the film.

Marshall Fine's biography of Peckinpah corroborates the account of *Dundee* star Charlton Heston's private journal that the screenplay of the film was always problematic. Despite months of preproduction rewriting there was still no finished script on hand when shooting began.[75] No amount of on-location work on the screenplay seemed to remedy the piece's defects, one of the most prominent of which was the role of the principal female: Teresa (Santa Berger). And while this again was a story begun before Peckinpah's hiring, *Dundee* was a film on which he contributed enough to the screenplay to earn an on-screen shared screenplay credit with Harry Julian Fink (who had drafted the original story outline) and Oscar Saul. If one is to heap accolades on Peckinpah for his contributions to *High Country* on which he did *not* receive a writing credit, then one has to accept that some important measure of the creative failure on *Dundee* was Peckinpah's.

The crux of the problem is that while *Dundee* is more blatantly a Peckinpah film than the gently elegiac *High Country,* like the earlier film (as well as *The Deadly Companions)* it is Peckinpah with a foot in two worlds: the more acidic one of *The Wild Bunch,* and the more traditional one of Old Hollywood Westerns. It is a blend of the familiar (Western cavalry troop led by a square-jawed hero in pursuit of Apache raiders) and a new, harsher strain of contemporary storytelling (Union guards and Confederate prisoners partnered up in the pursuit; square-jawed hero is self-destructively flawed).

Teresa is a crucial element of the film and consequently one of its choke points since the script hangs so much of the title character's (Charlton Heston as Dundee) dramatic arc on his interaction with her.

More than any female character in any Peckinpah film, Teresa is a convention, and a clumsy one at that. Whatever deeper dramatic purposes Peckinpah, Fink, and Saul tried to give Teresa, the character can't overcome the blatant fact that her driving raison d'être, as Hollis Alpert wrote plainly in his review, is that "She's there for Major Dundee."[76] Casting the curvaceous Santa Berger in the role, surrounded by impoverished Mexicans in a village picked clean by occupying French troops, only emphasizes the poor conception behind a role that, ultimately, as Eugene Archer wrote, served as "an alien love interest."[77]

This doesn't invalidate what the writers unsuccessfully attempt to do with Teresa. Like so many of Peckinpah's women, Teresa's lot is the product of a male-dominated world. Like Kit in *The Deadly Companions,* Teresa is the only one of the film's major characters to have attempted a productive life (i.e., marriage [basis of a family]); the lead woman builds, while the lead men—Dundee and his Confederate counterpart Tyreen (Richard Harris)—are professional destroyers. Her widowhood is the result of the male-perpetuated unrest in Mexico. She will suffer another painful disappointment at the hands of Dundee to whom she reaches out in the traditional role of "earth mother," a ministering angel providing "security in a hard, uncertain world."[78] That is her great strength; that despite being spiritually wounded by the internecine conflict of Mexico, she still has the willingness to reach out tenderly for Dundee. As poorly rendered as she is, she is a typical Peckinpah hero/heroine, "damaged goods with saving graces that, for Peckinpah, was the state of being bravely human."[79] But where she offers honest interest, Dundee and Tyreen can initially only respond with machismo jousting for her attention: She is, for them, an objective with which to one-up each other in their ongoing duel of egos, another form of war.

As for the motive behind Teresa's willingness to engage Dundee, there is room for debate. The most obvious ascription is it's simple contrivance. They are attracted to each other almost immediately because the movie needs a romance.

Some of Peckinpah's more supportive critics attribute more depth to the relationship. Critic Jim Kitsis writes that Teresa needs Dundee to "feel alive, to escape the destruction that is everywhere."[80] Paul Seydor's minute examination of Peckinpah's work feels that Teresa is drawn to Dundee out of sympathy and a need to "feel something besides hatred."[81] While these are both intriguing possibilities, the character is so awkwardly built into the film that any high-flown ambitions for Teresa are undercut by a near-total lack of credibility in the execution.

Still, there are levels at which the character *does* work, in ways that appear in other Peckinpah films so regularly that it seems an almost reflexive point of the director's view. Teresa *does* illustrate the recurring Peckinpah dichotomy between men and women. She is loving, generous, and supportive. Against this is Dundee, symbol of "the implicit militarism of the male group in our society,"[82] an image Peckinpah will later expose through characters like Mapache in *The Wild Bunch,* the Cornish louts of *Straw Dogs,* El Jefe in *Bring Me the Head of Alfredo Garcia,* the German military aristocrats in *Cross of Iron,* and even in the mellow elegy of *The Ballad of Cable Hogue* through the vehicle of the title character's obsessive revenge.

Teresa is puzzled by the energy men devote to fighting, particularly as the current conflicts—both the unrest in Mexico and Dundee's pursuit of the Apache raiders—seems to so little purpose. Dundee's answer is that men are drawn to the simplicity of military life, and, by unspoken extension, the uncomplicated existence of kill or be killed.

Dundee is that half-developed Peckinpah man-child, the boy (or rather, *boys* since his troops are no different) playing Army, functionally unable to make the adult commitment to marriage and family—to society-building—that Teresa can. Dundee is an icon of male self-destructiveness, conceived, as the director once stated, as a man who "kept failing in what he was doing."[83] Assigned to command a prison camp as a punishing exile from combat because of some unspecified, unauthorized action at Gettysburg, Dundee seeks to redeem himself by chasing after the Apache Sierra Charriba ostensibly to rescue captive white children. This leads Dundee on an illegal incursion into Mexico, but even when Charriba releases the children, Dundee obsessively continues, as Seydor sees it, on an Ahab-like chase after the Apache that leads him into an ambush (another failure), a schism in his command when he executes a deserter (still another), and then a dalliance with Teresa that leaves him open to wounding by an Apache sniper (and yet another).

In contrast, Teresa, in true earth mother fashion, offers unconditional love. Dundee is unequipped for love. He fights, however unsuccessfully, because it is all he knows; it is all he *is*. It is fitting that his consummating act with Teresa is interrupted by an Apache arrow; the violence Dundee has provoked literally follows him into Teresa's arms. It is also fitting that Dundee reassumes his self-control and his command only when shorn of Teresa; he is strong, again, once more contracted within the protective shell of his military mission, his single-minded, immature pursuit.

Dundee's parade of failures leads him, in his wound-induced delirium, into the embrace of a prostitute. Though it is a small sequence—just a few seconds of screen time—and the role of Dundee's whore a nonspeaking cameo to boot—it is storytelling more well-integrated into the film and more solidly formulated than the costarring role of Teresa.

Like the bodacious Kate, the silent Mexican whore is portrayed as neither good nor bad: She simply *is*. The whore is a safe harbor for Dundee, offering the same consoling arms as Teresa sans Teresa's moral judgments. Teresa may give unconditional love, but she still judges the object of her affection. The whore's profession is to be blind to the character of the man who comes to her.

In this, while Peckinpah holds no pejorative view of the whore, Dundee's retreat to the whore is viewed as yet another failure; in fact, it is his final, ultimate collapse of character. The short scene says it all: the squalid surroundings, Dundee's bearded and unwashed state (out of uniform: He came to Teresa as a military man, and will resume his uniform afterward, but his retreat to the whore is a fall from the grace of his profession). On balance, then, the whore holds the higher moral ground than Dundee.

It is typical Peckinpah that when discovered with the whore by Teresa, there is no attempt on Dundee's part to apologize or gain Teresa back. All things considered, Dundee is better off without Teresa for he has no capacity for the mature relationship she offers. He is at home in his self-pity and disgrace.

The whore ministering to damaged men, and the woman—Teresa—damaged by damaged men offer a pair of bleak man/woman equations. But Peckinpah offers a third track in another briefly limned relationship, this one between Dundee's young bugler Ryan (Michael Anderson Jr.) and a pretty, unidentified young Mexican girl in Teresa's village.

Like the episode with the whore, the relationship between Ryan and the Mexican girl is a bare sketch. Also as with the whore, possibly free of the burden of having to develop a credible, full-fledged portrait of a relationship that, in full, might seem as contrived as that of Dundee and Teresa, the tale of the duo is well-crafted and smoothly integrated into the background of the film.

The brief images of the naifish bugler and the girl faintly echo the relationship between Elsa and Heck in *High Country* in that it presents a connection between two comparably innocent people, still untainted by conflicts around them. The two young people are tender and respectful of each other. There is none of the mannish competition for her attention that marks the Dundee/Tyreen/Teresa sparring, none of the soul-baring wooing that bespeaks the Dundee/Teresa scenes. The Mexican girl does not need to minister to Ryan as Teresa (and later, the whore) must to Dundee, because of his purity of thought and purpose (Ryan has no past failure we are aware of to drag the troop through hell for personal redemption; he is the good guy, the Apache is the bad guy, and his involvement is that simple/pure). Though the film implies that the relationship achieves a sexual consummation, the nature of the two people keep it an act of purity; the two remain innocents.

Several times the script draws attention to Ryan's youth and innocence. At the village fiesta where Dundee and Tyreen duel for Teresa, Dundee sees Ryan with the village girl and wonders aloud to Tyreen, "Is he even old enough to shave?" More pointedly, it is Ryan who fells Sierra Charriba with a single shot—the only shot we see Ryan fire in the whole film. Dundee is the fallen Lancelot, warrior by inclination and training, but tainted with his failures. Like Lancelot, Dundee can reach the grail (he plans the ambush that destroys Charriba), but cannot pass through the door of the chapel. Ryan, the pure-of-heart Parsifal, has the honor.

Standing over the dead Apache chief, Ryan says, "He seems so small." Dundee replies: "He was big enough, son." There is a spiritual truth here: To Ryan, with the strength of his good nature, the Apache warrior *is* small, while to the more soldierly, more overtly masculine Dundee, Charriba would always be too big for the major's flawed grasp to attain.

While the film is obviously more about the men than their women, and therefore more about Dundee's failures (and distantly the strength of Ryan's purity), Ryan and his village senorita offer an option of promise in a ravaged landscape: Good men and good women can find each other. It's just that under such horrible circumstances, undamaged goods are of jewel-like rarity.

In Peckinpah's next film, the circumstances would be even more extreme, and the vein of goodness long played out.

★   ★   ★

Even when on top of his game, throughout this opening phase of Peckinpah's big-screen career his films bore traces of the generations of Western films that had come before. Still learning his craft, and short of the creative latitude he would have at his peak, these early films struggle in a tug of war between old and new. This is most clear in their women.

Their appearances, their relationships with Peckinpah's male characters, their predictable arcs carry the air of tradition, convention, device, and cliché. Sometimes they are a well-used cliché (Elsa Knudsen in *High Country,* for example), and other times, as with *Major Dundee*'s Teresa, they are so ineptly executed as to be crippling.

But even in these sometimes flawed works, there were developing strains that would come to more full flower in Peckinpah's remaining three period Westerns, and even half-matured those strains stand in refute of feminist criticism.

The Deadly Companions, Ride the High Country, and *Major Dundee* are clearly masculine films, their themes and main characters all concerning and concentrating on men. But there is no glorying in manliness in them, no salute to manly virtues. Left to their own machismo devices, men are self-destructive, short-sighted children, ids with access to firearms. It falls to women to mend their wounds, both physical and psychological, and to try to preserve some sort of life worth living by picking out some path of survival through the wreckage.

As we shall see, in the latter part of his career Peckinpah hit his stride by casting aside convention. In both structure and theme, Peckinpah would come back from his idle years with a film that was a "revolutionary masterpiece" because it violated so many conventions not just of the movie Western, but of traditional Hollywood storytelling in general.[84]

No Peckinpah film would more marginalize his on-screen women, and, paradoxically, in doing so be more honest.

The Wild Bunch

While many consider *The Wild Bunch* the quintessential Sam Peckinpah film (Peckinpah fans invariably fawn over even the stark director's credit during the chiaroscuro opening titles), and the film boasts themes, characterizations, and images that are veritable Peckinpah trademarks, the film is, ironically, not wholly a Peckinpah story. The story began as a rough outline by Roy Sickner, which was fleshed out and turned into a screenplay by Walon Green.[85] Peckinpah would, eventually, contribute enough to the script to share the on-screen screenplay credit with Green. However, while Green concedes that Peckinpah "made a number of noteworthy changes," the final screenplay of *The Wild Bunch* remained "faithful" to Green's original script.[86]

While no Peckinpah film offers a sequence to equal the extended agony of Amy's rape in *Straw Dogs,* on a quantitative basis the director helmed no other film that presented so much physical harm against women: one is trampled to death by a horse, and four are shot to death (a fifth in a sequence excised from the initial release print), one repeatedly while being used as a shield. It may have been *Straw Dogs* that catalyzed feminist criticism against the director, but having done so feminists had only to go back as far as *The Wild Bunch* to declare that the abuse in the later film was neither singular nor extraordinary.

Here again, Peckinpah takes a multiple-track approach, laying out several groups of women each emblematic of a particular mindset. Typical of his best works, these renderings blend academic and social history, cultural myth, and the director's own biography. In the cut of the film most often seen, there are three such groups: prostitutes; an innocent ideal; and the repressives of the new Western-taming society bringing the Wild West to heel. The three groups neatly present themselves in the film in reverse order.

The (literally) banner-carrying matrons of the new proscriptions appear in the film's opening scenes wherein the Bunch attempt to rob railroad offices in the town of Starbuck. Though the women represent a variety of ages, Peckinpah only focuses on a few middle-aged faces, most of whom are participating in a temperance rally. None of these focal women in the opening sequence are pictured with husbands or any sign of family. The overall impression is one of stultification, an emotional constipation. Peckinpah focuses on that which typically represents nurturing, motherhood, promulgation of the species and presents it in its infertile decrepitude. This is not so much misogyny as a potent symbol—combined with the repressive air of the temperance march—of the aridity the new society offers. The Old West is not growing up: it's drying up.

The Starbuck robbery goes awry and a bloody massacre— possibly one of the two most violent sequences in all of filmdom (the other being the film's climax)—ensues. In the Bunch's breakout attempt, one member, Crazy Lee (Bo Hopkins) is left behind in charge of several hostages: two clerks and a customer, another of Peckinpah's middle-aged dowagers.

The matron, disgusted at Crazy Lee, sneerily defames him: "You trash!" Crazy Lee responds with a mischievous look, comes up to the woman purring, "Aww, hush now," and swirls his tongue in her ear. On Lee's part, there is nothing sexual to it. This is simply the most egregious insult he can come up with to taunt the woman: assault the infertile with the overtly sexual. Petite violation it may be, Crazy Lee will nevertheless answer for it in typical Peckinpah fashion, going down in a hail of bullets.

The Bunch escape Starbuck, cross into Mexico and hole up at the village of one of their members, Angel (Jaime Sanchez). It is here that Peckinpah revisits the idea of innocence he depicted between *Major Dundee*'s Trooper Ryan and a young Mexican girl. But this time Peckinpah avoids the tactical mistakes of the earlier film. The village, picked clean by corrupt *Federales,* is a place of privation with starving dogs picking through dusty streets. There are no voluptuous European women tucked away here, and no obligatory love interest shoehorned into the visit. Similar to *Dundee* the few connections some of the Bunch make are sketches, generally wordless, virtual pantomimes of sweet idylls sans even the good-natured macho dueling of Dundee and Tyreen vying for Teresa's attention. When Old Sykes (Edmond O'Brien) decides to "steal his girl," referring to the Reubenesque village woman dancing with fellow Bunch member Dutch (Ernest Borgnine), there is none of the competitiveness of the Dundee/Tyreen pairing: Sykes politely cuts in and Dutch, just as politely, cedes the dance to Sykes. Here in Angel's village, all is in good fun and there is no place—no *cause*—for masculine jousting. Where Dundee and Tyreen always seem to be maneuvering for dominance, in Angel's village a salving equanimity reigns.

And that is the essence of the village sequence. This small distressed group of ramshackle adobe homes stands as an island of bucolic peace and goodwill in a film that is otherwise fraught with violence, tumult, betrayal, desperation, amorality, and violence. As with *Dundee,* the Bunch bring along a feeling of liberation to the village and a fiesta ensues, most of which Peckinpah shoots amid lush greens to distinguish the village from the arid browns and yellows of most of the rest of the film. Where the people of Starbuck marched for temperance, Angel's village residents dance free-spiritedly; the matrons of Starbuck are pursed-lipped middle-aged women, but many of the village women—particularly those who dance and dally with the Bunch—are young and playful. Where the aftermath of the Starbuck massacre shows a place of no clean moral order—with the town's mayor and ranking citizens in a shouting match with the ambushing railroad posse over who represents the law—Angel's village has no apparent authority at all, its people evidently living together in a communal purr. Poor and stripped bare, the village remains more vibrant and alive than the physical and emotional desert around it.

The Gorch brothers, Lyle and Tector (Warren Oates and Ben Johnson), are the most boorish of the gang: loud, crude, blithely violent, passing the time between robberies by "running whores in Hondo." But in Angel's village they play cat's cradle with childish abandon with one of the village's young girls. Fawning over her like schoolboys they follow her off while one of the village elders, Don Jose (Chano Urueta), comments to other members of the Bunch, "Even the worst of us wish to be children again. Perhaps the worst of us most of all."

The Gorch brothers are not the only ones taken with the pleasures of innocent company in the village. In a sequence that *is* pure Peckinpah, created on the spot during the shoot, the director came up with the Bunch's dreamy exit from the village, its residents lined up on either side of the road out of town to bid farewell to the gang.[87] The woman who had danced with Dutch steps forward to offer him a flower. Dutch accepts the flower self-consciously, like a schoolboy shown interest by a girl in front of his friends. Pike, the leader and elder statesman of the Bunch, does not mock, but smiles apprecia- tively. *Dundee* suggested a sexual consummation between young Ryan and his village *amour,* but the Bunch's visit to Angel's village hints at nothing but joyful yet chaste connections.

The people of the village—more particularly its women—are a recurring symbol in nearly every Peckinpah film. The director regu- larly uses a certain stripe of women to "provide an innocent, un- spoiled counterpoint to the rampant male madness"[88]; a what "should/could be" versus the bleaker "what *is.*"

After Angel's village, it is on to Agua Verde ("Green Water," ironically named as this nest of corrupt *Federales* is almost devoid of color), headquarters of Mapache (Emilio Fernandez), an old-style *ban- dito* staving off his own obsolescence by becoming a uniformed thug for the Juerta government. Mapache's Agua Verde is the antithesis of Starbuck. The town seems always in an unending, liquor-sodden party, and nearly all the women appear to be gay, dancing, freewheel- ing whores. It also stands in opposition to Angel's village. Where Angel's people engaged in a fiesta of clean fun, the Agua Verde gang revel in drunken debauchery; the engagements with the village girls are one of innocence while Mapache's are steeped in carnality. Star- buck is inhibited, Agua Verde morally bankrupt, but Angel's village Edenesque.

By strict definition, it is not quite on point to consider Mapache's women classically defined whores. "Camp followers" may be a better description. Mapache and his men do not exchange money for sexual favors; the women seem to have willingly thrown their lot in with Mapache and his cohorts. The foremost example is Aurora (Aurora Clavel).

Angel's fiancée, she had abandoned the village to follow after Mapache—willingly. When the Bunch arrive at Agua Verde it is in time to see Aurora give the gift of a beautifully appointed saddle horse to Mapache. A whore, by definition, does not give gifts to her patron.

While superficially this may be taken as a Peckinpah jab at the faithlessness of women, all he has done, in actuality, is put Aurora and the Bunch on an unappetizing plain of equivalence. It is only Angel who is hurt by Aurora's act. The Bunch find no insult in it, and are, in fact, amused by the way Aurora dotes on Mapache. Why not? Mapache's women find, in his circle, security, comfort, and a power unseen anywhere else in the Mexico of the film. For Aurora—as well as the other women in Mapache's camp—the general is "a way of getting out of her village and also a way of surviving."[89] Those very same attractions have brought the Bunch to Agua Verde, first to try to peddle their excess mounts to the general and to find safety from the bounty hunters dogging them, and eventually to become—in more literal fashion than Mapache's women—his whores.

It is the Bunch who will trade service for money, taking on the job of stealing U.S. Army rifles for Mapache for $10,000. The whoredom of the arrangement is made all the more emphatic when Angel balks at participating, knowing that the rifles will ultimately be used against his people. "Would you steal guns to kill your mother or your father?" Pike replies in a prostitute's motto: "Ten thousand cuts an awful lot of family ties."

Even the comparatively idealistic Angel whores himself. He has left his village not to join up with the anti-Juerta revolutionaries with whom he is simpatico, but to rob and kill with the Bunch. He warns the Bunch against committing any dishonorable act in his hometown since his neighbors are unaware of the particulars of his life since his leaving; he is the whore preserving his name at home, while prostituting himself everywhere else. The Bunch points out Angel's hypocrisy later while trying to cajole him into joining in the gun theft. When Angel balks, his ruthlessness in dealing with the people of Starbuck is pointed out to him. "Those were not my people," he rationalizes. "I care only about *my* people, *my* village." And even then, Angel will still whore: He *does* go along with the robbery in exchange for a crate of rifles he will turn over to the revolutionaries. Angel is the punch line to the bawdy old joke: "We've already established *what* you are; now we're just arguing price."

Angel's ultimate hypocrisy is in his killing of Aurora. As Aurora sits on Mapache's lap, baiting her ex-fiancé by sexually teasing the general, Angel begins to boil, pushed still further by the Bunch's unsympathetic comments. In declaration he shouts *"Puta!"* ("Whore!") and shoots her.

Angel kills her for the same sin he has committed. Abandoned by Angel who had gone off to join the Bunch, she aligned herself with Mapache; as harshly pragmatic and guiltless a decision as Angel's career choice. Angel's double standard is reminiscent of a similar interaction in Sidney Kingsley's stage play of tenement life in the 1930s: *Dead End*. In the play, a wanted gangster returns to the slum neighborhood of his youth to meet a girlfriend from past days. He discovers that in his absence she has become a diseased prostitute. The gangster recoils. "Why didn't you starve first?" he condemns. Her response: "Why didn't *you?*" And both are equally doomed for their choices.

The man who leads the pursuit of the Bunch—Pike's one-time friend Deke Thornton (Robert Ryan)—also whores himself for the same reason Mapache's women do: safety, security, and so on. Deke is pledged to pursue his old friend to the finish in exchange for parole from hellish Yuma Prison. Underlining the prostitutive nature of the arrangement is the fact that Deke has not made that pledge to the law, but to the railroad that arranged the bobbled Starbuck ambush.

The reaction of Mapache's henchmen after the killing of Aurora—beating Angel to the ground—is based on their mistaken assumption that Angel had attempted to kill Mapache. It is the measure of Mapache's pathological indulgence, as well as the lack of any moral structure among his troops, that, when told Angel was only reacting to the girl, Mapache laughs and is joined by his minions. One hand still covered with fresh blood, Mapache can find only amusement in the mistake and will later free Angel to help in the robbery: "He is not important to me." And neither, evidently, is Aurora. Later, as the girl's solemn funeral procession marches past the meeting between the Bunch and Mapache's advisors, Mapache's second-in-command Zamorra (Jorge Russek), in an image of near-Felliniesque grotesqueness, roughly hurries them along so as not to disturb the planning session. To Mapache and his horde, Aurora and the other women who come to them are dispensable toys, like the incessant mariachi band, the shiny new automobile he tours round the village plaza, and the Browning machine gun that he will use to spray that same plaza for the malevolent, sociopathic pleasure of it. Mapache is an extreme symbol of the "rampant male madness" Peckinpah regularly depicts as being innate as well as inescapably self-destructive. That madness is there in almost every Peckinpah hero/antihero, to one degree or another, as well as in his villains, and frequently his women have the price of it forced upon them as they find themselves both literally and figuratively in a crossfire. For example:

In *Straw Dogs,* Amy's rape comes as a consequence of the competing imperialisms of the low workmen and her tweedy husband;

Junior Bonner's mother is reduced to selling trinkets at a gift shop after her husband's endless schemes have left her financially depleted;

Elita in *Bring Me the Head of Alfredo Garcia* is murdered by one of Bennie's competitors for the aforementioned head.

Every Peckinpah film has them, but nowhere is that crossfire as intense as in *The Wild Bunch.*

Like the repressed women of the Starbuck sequence, Mapache's women throughout the Agua Verde sequences, and in the violent climax particularly, women will suffer in the killing zone between two groups of single-minded, sociopathic men. There is the woman hostage shot by Crazy Lee when she tries to escape during the botched Starbuck robbery, and a temperance marcher trampled to death by Pike's horse as he flees the main street ambush. There will be Aurora, and then later, in the bookending apocalypse that climaxes the film, two more will die, one of them in a manner that goes right to the heart of the feminist critique against the director. The woman that Dutch grabs during that final battle and uses as a shield is another crossfire victim, but the other instance is a touchstone of anti-Peckinpah feminist railing.

During the closing shoot-out, Pike barges into a room off the gunfire-filled plaza. He spies a young woman and for a moment it seems Pike might shoot her. But then he notes she's looking not at him, but at a standing mirror. Pike swivels his shotgun away from her and blasts the mirror. His suspicion is confirmed as a soldier falls dead from behind the shattered glass. He turns his back on the woman, she produces a pistol and shoots Pike in the back. Spitting, "Bitch!" he turns and fells her with another shotgun blast.

The brief, violent, abrupt sequence succinctly covers every feminist indictment of male paranoia: woman as back-shooting betrayer (corroborated by Aurora's betrayal of Angel, and Angel's betrayal to

Mapache by Aurora's mother); woman as whore (the obvious conno-
tation in the woman's relationship with the soldier she shares quarters
with); woman as a deserving recipient of male violence. In short,
woman as—in Pike Bishop's word—"Bitch!"

It is an easy enough reading to draw from the film, particularly
since *The Wild Bunch* only presents its women in brief sketches. Unlike Peckinpah's previous three features, *The Wild Bunch* offers no
major female anchor character. The women in *Bunch* are marginalized, out of the mainstream of the plot, but for good reason. There
may have been women who achieved positions of note in the Old
West, but in the particular environs presented in *Bunch,* such an intrusion is realistically unthinkable.

The Wild Bunch is a story *about* marginal people. The Bunch are
the detritus carried along before a wave of Progress flooding the Old
West, a world where the establishment and enforcement of law are
arbitrary (the Bunch are hunted not by lawmen, but by a posse of
"railroad deputies"—the law has been usurped by another male im-
perialism in the flux state of the New West: capitalism). The Bunch
come from nowhere and are going nowhere. There is no place they
call home, no ties, not even an aspiration of one. (When Pike muses
he'd like to make one more big score and "back off," Dutch snaps
back, "Back off to *what?*" to which Pike has no answer.) Despite
being etched with the abrasive realism of 1960s filmmaking and Peckinpah's own hunt for authenticity, in this sense the Bunch are classic
Western characters. As Robert Warshow wrote:

> The Western hero . . . resembles the gangster in being lonely, and
> to some degree melancholy . . . his loneliness is organic, not im-
> posed on him by his situation but belonging to him intimately and
> testifying to his completeness.[90]

They are men of the road, outlaws to boot, and have neither the
time nor the temperament nor the *nature* to make anything more than
a transitory connection with other people as they drift from one caper
to another. Those people may be the innocents of Angel's village, but
for men of the Bunch's low caliber, they're more likely—and understandably—to be prostitutes, or, in Agua Verde, Mapache's whorelike
hangers-on.

This is equally true of the men in Peckinpah's earlier films but it is the mark of the conventions that heavily influence those pictures that women find a prominent place in those films. *The Deadly Companions* is built on a contrivance to throw a man and woman together, and Elsa Knudsen in *Ride the High Country* and Teresa in *Major Dundee* are obvious romance ploys. It would be a mistake to interpret the minimalization of women or their relegation to the status of appurtenances in *The Wild Bunch* as a misogynistic jibe. Their place in the film is true to the film's milieu and even more so to the base characters that inhabit the film. These are men *incapable* of involving women any more deeply in their lives than is represented in *The Wild Bunch*.

Again this goes back to Peckinpah's ongoing theme of men as oversized children. The Bunch squabble among themselves like kids, play sometimes sadistic pranks on each other, and their fleeting contacts with women are, at best, adolescent. If we are drawn to the Bunch at all, it is out of a dynamic of comparable values. Flawed and base as the gang members are, they seem honorable and dignified when measured against Mapache and his troops, or against the bounty hunters who pursue them.

Even more animalistic and profane than the Bunch, the bounty hunters, subsidized by the pathological railroad authorities, are never in the presence of women, even whores. They squabble and pick over the bounty-carrying dead in Starbuck's streets like children arguing over a shiny dime: "I saw it first!"

There are *true* whores in the film and as is the usual Peckinpah trope, without implying anything pejorative toward the women, they signal a failing in the men who take their company.

Whores complete an arc for the Gorch brothers begun in the innocent play in Angel's village. When first contracted by Mapache, as a kind of "signing bonus," the Gorches are "assigned" several of Mapache's women. They skip and dance through a wine cellar and later cavort in a barrel hot-tub style. The conduct of the two men retains some of the childish playfulness of the village scene, only now there is something corrupt about it. Where the earlier scene had been one of innocent pleasure, this latter scene, with nudity and free-flowing wine, is one of childish self-indulgence and carnality. Last, before rousing what's left of their dignity to face off with Mapache and his troops in the final battle, the Gorches are cloistered with a true whore, Tector (Ben Johnson) disinterested while Lyle (Warren Oates) is engaged in a schoolyard bicker session with the irate whore over price. It is an arc—from innocence to corruption to indignity—that describes the dramatic course of the Bunch en toto through the film.

It is not a lack of allusions that brings up constant references to the schoolyard in reference to the Bunch, but a consistent theme Peckinpah/Green/Sickner have set in their characters and that can be found in nearly every Peckinpah film: men as children—immature, unrestrained, short-sighted, living in the moment, and then suddenly finding their moments have run out. The women, with few exceptions, and even when they are out of the main flow of the story, are the gauges that demarcate the immaturity of the men.

As in *Dundee,* the Bunch's retreat to whores in the film's final act is a mark of failure and collapse. Whereas the whore arguing with the Gorches comes off as something of a harridan, in the next room a glum, self-admonishing Pike keeps company with a silent, Madonna-like prostitute who keeps her infant child nearby. Even a whore can produce life—because women *are* life—and evidences that fact here at the moment when Pike realizes he and his companions have no life left.

The scenes leading up to the whorehouse scene are ones of retreat and failure. Though they succeed in pulling off the gun heist, Angel has been turned in to Mapache who delights in torturing him and the bounty hunters who have pursued the Bunch since Starbuck continue to hound them and seem to have picked off Old Sykes. The Bunch retreat to Agua Verde to hide from the bounty hunters, back down from Mapache in trying to buy Angel's freedom, and then retreat to the whorehouse. As in *Dundee,* the whores offer a nonjudgmental shelter from the misfortune brought on the Bunch by their own failings. Peckinpah's whores are often a balm, a salve, a lifeguard, but their presence signifies in the man who comes to them a hurt, a wound, someone in over his head.

Where in those earlier films Peckinpah ceded the moral high ground to his women, he takes a more honestly ambivalent tack in *Bunch.* He still posits a higher moral plain in the village idyll, one that men may visit but, by nature and circumstance, eventually leave (even the sage Don Jose, who was once a *bandito* himself, will, at the end of the movie, leave the peaceful coexistence of the village to join up with the rebels—a way of extending the dead-end existence of the outlaw). But Peckinpah also offers a more troubling alternative as well. Women may be able to morally trump men, but in *The Wild Bunch,* for the first time they are just as fallible. Rather than misogyny, this represents a harsh, uncomfortable, and unflattering equivalence, but it is an equivalence nonetheless. "When Pike Bishop shoots an armed woman in the final shoot-out, it is not an armed woman to him; just an enemy with a gun. . . . During the (Starbuck) getaway, Bishop accidentally tramples a woman with his horse as he tries to escape. He does not seem to regret this at all. She got in his way."[91]

To cite the death of these women as something extraordinary and somehow different from the multitudes of men dying all about them is a dishonest self-serving brand of feminism. Equality, parity, equivalence—whatever term one chooses to use—is a double-edged sword. To label these acts misogyny is to selectively break them out of a larger, brutal but fair distribution of favor and disfavor. This is not to diminish the *noir*ishness of Peckinpah's version, but "misogyny" is an unfairly limiting term. The more expansive vision at work in *The Wild Bunch*—and throughout Peckinpah's work—would more accurately be described as *misanthropy.* It's not that Peckinpah's films show the director with a low opinion of women, but with a low opinion of humankind in general.

A parallel can be found to a condition that arose in the career of filmmaker Robert Aldrich. With brawny adventure films like *The Dirty Dozen* and *Flight of the Phoenix* (1965) mixed with films like *Hush . . . Hush, Sweet Charlotte* and *Whatever Happened to Baby Jane?* Aldrich saw his reputation whipsaw from "a director who dealt a lot with women" into one where he was "sometimes called 'Mr. Macho.' " Aldrich's response to the situation touches on this issue of equivalence:

> I get asked that question all the time. . . . 'Why do you downgrade women?' In point of fact, I always thought of myself as a guy who was very fond of ladies, and I thought I worked with them very well. . . . Long before liberation, I thought they were to be reckoned with. They're not docile, they're not subservient, they're not secondary citizens. They kill you as much as you kill them![92]

So it is for the woman who turns a gun on Pike Bishop. She has decided to participate in what, in Peckinpah's cinema, is normally a male's game of destruction. Infected by the male fever, she shares the male fate.

In its uncut form, *The Wild Bunch* offers still another track. In one of the deleted sequences, flashbacks show us Pike involved with a married woman. The impression is of a serious affair, that both Pike and the woman care for each other, and that it may have been Pike's one opportunity to change the direction of his life. The couple are interrupted by her husband who kills the woman and wounds Pike who escapes.

Like Dundee, no matter his intention, Pike ultimately can consummate the relationship only in violence. Whereas with Dundee the violence is visited upon himself, with Pike—on the more unrestrained turf of *The Wild Bunch*—it falls on those he touches. Pike—and men like him—are like typhoid carriers, infecting others with a disease that will eventually claim the carrier. And the nature of the relationship—the woman being married to another—confirms that element in Pike shared with all Peckinpah men; an inability to plant a lasting root. By its very nature the relationship is damned, the only question being the degree of tragedy that will finish it.

The deleted sequence changes Pike from a more pathological version of Owen Wister's Westerners who won't grow up to a more tragic figure. Pike, like Dundee but unlike the other members of the Bunch, is not a man without ties, but a man who *cannot* have ties; a man who had access to a more life-affirming option, but was predestined to be denied the exercise of that option. It is yet another sequence confirming a pattern in the film and in other Peckinpah films: that of the woman victimized by competing masculine imperialisms.

The narrative thrust of the film loses nothing with the loss of the sequence, and though Pike's character benefits slightly from the added color, in many ways it is thematically redundant. In the Starbuck women left dead after the botched robbery, Aurora's "execution," and the women felled during the final shoot-out, the case has already been abundantly made. Pike's love affair only provides another paradigm producing the same, horrible result.

$\star$ $\star$ $\star$

The violence suffered by the women in *The Wild Bunch* is a large part of what makes the film such a Peckinpah milestone. This is a West completely shorn of romantic myth, the image of cowboys and gun-fighters as some sort of American knight errant replaced with the more unsavory truth. *The Wild Bunch* portrays hardscrabble characters scratching around in the chaos at the edge of an amoral "civilizing" deluge. Survival is not guaranteed, and only offered—but not prom-ised—by drastic actions producing drastic consequences.

Women are not deeply involved in the goings-on of the film, which makes *The Wild Bunch* more true to its story than Peckinpah's earlier films. Yet, they serve as enormously important markers. Dis-cussion of Peckinpah's women invariably becomes about his men, be-cause the women stand as the gauges of the sundry failings and failures of the men.

But where the men of *The Wild Bunch* are dominated by their nature, the hero of Peckinpah's next film would be at war with his, and as a consequence a woman would come as close to center stage as ever occurred in a Peckinpah project. For the only time in the di-rector's career, what had usually been an undertone in his films would become the front story. Peckinpah's next film would be about women/love/life versus men/violence/death, a story Kathleen Mur-phy would laud as "celebratory and elegiac, raunchy and metaphysi-cal"—a grand description for a romantic comedy.[93]

The Ballad of Cable Hogue

The Wild Bunch may generally be considered *the* Sam Peckinpah film, but many aficionados consider *Cable Hogue* his best work and Peckin-pah himself called it his personal favorite.[94] In the honeymoon period after completing shooting of *Bunch,* while the director, his producers, and studio Warner Bros. were still happy with each other enough to look for a second project to do together, Peckinpah took a 180 degree career turn away from the cataclysmic *Bunch* to bring *Cable Hogue* to the same production team.[95] Though another iconographic Peckin-pah film, *Cable Hogue,* like *The Wild Bunch,* is not wholly an auteur original, having originally been drafted, as the screen credits testify, by John Crawford and Edmund Penney.

Still, according to cinematographer Lucien Ballard, "Peckinpah did a lot of rewriting on the set." Costar Stella Stevens says "that Peckinpah reconceived the part [of Hildy] for her as soon as she was signed." At one point, "early advertisements for the film that appeared in the trade papers [gave] Peckinpah partial scriptwriting credit."[96] So, despite the lack of an on-screen credit, and that the basis of the story lay elsewhere, Peckinpah seems to have made substantial contributions to the screen story, particularly to the woman's part. It is of special interest, then, that the film presents one of the most complete female characters in his body of work.

The film is actually the twining of two elegantly simple and traditional tales: a revenge story and a boy-meets/loses/regains-girl love story.

Cable Hogue (Jason Robards), a desert scavenger, is abandoned to die in the waterless expanse by his partners Bowen (Strother Martin) and Taggart (L. Q. Jones). Hogue stumbles across a water hole, which he ultimately builds into a prosperous stagecoach rest station. However, he never loses hold of the idea of eventually meeting up with Bowen and Taggart and exacting revenge. When their paths do cross, Hogue kills Taggart but spares Bowen, even giving the station over to him as he prepares to leave the desert with his love.

That love is Hildy (Stella Stevens), the town prostitute in nearby Dead Dog. Having discovered "water where it wasn't," Hogue hikes into Dead Dog to enlist financing for his water station and there he finds Hildy. Hogue goes to Hildy initially out of simple sexual attraction, but the two genuinely come to like each other, and consequently fall in love. But where Hildy wants the two of them to leave the desert and see the world that lies beyond the horizon together, Hogue is unwilling to give up his station and his certainty that he will eventually meet up with Bowen and Taggart. After Taggart is killed, Hildy returns to the water station. She has married into money, seen the world, her husband has passed away, and now she has returned for Hogue. Hogue agrees to go off with her, but when the brakes slip on her novel automobile, Hogue tries to stop the car and is mortally injured.

These two threads—the "male" element (the revenge story) and its distaff partner—follow the archetypal romantic pattern of its main characters, Hogue and Hildy. Like the "desert rat" and the town prostitute, the two stories meet, grow together, break apart, then ultimately rejoin. Peckinpah lays these traditional forms against a background that is patently *non*traditional. Here is a romantic comedy about revenge and the fade-out of a way of life (that *Bunch* theme of the extinction of the Old West again), set against the near-lunar background of the southwestern American desert and the town of Dead Dog, which appears barely scratched out of the inhospitable wastes. And, it being a Peckinpah romance, it ends in an *almost* happy ending, not with Cable Hogue and Hildy going off together, but with Hildy burying Hogue.

There are other women in the film besides Hildy, and they provide a superficial structural resemblance to Peckinpah's other films. The repressed matrons that had marched for temperance in *The Wild Bunch* seem to have returned, attending an evangelical tent meeting that seems always in session in Dead Dog just down the street from where Hildy maintains her quarters; there is a stage passenger, a pushy, middle-aged wife turning up her nose at the rustic quality of Hogue's newly settled "Cable Springs"; and there is Mrs. Jensen, a naïve young thing seduced by the libidinous—and bogus—preacher Joshua Sloane (David Warner). But none of them have the weight such sketches had in previous Peckinpah films. They exist on the periphery, no more than curlicues dressing the frame of a larger picture, crowded out by Peckinpah's attention that is set squarely on Hildy. With Hildy, Peckinpah took all the disparate elements of women he had spread across separate tracks in his earlier films, and blended their more positive aspects together into a single, whole, shaded, fully realized character.

Though Peckinpah detractors might focus on the fact that Hildy is another one of the prostitutes the director was often accused of being enamored with, the character is skillfully built to avoid both the romantic clichés and more cynical neorealist notions of movie whores. Hildy is neither golden-hearted whore, nor hard-bitten sexual mercenary. She neither ministers to the outcast and unloved out of a soft heart, nor engages in ruthless pursuit of profit. Hildy exists as a careful balance of traits that, in the context of her time and place, are both credible, understandable, and even admirable.

She is as opportunistic as Mapache's women. In a man's world, her one, viable asset is her body and she has no compunction about using it to better herself and to ensure some future security. Her conduct—independent, unapologetic, ultimately pragmatic—hearkens to such real-life prototypes as Maimie Pinzer and Mattie Silks. At the same time, she is not so mercenary that she cannot establish an earnest, "clean" love for Cable Hogue. Nor is she so jaded as not to be concerned about how she is thought of, though it is only the thoughts of the man she comes to care about that matter. When she asks Cable, "Never bother you none what I am?" he replies, "No, I enjoyed it. What the hell are ya? Human being. Try the best we can. We all got our own ways of livin'." "And lovin'?" she asks. He answers, "Gets mighty lonesome without it."

The Ballad of Cable Hogue is very much about two people about whom one could equally say that what each *does* is only dimly related to the person that each *is*. Circumstances may dictate less than admirable actions by both characters, but they do not alter their essentially positive nature. Both Hildy and Cable Hogue are the only two people in the film who can see beyond each others' outer self: Hildy's being that of the self-possessed, independent prostitute; Cable's that of the crude, unlettered desert rat. The pair represents the only heart-built bridge of mutual respect and consideration in the entire film.

As per the usual Peckinpah dynamic, however, the director grants the woman a moral aerie above the man. Hildy may prostitute herself for material security, but she is willing to sacrifice that security and station for Hogue . . . but not for Hogue's vengeance quest. Given the choice of a life with Hildy or a path that may be spiritually—if not physically—self-destructive, Hogue chooses the latter (Gil Westrum and Steve Judd chose a life by gun, Dundee and Tyreen chose soldiery, the Bunch a life of violence and lawlessness). But Hildy is not like *Dundee*'s Teresa or Pike's Teresa in the deleted sequence from *The Wild Bunch;* Hildy is strong enough to protect her moral high ground and not allow Hogue to drag his violent baggage into their relationship. Instead, she leaves.

Where Hildy operates from a place of moral certainties, Hogue fumbles with doubts and missteps. He loses Hildy, and when finally faced with Bowen and Taggart, whom he kills, Hogue realizes how empty has been living based on nothing but the goal of a bloodletting.

Having led, for a while, the material life she'd dreamed of, Hildy returns to Hogue. She is the ultimate pragmatist. Unable to fulfill herself with the man who chooses his revenge over her love, she opts for incremental attainment. She leaves Dead Dog, marries a rich man who eventually dies, then having satisfied her material ambitions, returns to—hopefully—do the same for those of her heart. The mutual affection and respect is still there between the two of them: neither judges the other by what has transpired since Hildy's leaving. Her marriage, his killing of Taggart, the choices they've made, for good or for ill . . . both echo Hildy's question from early in the film, "Never bother you none what I am?" "What the hell are ya? Human being. Try the best we can." These two wisest of all of Peckinpah's characters understand this. There is nothing to forgive. It is done, they will take up with each other again and move on.

Hogue is the first Peckinpah male to turn his back on a fruitless existence, the first to overcome that violent, ultimately unproductive nature that appears in every Peckinpah film; that "rampant male madness." That it comes too late does not lessen the victory, but Hogue's demise is also a warning of the toxicity of that madness. Had Hogue left the desert with Hildy she would not have had to come back for him, a circumstance that produces Hogue's unfortunate encounter with her automobile. Hogue's triumph is in his willingness to change; his defeat in that he triumphs too late.

It is no accident that he is visually and thematically associated with the desert. As in all his southwestern-set films, Peckinpah finds a haunting beauty in the unforgiving landscape, and imbues Hogue with the same appreciation. But it is still a desert and in films like *Deadly Companions, Major Dundee, The Wild Bunch, Cable Hogue,* and the later *Bring Me the Head of Alfredo Garcia,* the desert is a twilight zone of fringe dwellers and atavistic backwaters. It is where the mainstream pushes off those moving against the current, or where those mavericks retreat to hide. It often acts like an elephant's graveyard of characters and ideas being left behind by larger forces.

It is no surprise, then, that Hildy—the half of the couple willing to engage life, to *live*—leaves this place where things come to die. Hogue, like so many Peckinpah males, holes up in the scabrous landscape. Cable Hogue does find "water where it wasn't," both on the road to Dead Dog and in the usually violent, destructive male heart, but both are isolated outposts in a harsh, lethal terrain. The automobile will make stage stations like Cable Springs obsolete, and the same obsolescence literally rolls over Cable Hogue who waits too long in his beloved desert to move on.

★   ★   ★

Hildy marks a quantum leap for Peckinpah. Thereafter, his female characters are no longer constituted by a variety of choruses, each singing a different note of a chord. From Hildy on, Peckinpah's women are increasingly represented by a single, multitoned voice, a complete woman. They will combine both positive and negative traits as they continue to attempt survival in a world governed by competing male forces.

After *The Ballad of Cable Hogue,* for the first time in his film career Peckinpah would essay a film both contemporary and far removed from the West that had hosted his first five features: *Straw Dogs.* While *Straw Dogs's* Amy may not at first seem to have much in common with Hildy, she is very much a product of the same vein. Both try to make do with the few assets allowed them by a male-dominant society. Both attempt to be pragmatic opportunists. The difference is that Amy is forced to operate in an increasingly vile war zone between her husband David and the gang of low workmen whereas Hildy's environs—the Bible-thumpers aside—is easily more hospitable.

To construe Amy as yet another Peckinpah "Bitch!" because of the manipulations she executes (and ultimately suffers for) is to ignore the horrid situation she's put in by the men around her. She is a willing trophy wife (shades of Hildy's prostitution) but that doesn't deny an obvious affection between her and David (Hildy/Hogue). And it doesn't justify David's occasional condescension toward her, or his unwillingness not to give himself more fully to matters of love (i.e., a then infamous scene of David putting off lovemaking to set his alarm clock). And neither does her understandable bridling at David's off-putting manner justify the ogling and her eventual assault by the workmen. Whipsawed between two unsympathetic imperialisms, Amy suffers circumstances Hildy never has to face. If Amy in any way qualifies for an interpretation as a bitch, it is only because being a bitch is how one survives when surrounded by bastards. Hildy and Cable Hogue are rare Peckinpah heroes, ultimately ceding control to the better angels of their nature. David and Amy, on the other hand, represent their more flawed opposite numbers, a victory for the dark angels.

*   *   *

Peckinpah returned to the American West, this time in modern times, in a tale both masculine and gentle, *Junior Bonner*. Again, the distaff side of the equation is housed in a single woman, Elvira Bonner (Ida Lupino), mother of the title character. Like Hildy and Amy, Elvira pays the cost of a man's foolishness.

The boyishness of so-called manly pursuits is never more evident than in Ace Bonner (Robert Preston), Elvira's divorced husband. Like a kid flitting from one game of Let's Pretend to another, Ace has gone from one get-rich-quick adventure to the next. His wife has divorced him, he's flat broke, yet he continues to comport himself like some knight errant, off to the next joust as soon as he can raise some stake money. He is oblivious to his own self-destructiveness and to the pain and embarrassment it's caused his family.

Minus the lethal elements of *Straw Dogs* that push Amy to unpalatable extremes, Elvira, like Hildy, can maintain an admirable independence. Forced by Ace's failures into the humiliation of hawking cheap trinkets in a souvenir shop, Elvira still maintains her dignity (no doubt aided by the casting of the dignified Ida Lupino). There is no despair to the woman, not even rancor. She may not think much of Ace Bonner, but revenge and bitterness are traits Peckinpah reserves for men like Cable Hogue; his women go on with the business of life.

It is that very wisdom that allows Elvira to have what may be her last tryst with Ace. For a brief moment, both can long for what was best about the other and revisit a loving past for an intimate afternoon in what stands as one of the few genuinely sweet scenes Peckinpah put on film. Implicit is that neither has any illusions about the encounter signifying more than an interlude. Like Hogue, Ace is pledged to his "desert" of half-baked schemes, while Elvira, like Hildy, will move on.

*   *   *

Following came *The Getaway*, Peckinpah's biggest commercial hit, but a film widely acknowledged to be artistically empty. At best, *The*

Getaway is grand, skillfully rendered entertainment, but little more. In effect, it's a bit of escapism (if one can consider a film with such a high body count as escapist).

Therefore, it is curious that the first happily married main characters in Peckinpah's films appear in his most lightweight work to that point. Carol and Doc McCoy (Ali MacGraw and Steve McQueen) are as equal-partnered a pair as Peckinpah put on screen. A professional bank robbing team, they plan their jobs together, she participates in the caper, and will even take up a gun when the occasion arises. They are the first Peckinpah couple to end a movie driving happily off over the horizon together. Whether Peckinpah intended it or not, in the context of his body of work, *The Getaway* indicates that Peckinpah thought happy endings were only possible in escapist fantasies. Like Hemingway, Peckinpah seemed to think that any story containing an element of truth would end in death.

Yet even here, in this fast-paced chase picture, Peckinpah tropes emerge. Carol McCoy gains her husband's release from prison by sleeping with Benyon (Ben Johnson), a corrupt member of the parole board whom Doc had sent her to meet and cut a deal with. When Doc discovers how much Carol gave up to secure his freedom, he reacts with anger and abuse. While Carol's sacrifice was made out of extreme love, he can see it only in terms of betrayal, even though he was the one who sent her to Benyon. She taunts him: "You'd do the same for me, wouldn't you, Doc?" It will take much of the movie for Doc to come to terms with what Carol has done on his behalf. Unlike Cable Hogue, Doc McCoy is too territorial to accept the bumps and lumps that go with being a human being and trying "the best we can."

Even in Peckinpah fantasies, a little ugly reality intrudes.

⋆   ⋆   ⋆

With each film to this point, Peckinpah's mastery of the medium grew substantially. Despite its dramatic hollowness, from the point of technique *The Getaway* displayed Peckinpah at the top of his directorial game. While he always seemed to have a handle on the complexities and ambivalences, the inevitabilities and ambiguities of manhood, those last few films saw an enormous development in his ability to render women characters with as much dramatic heft as his men.

Hildy, Amy, Elvira Bonner, and even Carol McCoy—to one degree or another—showed an evolving Peckinpah archetype quite different from the whore and bitch categorizations critics ascribed to him, and that trace their spiritual roots to the multitracked renderings of his earlier films, as if all those disparate threads had been finally woven into whole cloth. These are self-determining and independent women who will opt to stay with a man out of love rather than need. They each have the earth mother's ability to nourish and succor, and the self-respect to deal with their men frankly, without resorting to stock "feminine wiles." They all also have the strength of will to leave when their men cross some moral line as Hildy leaves Hogue, Amy tries to leave David during *Straw Dogs*'s bloody finale, Elvira has already left Ace, and Carol threatens to leave Doc if he can't accept what she's done on his behalf.

Sam Peckinpah was not one to lead his personal or professional life in half-measures. In that respect, it was unsurprising that his next film seemed, in the space of its running time, to unravel the aesthetic progress he'd made to date, and that the film that followed his biggest success would be his biggest failure.

Pat Garrett and Billy the Kid

Bleak, unremittingly grim, slow-paced (or lethargic, depending on your view), *Pat Garrett* revisits (or, again, depending on your view, rehashes) much of the themes and story of *The Wild Bunch*. *Pat Garrett* refocuses the *Bunch* story away from the gang on the run and more on the Deke Thornton–like character in pursuit, in this case Pat Garrett (James Coburn). Though the circumstances facing Garrett are less directly threatening than those of Thornton, this is still a case of an outlaw turning on his friends to buy the good graces of the new social order paving over the Old West.

But *Pat Garrett* has none of the energy nor freshness of the earlier film. *The Ballad of Cable Hogue* and *Junior Bonner* also revisited central concepts of *The Wild Bunch* but skillfully transposed them to different circumstances, whereas *Pat Garrett* comes off as a tired retread of

Bunch. With its redundant treatment of those same theses, *Pat Garrett* has a tired, perfunctory feel.

Like its two title protagonists, the film seems to unhurriedly wander hither and thither, the two plot lines occasionally bumping into each other for a few moments of spark. Both muddled and pedantic, where *Bunch* let the themes of aging and obsolescence organically emerge from its characters and their actions, those same theses are flatly presented early on in *Pat Garrett*, then hammered repetitively throughout the remainder of the film. Where the characters in *Bunch* came to signify certain types of people, the characters in *Pat Garrett* begin as types that only sporadically become characters.

Despite Peckinpah's tussling with MGM over the production and editing of the film, and while MGM exec James Aubrey can certainly share the blame for the film's aesthetic and commercial failure, Peckinpah must also carry a large measure of responsibility for the fate of the film. Though he did not get a writing credit, billed writer Rudy Wurlitzer exasperatedly complained about the incessant rewrites Peckinpah had commanded of him and the deleterious effect the constant reworking was having on the screenplay. One can see this in the way individual scenes are stronger than the film as a whole (some as strong as anything in Peckinpah's better works), as if Peckinpah and Wurlitzer concentrated on small sections at a time with no sense of an overall architecture of how the pieces would fit together.

The sense of tired familiarity and regression that plagues the film certainly comes across in those parts of the film dealing with women. For the first time since *Bunch,* there is no major female voice in *Pat Garrett*. Peckinpah returns to his old pattern of parceling out different elements of that voice into smaller roles. In part, the nature of the story forces the treatment. As with *Bunch, Pat Garrett* is a story about fringe dwellers, people pushed to the margins by great, dynamic social forces. Attachments are necessarily going to be fleeting and mainly between fellow fringe dwellers.

But in Peckinpah's previous films, the multiple tracks acted in a compare-and-contrast mode as he simultaneously wove them around each other. In *Ride the High Country* we were presented with the contrast of Elsa versus the Coarsegold prostitutes, and in *Major Dundee,* there was the emotionally wounded Teresa versus the wholesome buoyancy of the young village girl who fancies Trooper Ryan versus the whore with whom Dundee eventually finds refuge. In *The Wild Bunch,* there was a careful gradation as the Bunch moved from the repressive air of Starbuck to the morally bankrupt Aqua Verde with Angel's idyllic village in between.

But in *Pat Garrett,* as with the rest of the film, that introspection and sense of organization doesn't exist. Here, the plot wanders along caroming off one event to another with no real rhythm or cumulative effect. The final sense, for not only his presentation of women in the film but with the film as a whole, is one of dissipation.

A number of the usual Peckinpah feminine touchstones are in the film. There are, naturally enough for the milieu of *Pat Garrett,* whores. As usual, the whores are presented as a moral neutral, but mark some failing on the part of the men who partake of their company.

One prostitute is offered to Billy the Kid by his gang after his escape from jail. She is treated with no more respect than an offered drink. It is one of the few moments when the film breaks free of the myth of the Western outlaw as knight errant and shows something of the callow, self-indulgence of men who live outside *any* law, old or new. "Billy's gang, including to a large extent Billy himself, bear a far greater *physical* resemblance to the Hammond brothers [of *Ride the High Country*] and to the egg-sucking, chicken stealing, gutter-trash pack of bounty hunters that Thornton is forced to lead [after the Wild Bunch]."[97]

There is Ruthie Lee (Rutanya Alda), a prostitute who evidently has known both The Kid and Garrett for some time but now sides more with the renegade Kid than lawman Garrett. Garrett goes to her for information on Billy's location, and when she does not cooperate he physically abuses her.

But the scene has no heft, indicating little about women in this hard-baked world of outlaws and amoral lawmen. Rather it plays out as just another in the film's endless parade of scenes showing Garrett turning on old friends to pursue another old friend, and being subject to yet another condemnation as to what a soulless sellout he has become.

Of somewhat more note are a pair of prostitutes engaged by Garrett (in a scene running longer in the restored print of the film). It is, unsurprisingly, one of the few times Garrett evidences pleasure in the film. Garrett is a man who has betrayed every connection with his past for survival, and in so doing attained a rather joyless, pointless existence. He "is the only fully alienated character in the story . . . caught between a life that has lost even the meaning that pleasure might confer upon it and a life devoted to make the territory safe for the very entrepreneurs he loathes."[98] Where better, then, to find a momentary respite of superficial enjoyment then in the nonjudgmental arms of whores a la Dundee and the Bunch before their final resurgence.

Another familiar Peckinpah trope is the woman caught in the crossfire of male agendas. For one, there is the daughter of one of Billy's Mexican friends who is almost raped by those hunting The Kid, but the scene is nearly a throwaway.

More intriguing is the character of Ida (Aurora Clavel), Garrett's Mexicana wife. In a scene present in the restored version, we see a bitter, emotionally empty relationship. It is a relief for Garrett to take to the road after The Kid. Ida is no harridan wife, however. She is a woman Garrett has married less out of love than for the sake of conformity; the patina of social norm domesticity. Ida is cut off from her husband who holds no emotional bond to her, isolated from the townspeople who look down on her presumably because she is Mexican, and shunned by her fellow Mexicans because her husband—one time simpatico as Billy remains—has become "too much of a gringo" by operating on behalf of the big ranchers and other business interests behind the hunt for The Kid.

There is also the now-familiar image of joyous innocence as well. Toward the end of the film, Billy makes an almost shy connection with Maria (Rita Coolidge), another in Peckinpah's line of young Latina village naifs. Shot as similar relationships were done in *Dundee* and *The Wild Bunch,* the relationship proceeds sans dialogue, a cinematic riff on childlike guiltlessness.

But here the scene feels hollow, as if done by rote. There is no offer of redemption (Elsa/Heck, *Ride the High Country),* nor does it exemplify a purity of purpose (remember how Ryan's relationship with the village girl in *Dundee* emphasized the goodness of heart in the Parsifal-like soldier), or carry the wistfulness of lost youth (the Gorch brothers/village girl in *The Wild Bunch,* recapturing a moment when all one's choices and possibilities are still ahead, and there is no burden more than play).

In *Pat Garrett,* the scene is more ritualistic. It provides a condemned man a last moment of bliss before his execution, which is soon to follow. In such a comparatively banal context, the relationship carries none of the resonance or piquancy of similar scenes in Peckinpah's earlier films.

There is one scene in which Peckinpah does equal his best work, and that is with the characters of Sheriff Baker (Slim Pickens) and his wife (Katy Jurado). Garrett goes to Baker to help flush out Black Harris (L. Q. Jones) and his amigos, all associates of The Kid. Baker, another of those characters who populate the film who've known both Garrett and The Kid for some time, now thinks little of Garrett, or the business interests he's working for. In fact, Baker seems to think little of the changing world around him in general, and his present concern is to finish building a boat with which he hopes to leave the tumult behind. Baker may wear a badge, but, perhaps more disillusioned than Garrett, he's just biding his time until his boat is done. When Garrett requests Baker's help to go after Black Harris, Baker says no . . . unless Garrett pays him.

It is Mrs. Baker who maintains the integrity and carries out the duties associated with a lawman's badge. It is she who runs the jailhouse with an efficient, iron hand. When Baker demands coin from Garrett for his help in going after Black Harris, it is his wife who shames him into living up to the obligations of his badge. The badge entails an obligation and risks, and the honorable person lives up to them, disillusioned or not. Were not Mrs. Baker an honorable person, she would not shame her husband, and had he still not some sense of honor, he could not have been so shamed.

Mrs. Baker is not simply a wife who pushes her husband out the door and says, "Go do your job." Shotgun in hand, she is the one who takes the reins of the wagon that takes Garrett and her husband out to Black Harris's hideout, and she trades shots with the dug-in outlaws right along with her husband.

In the shoot-out, Baker is mortally wounded. He crawls to the bank of a creek as the day wanes. Mrs. Baker tearfully sits close by while her husband dies.

It is one of the few times in the movie that all the elements come together: John Coquillon's cinematography, setting a sunset of deepening crimson against the southwest wastes; Bob Dylan's normally intrusive score mournfully delivering up "Knock Knock Knockin' on Heaven's Door"; Slim Pickens, an actor usually associated with broad character roles, deftly taking the dying Baker through an initial daze, to resignation, then to sad farewell; and Katy Jurado's grieving soon-to-be widow.

It is a rare image in the Peckinpah pantheon. It bespeaks a long, loving, respectful relationship that has weathered good times and bad, a husband and wife in true, tested partnership. Devoid of the bitterness and frustration that marks the inequity, the immaturity, or the missed opportunity of previous Peckinpah man/woman pairings, it is a Valentine to the pledge of "until death to us part." In better works Peckinpah never showed such heart, and in *Pat Garrett* he indicates that he is keenly aware of what a rare quality he is portraying. He has Garrett looking on, mournful both for Baker's death and for the idea of a deep and abiding love he can never know and only envy.

Were Baker's death to benefit from the strategic positioning that enhanced men/women scenes in earlier Peckinpah films, it would have had a telling impact measured against the void that is Garrett's life and the hollow relationship he has with Ida. But the sequence is just another in the random chain that comprises a film that while being technically proficient (it may be one of the best looking Westerns ever made) remains artistically crippled.

Unfocused as the film is, and perhaps because of it, *Pat Garrett* shows Peckinpah's sense of women's moral superiority to be almost reflexive. Pushed aside by the society-changing dynamics altering the West (much like the film's Mexicans), caught in the habitual cross fire of conflicting male agendas, whore and housewife, bystander and active participant, none of the film's women indulge in the opportunism, rootlessness, callowness, and casual violence that marks nearly every male in almost every scene of the film.

Even the ostensible hero, Billy the Kid, presented as the last vestige of the free spirited Old West (the script conveniently mislays Bonney's own history riding as a hired gun for the big ranchers who co-opt Garrett), is a mix of aggrandizing legend and unsavory truth. In his jailbreak, The Kid shoots one of the deputies in the back—an execution, actually—even though the deputy is an old friend, unarmed, and can do nothing to stop Bonney. At another point in the film Bonney bumps into another deputy Alamosa Bill (Jack Elam) at a stagecoach station and calls him out to "step off the ten paces" simply because Bill wears a badge.

Like the ants and scorpions under the opening credits of *The Wild Bunch,* these dying members of the old Western breed turn on each other because it's all they know how to do. Pushing aside common sense and compromise, they almost hunger for the grave. The role left for their women is as victims of the cross fire . . . or as mourners.

★   ★   ★

Peckinpah would follow the disastrous release of *Pat Garrett and Billy the Kid* with *Bring Me the Head of Alfredo Garcia.* Easily his most bizarre work, the near-surreal effort is actually more cohesive than *Pat Garrett.* With a clear, dramatic arc, and the impetus of being, in the main, a "road" movie, *Alfredo Garcia* has that clear sense of architecture missing in *Pat Garrett.* This did not offset the fact that many found the incredibly grim story unpalatable and, to some critical eyes, outrageous.

But Peckinpah returns to anchoring the distaff side of the film in a single voice, Elita (Isela Vega), the prostitute girlfriend of saloon pianist Bennie (Warren Oates). Elita and Bennie are a more harsh version of Hildy and Cable Hogue, two members of the demimonde desperate for a break that will take them some place better.

Elita and Bennie have a bumpier road to follow than Hildy and Hogue. In a moment of weakness Elita had slept with the charming yet callow Alfredo Garcia, and Bennie uses that sin as a whip to coax her into leading him to Garcia's grave and the head on which a South American *jefe* has placed a bounty. But Bennie soon lets the sin go and the trip becomes almost a picnic excursion. They are both too riddled with flaws, and too understanding of them, not to forgive them.

They stumble through a bigger crisis, the attempted rape of Elita. Bennie's anger at his own impotence—and that it is *his* quest that put them into this situation—comes out at Elita. But later, remorseful, he goes to the traumatized Elita, sitting numb under a shower, and takes her in his arms. It is a scene of astounding sweetness in a film so relentlessly macabre and grotesque. Like Hildy and Hogue, they weather missteps because they truly do love each other.

It is also Elita who decides that Bennie has gone too far in dedicating himself to returning the bountied head. She will show Bennie to Garcia's grave, then leave him, as Hildy left Hogue to his revenge quest. But Elita's agreement to take Bennie to the grave is one participating step too many and she is killed by men seeking to rob Bennie of his trophy.

Whatever any viewer's feelings about *Alfredo Garcia* may be—and the film is extreme enough in almost every way to justify nearly any intelligible take on it—Elita is, after the diffuse *Pat Garrett,* a return to the strong women characters Peckinpah had begun evolving with *The Ballad of Cable Hogue.*

★   ★   ★

The back-to-back commercial failures of *Pat Garrett* and *Alfredo Garcia* signaled the end of Peckinpah's career as a personal filmmaker. His remaining works were of uneven quality, rarely showing the cinematic heat of a filmmaker's passion.

With moderate success, *The Killer Elite* incorporated some of the undertones of *The Wild Bunch* into a contemporary espionage tale. The freelance agents in the story are a small clique disappearing in the face of corporate management. The most prominent woman's role is the physical therapist (Kate Van Heflin) who helps rehabilitate Mike Locken (James Caan), an agent left crippled by one-time partner George Hansen (Robert Duvall).

Done with a minimal amount of dialogue, in almost documentary-like fashion, Peckinpah admirably fashions a sweet relationship between the two, taking them from rehabilitation sessions to arm-in-arm walks and finally to cohabitation. While much of the rest of the film is dramatically muddled, it is remarkable how Peckinpah, with his reputation as a macho action direction, so easily captures the growing togetherness of these two people. But then, in true Peckinpah fashion, Locken, as his Old West predecessors like Major Dundee and Cable Hogue, leaves in the mistaken assumption he can make his torn body and soul whole again by revenging himself against his one-time partner.

★ ★ ★

Women are understandably scarce in *Cross of Iron*. Sister Eva (*Major Dundee* veteran Senta Berger used here to much better effect) has a brief affair with Corporal Steiner (James Coburn) while he recovers from a wound suffered at the front. But Steiner leaves her to return to his comrades. It is neither a strong nor weak interlude, but the kind of scene that seems de rigeur in many war films.

Of more potency is a scene later in the film where Steiner's platoon, trying to thread its way back to its own lines, encounters a unit of female Russian soldiers. Starved of female companionship, many of the men try to initiate something with the women, but the firm hand of Steiner keeps most of them in check.

However, Private Dietz (Michael Nowka), left in charge of several of the women, lets one approach him. Tearfully, having distracted him, she stabs him and he dies. The impetus of war—the most mad of rampant male madnesses—compels her to take advantage of young Dietz's naiveté, but she cannot do it with the casualness of the men.

Simultaneous with Dietz's assassination, the platoon's once card-carrying Nazi, Kruger (Klaus Lowitsch), tries to force himself on another of the Russian women. When she maims him he clubs her to death. When Steiner sees the hobbled Kruger, he balances Kruger's sin against Dietz's death, turns Kruger over to the women and announces, "Now we're even." Steiner leads his men away as the Russian women descend on Kruger. It's almost as if the rage built by every aggrieved Peckinpah woman was turned against the egregious Nazi as another Peckinpah sexual predator meets his ritualistic fate.

★ ★ ★

There is little worth saying about the horrid *Convoy* and one is reluctant to peer too studiously at what is a mishmash of Peckinpah's grand themes ham-handedly jammed into an inane trucker comedy. Still, Peckinpah's instinct to put women above his men carried through. There is Melissa (Ali MacGraw), a photographer caught up in the trucker rebellion led by Rubber Duck (Kris Kristofferson), who seems one of the few participants in the rebellion with an ability to see the constructive possibilities it creates. Widow Woman (Madge Sinclair) is a feisty trucker, every bit the equal of her male counterparts and accepted as same. And there is Violet (Cassie Yates), the truck stop waitress who sweetly offers herself up as a birthday present for Rubber Duck, only to be abandoned by him as he joins the café brawl that instigates the renegade truck convoy.

Something earnest fleetingly alights in *Convoy,* in the respect shown for Widow Woman, and for the pitiful attempt Violet makes to touch Rubber Duck, but the film, as a whole, is so ridiculous and badly written that it is all rather unforgettable.

★   ★   ★

Last, there is *The Osterman Weekend.* More slick and polished than *Convoy,* the improbabilities of Robert Ludlum's novel that were acceptable on the page become all too crippling on the screen (a similar fate befell John Frankenheimer's attempt at Ludlum's *The Holcroft Covenant* [1985]). Though not as silly as *Convoy, Osterman* is as dramatically vapid and, again, one hesitates to give more attention to the film than it is worth.

There are a variety of women in the film, wives of the friends of newsman John Tanner (Rutger Hauer) who may or may not be Soviet agents. There is sluttish, cokehead Virginia Tremayne (Helen Shaver), and superfluous Betty Cardone (Cassie Yates), but they, like most of the other characters in the film, never become more than types and barely that. Of note is Ali Tanner (Meg Foster), portrayed as a strong-willed, self-possessed woman as capable as her husband of defending her family in a fight. But the film is, ultimately, a cartoon and one is inclined to think of its characters similarly.

★   ★   ★

Every woman in a Peckinpah film can trace her roots to characters and concepts in the director's period Westerns. With *The Deadly Companion* an atypical first feature, and *Pat Garrett and Billy the Kid* a confused last visit to the genre, one could go further and say those roots are confined to the four period Westerns that seem to codify the tenets of all Peckinpah films: *Ride the High Country, Major Dundee, The Wild Bunch,* and *The Ballad of Cable Hogue.*

In those four films Peckinpah rose above—or maneuvered around—the limitations imposed on him by the strictures of corporate moviemaking and managed to make some essential statements about the world as he saw it, and the men and women who populated it. The thematic lines of the women in those films not only run forward into all of the women in his films, but back as well, straight and true not to Western fiction traditions and myth, but to the historical true West. And history, as any good historian knows, not only tells us how we got to where we are, but where we might be going.

NOTES

1. Henry James, *The Bostonians* (New York: Vintage Press, 1991), 225.

2. Joel W. Finler, *The Movie Director's Story* (New York: Crescent, 1985), 42.

3. Michael Parkinson and Clyde Jeavons, *A Pictorial History of Westerns* (London: Hamlyn Publishing, 1973), 164.

4. Parkinson and Jeavons, *A Pictorial History,* 166.

5. Parkinson and Jeavons, *A Pictorial History,* 170.

6. Finler, *Director's,* 89.

7. Alice Kessler-Harris, *Out to Work: A History of Wage-Earning Women in the United States* (New York: Oxford University Press, 1982), 50.

8. Joan Swallow Reiter, *The Women. The Old West* (Alexandria, Va.,: Time-Life, 1978), 18.

9. Robert Hine, *The American West: An Interpretive History* (Boston, Mass.: Little Brown, 1973), 174.

10. John Myers, *The Westerners: A Roundup of Pioneer Reminiscences* (Englewood Cliffs, N.J.: Prentice, 1969), 187.

11. Myers, *The Westerners,* 136.

12. Time-Life Books, *The Gamblers. The Old West* (Alexandria, Va.: Time-Life, 1978), 60.

13. Reiter, *The Women,* 7.

14. Reiter, *The Women,* 129.

15. Hine, *The American West,* 161.

16. Kessler-Harris, *Out to Work,* 53.

17. Christiane Fischer, ed., *Let Them Speak for Themselves: Women in the American West 1849–1900* (New York: Dutton, 1978), 29.

18. Fischer, *Let Them Speak,* 153.

19. Reiter, *The Women,* 47.

20. Keith Wheeler, *The Townsmen. The Old West* (Alexandria, Va.: Time-Life, 1978), 38.

21. Time-Life Books, *The Gamblers,* 87.

22. Robert Wallace, *The Miners. The Old West* (Alexandria, Va.: Time-Life, 1978), 153.

23. Wheeler, *The Townsmen,* 38.

24. Fischer, *Let Them Speak,* 155

25. June Sochen, *Herstory: A Woman's View of American History* (New York: Alfred Publishing, 1974), 112.

26. Kessler-Harris, *Out to Work,* 104

27. Sochen, *Herstory,* 115.

28. Wheeler, *The Townsmen,* 172.

29. Nancy Wilson Ross, ed., *Westward the Women* (New York: Random, 1944), 135.

30. Wallace, *The Miners,* 157.

31. Reiter, *The Women,* 141.

32. Ross, *Westward,* 128.

33. Wallace, *The Miners,* 157.

34. Sochen, *Herstory,* 116.

35. Reiter, *The Women,* 141.

36. Hine, *The American West,* 312.

37. Rita Parks, *The Western Hero in Film and Television: Mass Media Mythology.* Studies in Cinema (Ann Arbor, Mich.: UMI Research Papers, 1982), 14.

38. Parks, *The Western Hero,* 104.

39. Philip French, *Westerns: Aspects of a Movie Genre.* Cinema One (New York: Viking, 1974), 48.

40. James Folsom, ed., *The Western: A Collection of Critical Essays* (Englewood Cliffs, N.J.: Prentice, 1979), 58.

41. Paul Trachtman, *The Gunfighters. The Old West* (Alexandria, Va.: Time-Life, 1978), 17.

42. Trachtman, *The Gunfighters,* 62.

43. Trachtman, *The Gunfighters,* 190, 183.

44. Reiter, *The Women,* 158.

45. Hine, *The American West,* 270.

46. Folsom, *The Western,* 66.

47. Harold Schecter and Jonna Gormley Semeiks, *Patterns in Popular Culture: A Sourcebook for Writers* (New York: Harper, 1980), 115.

48. Robert Warshow, "Movie Chronicle: The Westerner," in *Film Theory and Criticism,* ed. Gearld Mast and Marshall Cohen, 2nd ed. (New York: Oxford University Press, 1979), 471.

49. Warshow, "Movie Chronicle," 158.

50. Warshow, "Movie Chronicle," 471.

51. Schecter and Semeiks, *Patterns in Popular Culture,* 115.

52. Warshow, "Movie Chronicle," 471.

53. Jim Kitsis, *Horizons West. Cinema One* (Bloomington: Indiana University Press, 1969), 14.

54. French, *Westerns,* 48.

55. Fischer, *Let Them Speak,* 21.

56. *Four Fallen Women,* Introduction (New York: Dell, 1953), 6.

57. French, *Westerns,* 63.

58. French, *Westerns,* 64.

59. Hine, *The American West,* 271.

60. Fine, 356, 347

61. Parkinson and Jeavons, *A Pictorial History,* 89.

62. Marshall Fine, *Bloody Sam: The Life and Films of Sam Peckinpah* (New York: Donald I. Fine, 1991), 227–228.

63. Fine, *Bloody Sam,* 335.

64. Fine, *Bloody Sam,* 350.

65. Charles U. Larson, *Persuasion: Reception and Responsibility,* 5th ed. (Belmont, Calif.: Wadsworth Publishing, 1989), 271.

66. Fine, *Bloody Sam,* 213.

67. Kathleen Murphy, "The Ballad of David Sumner: A Peckinpah Psychodrama," *Movietone News* (January 1972): 24.

68. Molly Haskell, *From Reverence to Rape: The Treatment of Women in the Movies* (New York: Holt, 1974), 63.

69. Quoted in *"Straw Dogs," Filmfacts* XV (February 1972): 3.

70. Paul Seydor, *Peckinpah: The Western Films* (Urbana: University of Illinois Press, 1980), 16.

71. Seydor, *Peckinpah,* 23.

72. Fine, *Bloody Sam,* 69.

73. Seydor, *Peckinpah,* 28.

74. Fine, *Bloody Sam,* 70.

75. Fine, *Bloody Sam,* 84.

76. Quoted in *"Major Dundee," Filmfacts* VIII (July 1965): 106.

77. Eugene Archer, quoted in *"Major Dundee," Filmfacts* VIII, 107.

78. Schecter and Semeiks, *Patterns in Popular Culture,* 160.

79. Kathleen Murphy, "Blood of a Poet: The Cinema According to Sam Peckinpah," The Film Society of Lincoln Center, The Walter Reade Theater Program (March 1995): 10.

80. Kitsis, *Horizons West,* 155.

81. Seydor, *Peckinpah,* 61.

82. Jack Nachbar, ed., *Focus on the Western. Film Focus* (Englewood Cliffs, N.J.: Prentice, 1974), 123.

83. Seydor, *Peckinpah,* 63.

84. Murphy, "Blood," 17.

85. Fine, *Bloody Sam,* 122–23.

86. Fine, *Bloody Sam,* 127.

87. David Weddle, "The Making of *The Wild Bunch,*" *Film Comment* (May/June 1994): 51.

88. Ron Shelton, *"The Wild Bunch,"* *American Film* (April 1989): 18.

89. Seydor, *Peckinpah,* 90.

90. Warshow, "Movie Chronicle," 470–471.

91. William Mesce, *The Wild Bunch: A Filmguide to Research.* Unpublished research guide. University of South Carolina, Columbia, 1976, 1.

92. Stuart Byron, "I Can't Get Jimmy Carter to See My Movie!" *Film Comment* (March/April 1977): 48.

93. Murphy, "Blood," 12.

94. Murphy, "Blood," 12.

95. Fine, *Bloody Sam,* 163.

96. Seydor, *Peckinpah,* 145.

97. Seydor, *Peckinpah,* 223.

98. Seydor, *Peckinpah,* 213.

· 5 ·

Conclusion: All Things Considered

Don't pretend to think I love your sex so little, when you know that what you really object to in me is that I love it too much!

—*Henry James*, The Bostonians (1885)[1]

IN ANSWER TO DR. FREUD'S QUESTION . . .

*A*ccording to a November 2000 report from the nonprofit Institute for Women's Policy Research, American women have gained substantially in education, income, and increased political involvement in recent years; their economic and social status, at this writing, is the best it's ever been. At the same time, such progress is not universal throughout the fifty states, and, in general, women continue to not have across-the-board access to the same professional opportunities or pay levels as men.[2] The point is that while a lot has changed for American women over the last thirty years—since *The Wild Bunch,* say—a lot still has *not*, including the sensibilities of a number of men. By way of example:

> Just a few years ago, during a Washington D.C. revival production of the stage musical *Bye Bye Birdie,* male audience members burst into applause when the character of Albert told his prospective fiancée Rose that, as his wife, it will be her duty "to cook, clean and care for him."[3]

> San Francisco activist Elenore Pred bemoaned consistent Federal underfunding of breast cancer research and opined, "If we told the

149

men in this country that one in nine were going to lose a testicle, they'd think it was an epidemic and do something about it."[4]

For the last few decades, American women have tried to balance on a cusp. If, in the "old days" women were subjected to a uniform message preaching subjugation and second-class status, today they must sift through a shifting blend of sometimes conflicting feminist ideologies and old-fashioned societal gender tropes. Women-targeted magazines like *Cosmopolitan* and *Vogue* offer workplace survival tips for the professional woman, while simultaneously promoting the "traditional" idea that her chief concerns should include a sense of fashion and physical beauty. This awkward hybrid of old and new is regularly displayed in mainstream media, such as the cover story for the July 31, 2000, issue of *People*. The issue's "special report" looked at a gallery of celebrity women —actresses, pop stars, models, and the like—all supposedly emblematic of the contemporary, empowered, self-determining professional woman. But the main thrust of the fifty-page piece was how such women maintain their physical beauty, particularly as they grow older. The report included individual celeb's "beauty tips" and featured a special "Red Hot Grandmas" subsection, the apparent message in one of America's most popular weekly magazines being that thirty years after women went into the streets demanding to be thought of as something more than sex objects and housewives, their long-term professional and creative contributions are not nearly as important as how to stay pretty.

Some feminists bridling at these atavistic elements go as far as to label such publications pornography "mediated" through more socially accepted vehicles, the tacit media message being, "This is what men want. . . . This is what you must be if you want to succeed as a woman."[5]

Equality ("parity" is probably a more accurate word) has not turned out to be quite the professional/emotional/social Eden so many leading edge feminists had postulated years ago. While American women have yet to reach true social parity with American men, the increased opportunities that have come their way have put women in a position to share men's ills and foibles along with their perks. Feminist rhetoric has often taken on a tone of moral superiority (as does the rhetoric of most disenfranchised constituencies), but the move toward parity has forced a ceding of the moral high ground.

Critics of feminist rhetoric (not feminism) contended that there had always been a certain amount of hypocrisy among feminist activists' calls for equality. In *The Myth of Male Power,* Warren Farrell pointed out the unpredicted cost of female empowerment: "Feminism suggested that God might be a 'she,' but not that the devil might also be a 'she.' Feminism articulated the shadow side of men and the light side of women. It neglected the shadow side of women and the light side of men."[6] *Time* writer Lance Morrow seconded Farrell: "Women must do their share, not just take the share they find attractive. Equality must be equality in all things, not just in the professional opportunities that white middle- and upper-middle-class women wish to exploit."[7]

Women in military service, for example, had long lobbied to be included in the ranks of front line units: infantry, fighter and bomber squadrons, warship crews, and so on. To be excluded from such units, the argument went, was to be denied the fast-track career paths open to combat officers. But inclusion in such units tacitly declared that women should be just as eligible as men to be put in a position to be killed and maimed, and that they were just as qualified as men *to* kill and maim and destroy.

On the corporate front, inclusion into upper-management circles meant exposure to the politicking and backbiting that are a part of any large corporation's environment, and the acquisition of such expertise as a survival skill. Bridget Potter broached the topic of the "myth of the 'level playing field' " aspired to by feminists in a speech to a woman's communications group in 1988 where she was being recognized for her accomplishments as head of original programming for Home Box Office, making her one of a then handful of decision-making female executives in television programming:

> Undoubtedly there are men—in any profession—that do not feel women are qualified managers because of their sex. However, any woman in business who feels that her progress is being limited solely because of her sex is operating under a gross misconception. Believe me: men do not treat male competitors any better than female competitors. . . . (There is) an assumption, not just on the part of women, but of any minority, that if you remove any hint of any kind of prejudice from the work place, equal opportunity will

reign. That was *never* the case and it probably never will be. Corporate America is not a fair and democratic place.[8]

While the 1960s explosion of feminism in the popular consciousness did represent an effective shift in the status quo for women, this did not mean that women were speaking with one voice. Feminist writer Gloria Steinem was decrying marriage as an institution that was oppressive to men,[9] and more radical lesbian elements of the movement were going a step further and espousing complete separation of male and female spheres,[10] while Marabel Morgan countered with the popular success of her book *The Total Woman,* which advocated (and gave the how-tos of) a wife's complete subjugation to male professional and personal needs. While Steinem and other feminist ideologues promoted the idea of women-run businesses as a way of gaining professional and economic parity with men,[11] conservative activist Phyllis Schlafly slammed the Clinton administration's School-to-Work Opportunities Act (intended to give both male *and* female schoolchildren practical job skills training) as, somehow, a "direct threat to individual students,"[12] and Randall Terry, leader of the anti-abortion organization Operation Rescue, wrote off the professional aspirations of working women—and the rising necessity of two-income households —as self-indulgence: "they want money, they want bigger homes, they want a boat."[13]

An issue illustrating the divisions even *within* the women's movement was provided by the magazine *Film Comment* in a special December 1984 "Midsection Debate" on pornography featuring essays written by a number of feminists, film aesthetes, and civil libertarians. Flash points for the discussion were the releases of two controversial Brian DePalma films—*Dressed to Kill* (1980) and *Body Double* (1984)—and an antiporn ordinance passed by the Minneapolis city council. Both of the DePalma films enraged feminists with what they considered gratuitous and demeaning sexual content and graphic violence against women (*Body Double,* for example, features a lengthy scene of exhibitionistic female masturbation, and later the murder of what appears to be the same woman by impalement by a massive power drill). Among the drafters of the antiporn ordinance was radical feminist Andrea Dworkin.

Debate over the Minneapolis ordinance had the likes of Dworkin and WAP (Women Against Pornography) in unlikely alliance with politically conservative and religious fundamentalist groups (unlikely in that such traditionalist groups had little use for much else from feminist circles[14]). Among the ranks opposing women in favor of the ordinance were *other* women's groups like FACT (Feminists Anti-Censorship Taskforce) and COYOTE (Cast Off Your Old Tired Ethics), a prostitutes advocacy group founded by unapologetic one-time prostitute and sometime erotic film performer Margo St. James, the kind of woman that groups like WAP contend are horribly exploited and debased.[15]

Over the years, the feminist compass needle has continued to swing in a variety of directions. What had seemed declarative became qualified. Gloria Steinem, who had decried marriage and who dismissed the value of a male partner saying, "A woman without a man is like a fish without a bicycle,"[16] married a businessman at age sixty-six in September 2000.[17] Norma McCorvey—the Jane Roe of the 1973 Supreme Court Roe vs. Wade decision that legalized abortion—joined Operation Rescue twenty-two years later. Pop star Madonna, who some considered a symbol of female empowerment in how she controlled her career, took on single motherhood, and gloried in her own sexuality—particularly in her controversial photographic book *Sex,* which featured her nude in a variety of sexual situations—settled in England and carped about nudie photographs in British tabloids: "My God, you see nothing but naked women in the newspapers here. I just have not been able to get used to the naked girls on Page 3."[18]

This maelstrom of mixed messages, confused goals, and out-and-out retrograde thought are equally evident in the entertainment arena. Whatever gains women have made socially far outstrip their deteriorating status in film and television. In *From Reverence to Rape,* Molly Haskell mapped a downward course for women in films beginning with the sexually repressed films of the 1950s and reaching a nadir at the time of her writing in the early 1970s.[19] Increasing violence against women on screen was, and continues to be, viewed by a number of observers as "a hysterical response to sixties and seventies feminism: The male spectator enjoys a sadistic revenge on women who refuse to slide neatly and obligingly into his patriarchally determined view of 'the way things should naturally be.' "[20] Susan Faludi, in her 1992 book, *Backlash: The Undeclared War Against American Women,* posits a male reaction against the women's movement that, in part, manifests itself in the poor quality of female images on television and in film.[21] Faludi cites, as examples, the psychotic nanny of *The Hand That Rocks the Cradle* (1992), the sexually obsessive Glenn Close character in *Fatal Attraction* (1987), and the cute prostitute that finds herself a rich husband in *Pretty Woman* (1990).[22]

Against this, one might thankfully note the surging popularity of modestly budgeted independent films over the last decade or so that have provided a venue for up-and-coming talent and veteran actresses in a refreshing stream of truly interesting, starring roles. Hillary Swank, Lili Taylor, Chloe Sevigny, Helena Bonham Carter, Laura Linney, and Christina Ricci are just a few of a burgeoning class of powerfully talented young women displaying their best thespian muscles in offbeat "indie" films like *Boys Don't Cry* (1999), *You Can Count On Me* (2000), and *The Opposite of Sex* (1999). The same venue also offers compelling roles for proven actresses past the age when mainstream development execs consider them commercially viable, for instance, Meryl Streep in *Dancing at Lughnasa* (1998), Sigourney Weaver in *The Ice Storm* (1998), Ellen Burstyn in *Requiem For a Dream* (2000), Emma Thompson in *Howard's End* (1992), and Frances Mc-Dormand in her Oscar-winning turn as a pregnant law enforcement officer in the decidedly un-Hollywoodish *Fargo* (1996).

Within the limited commercial opportunities mainstream cinema does offer, there are women who have graduated to the mega-million-dollar salaries that have previously been an all-male tier. Despite an iffy box-office track record, Sandra Bullock's per-film paycheck has risen from $1.2 million to $10 million,[23] and, with box-office blockbusters like *Erin Brockovich* (2000) and *Runaway Bride* (1999), Julia Roberts joined the small circle of $20 million per picture performers and is considered one of the industry's "most influential women."[24] *The Hollywood Reporter* described both Roberts's power and its rarity among her sex saying, "Julia Roberts is really the only actress in Hollywood who has the ability to have any project she's interested in made. She's the only one who can command that kind of power." The likes of Roberts, Bullock, Michelle Pfeiffer, Drew Barrymore, and others have even set up their own production companies to give themselves increased creative control and financial participation in their projects.

Women have also gained unprecedented entry to the elite circles behind the camera. Nora Ephron, Penny Marshall, Amy Heckerling, and Betty Thomas have all become familiar director's credits, and Kathryn Bigelow (*Near Dark* [1987], *Strange Days* [1995]) and Mimi Leder (*The Peacemaker* [1995], *Deep Impact* [1998]) helm the kind of big-budget action films previously the preserve of men. The ranks of female producers—such as *X-Men* (2000) producer Lauren Shuler-Donner, sci fi maven Gale Anne Hurd, and Steven Spielberg's usual producing partner Kathleen Kennedy—and studio execs, like Universal Pictures's chairwoman Stacey Snider, DreamWorks's Laurie MacDonald, Disney's Nina Jacobson, and Paramount's production exec Sherry Lansing—perhaps the most powerful woman in the movie business at this writing[25]—are likewise expanding.

TV has also seen a growing trend in sitcoms and drama series toplined by newcomers and veteran actresses, produced or executive produced by women like Oprah Winfrey, Barbara Hall ("Judging Amy"), and Marcy Carsey and Caryn Mandabach of Carsey/Werner ("Third Rock From the Sun," "Roseanne," "That 70s Show"), and overseen by female network programming execs like Nina Tassler and Wendi Goldstein at CBS, and Lisa Leingang at NBC. Television has gone from initial tentative steps in displaying the independent woman in such series as "That Girl" in the 1960s to a pantheon of strong women carrying their own series across the gamut of genres: "Murphy Brown," "Roseanne," "Cybil," "Ally McBeal," "Felicity," "Providence," "Judging Amy," "Buffy the Vampire Slayer," "Time and Again," et al. Women have also found parity with male authority in such ensemble pieces as "ER," "Law & Order," "Third Watch," and others.

Since 1991, *The Hollywood Reporter* has published a Women in Entertainment Power 50 list, and over the course of that time "the number of women in high-ranking positions increase tenfold—a list that was once only peppered with presidents of film and television entities is now dominated by them . . . our informal survey of the roster of the major film studios revealed that women occupy about 30% of the executive slots."[26]

For all this progress, these new opportunities are at least nega-

tively balanced out (and, at worst, offset) by the fact that the entertainment industry remains tilted heavily in favor of men. Most of the
major stars—and most of the better-paid stars—remain men. In the
circles of major studio feature film production, men still retain an
overwhelming dominance in administrative, production, and creative
posts, particularly at the senior and executive level. Most trenchantly,
the product on screen is still primarily about and for men.

While the *why* behind male-oriented film entertainment offered
by Susan Faludi might be arguable, the numbers show this long-
standing trend has accelerated precipitously in recent years, at least on
the creative side of the major studios. By the mid-1990s, just 29 percent of feature film roles were going to women, with screenwriters
contending that strong women characters didn't "sell," and production executives maintaining the old plaint that women couldn't carry
movies. Producer Joel Silver of *Lethal Weapon* fame went as far as to
say that the only practical role for women on screen was "either
naked or dead."[27] On television, "Men are powerful, authoritative,
dominant and aggressive; women are subservient and relatively unim-
portant except in family roles and as sex objects," and, despite recent
qualitative and quantitative upticks, men have outnumbered women
in TV over the years approximately 3-to-1.[28] Men's on-screen careers
seem resistant to the passage of time. Sean Connery in his seventies
could still be cast opposite Catherine Zeta-Jones, less than half his age,
in *Entrapment* (1999), but an actress's career remains governed by the
clock as much as anything else. Famke Janssen, actress *(X-Men* [2000])
and ex-model explained the fragility of a woman's Hollywood professional arc thusly: "If you play the pretty girl or the sidekick . . . your
career is a very short one, because the moment those looks start fading, you're over."[29]

Called to answer for creative decisions that favor men and such
male-oriented action fare as *Top Gun, Con Air, The Rock, The Hunt
For Red October, Goldeneye, Crimson Tide,* and so on along with teen
male-oriented sex fantasy fare like *American Pie* (1999) and the broad,
bawdy frat house humor of films like *There's Something About Mary*
(1998) and *South Park: Bigger, Longer & Uncut* (1999), production
execs point to the marked underperformance of such serious major
studio "women's pictures" as the Michelle Pfeiffer starrer *Deep End of
the Ocean* (1999), Jodie Foster's rendering of *Anna and the King* (1999),

and the still-more disappointing screen adaptation of Toni Morrison's *Beloved* (1999). If a big-budget film version of an acclaimed novel like *Beloved,* starring one of America's most beloved TV personalities— Oprah Winfrey—and directed by Academy Award–winner Jonathan Demme could flop—so the case is made—then why bother? Like-wise, big studio romances like *Random Hearts* (1999), *The Horse Whisperer* (1999), and *The Story of Us* (2000), which paired women leads with top male stars, also produced weak box office.

Actress Glenn Close provides a succinct summary to the situation: "I think women will always be problematic in film because it's a male-oriented and largely male-run business. They don't know what to do with us in life, so why would they know what to do with us in film?"[30]

★   ★   ★

Even among the limited but impressive successes in film and on TV that do feature women as headliners, the consensus on what constitutes strong, positive female imagery is nonexistent, very much reflecting the same sense of experimentation and confusion among women off screen.

Some films that do show women in a stronger, more independent and constructive attitude represent, in some critics' eyes, dubious progress. Susan Faludi points out that the strength of heroines like Sigourney Weaver in *Aliens* (1986) and Linda Hamilton in *Terminator 2* (1991), among others, grant women great strength and determination—but only in the traditional role of protective mother figure.[31] Film critic Roger Corliss also finds such heroines doubtful contributors to the image of the independent female but for different reasons, observing that they "are not strong women who use their ingenuity, humanity and mother wit. They are Rambo in drag. . . . Too many filmmakers strapped by the conventions of the shoot-'em-up genre think they are solving the problem of beefing up women's roles by turning them into beefcake. . . . [A filmmaker like James] Cameron *(Terminator 2)* wonders, Why can't a [modern] woman be more like a (mean) man? Then he makes her into one."[32]

Pertinent to the topic of this examination, another such example is provided by the 1994 remake of Peckinpah's *The Getaway.* In a conscious effort to put the role of Carol McCoy (Kim Bassinger this time) on a more equal footing with her husband Doc (Bassinger's real-life husband Alex Baldwin), the film makes them almost dramatically indistinguishable. Peckinpah's version opened with one of the picture's few scenes with heart; an almost documentary-like montage sequence of Doc in prison suffering the mind-numbing routine of road gang and machine shop work, and the boredom and celibacy of cellblock life. The 1994 version, on the other hand, begins with the McCoys target shooting together, the camera lingering almost fetishistically on chrome-plated weapons firing in slow motion. In this version, Carol McCoy is every bit the cool, steely killer her husband is, so much so that she wants his pet .45 automatic for her own. Gunplay and sexplay are two sides of the same coin with both partners equally adept at each.[33]

If such images are negatives, or at least only arguable positives, what *would* constitute a clear, positive, acceptable female role model? The Faludi school of thought labels the title characters of *Thelma and Louise* as positive feminist images, while Betty Friedan includes them in her complaint about "how far we have strayed from the autonomous, independent women in control of their lives . . . that used to be played by Katherine Hepburn, Barbara Stanwyck, Myrna Loy and Bette Davis."[34]

★   ★   ★

The point here is not to denigrate the women's movement or carp on the minor foibles and inconsistencies of those personages and images considered the movement's forefront representatives. The fact is that feminism has always been a sociocultural *movement*, not a political party with an agreed-upon agenda. Like other similar movements—that of African Americans, say, or the physically and mentally handicapped—there's more of a consensus on the unfairness of the status quo rather than universal agreement on what the template and measuring sticks of progress should be. More simply, it has been easier to get women to agree on what they are *against* rather than to agree on what they are *for*. The feminist explosion of the 1960s–1970s *did* succeed in jarring the status quo, and, in consequence, America continues to reevaluate and police itself on matters of fairness regarding women as well as other constituencies. But, unsurprisingly, in upsetting a mind-set that has been cultivated and ingrained into American society over more than three centuries, after just three decades women are still in the process of redefining themselves, a process made all the more difficult as American society and culture seem to evolve with ever-increasing rapidity. It's like trying to build a new building on shifting ground.

As we move further from that turbulent era when feminism went into the streets with what seemed like one, unified voice, there is greater confusion about what "feminism" is and should be, a circumstance that explains the Betty Friedan remark cited earlier in this volume that feminism is a revolution "stalled, stuck, stopped in its tracks."[35] That stumble evidenced itself in the statement of another feminist, Gloria Steinem, when, in a 1995 interview she was asked, "Why are so many women so scared to call themselves a feminist today?" Steinem replied, "Because they're not sure what the word means."[36] Of late, women seem more likely to politically coalesce around demographically relevant issues rather than abstract feminist ideological themes, as demonstrated in the Million Mom March for gun control and organizations like Mothers Against Drunk Driving.[37]

SLIDING SCALES

There is a relevant point to this extended digression into the trials and tribulations of feminism over the last few decades. In the context of that ongoing social flux, and the militancy of those early movement days of the 1960s–1970s, it isn't much of a reach to point out just how subjective the feminist criteria was that called the work of Sam Peckinpah to task. The claim of misogyny was based on a repetitive focus on a few select images subjectively interpreted in a volatile time, and that focused exclusively on the director without acknowledging long-standing industry trends and Peckinpah's own questionable authority over his films. While one might validly call into question the subjectivity with which those same images have been interpreted in this volume, that would only serve to underscore the point that we are here dealing with opinion that was neither set nor agreed upon by consensus, and that was as much a product of the heat of the moment as of insightful criticism. As film critic Marcia Pally wrote, "if an oil canvas of a nude hanging in a gallery is stolen and the thief jerks off to it, is that painting art or pornography? Implicit in the problem of definition is the question of who gets to decide."[38]

The feminist panning of Peckinpah—and this is pure surmise—came from an earnest enough—if, perhaps, inchoate—discontent, not just with Peckinpah, but with the general condition of women both on screen and off. Ann Snitow, of FACT, showed particular insight in this regard in her contribution to the *Film Comment* debate on porn:

> How many engaging grade-B entertainments have begun with a touch of intriguing emotional yeast only to end as the usual flat white bread because of that old, dreary motive-to-negate-the-female? What women feel most, I think, is disappointment. . . . Our present film culture does do violence of a kind to women—the violence of impoverishment. . . . I've been using the word 'violence' metaphorically, which seems fitting in a discussion . . . where what's at stake is consciousness, not actual torn flesh and blood.[39]

⋆   ⋆   ⋆

Feminist criticism of Peckinpah's work displayed no acknowledgment of how his work fit into the larger context of the industry. We have seen that Peckinpah's films fell into the currents of already entrenched and developing trends in the motion picture business. It would be disingenuous to write the director off as simply a point on a line. Were he that disposable, his work would not have retained the interest it does for both popular audiences and the critical community. His films *did* serve as benchmarks on their own artistic merits, within the evolution of their respective genres, and in the growing liberalization of film content. But as we've seen, Hollywood has long tended toward the male, and a growing reliance on such male-oriented genres as action and thriller films was already long in process by the time of Peckinpah's commercial coronation with *The Wild Bunch.* The howling over graphic on-screen sex and violence had begun years earlier with films like *Bonnie and Clyde, Point Blank,* and *The Dirty Dozen.* The success of Peckinpah titles like *Bunch, Straw Dogs,* and *The Getaway* may have pushed the industry a little further a little faster, sparking a multitude of clones as is the industry's wont, but in retrospect, the evolution they were a part of seems, in hindsight, inevitable.

Peckinpah was also derided for a perceived obsession with macho themes and stories, a criticism that, again, we have seen ignored a larger context, and was more perception than reality. A 1972 cover story by *Esquire* touting the production of *The Getaway* illustrates the point. "Here he is again, America," the intro to the piece began, "The last time Sam Peckinpah directed a movie *(Straw Dogs)*, Pauline Kael called it 'a fascist classic.' " Actually, Peckinpah's previous film had not been *Straw Dogs* but the amiable *Junior Bonner*. The piece went on, "It was a violent movie, America, and so was *The Wild Bunch* before it."[40] Another untruth: The film before *Straw Dogs* had been *The Ballad of Cable Hogue*. The theme of the entire story was what kind of filmmaker made this—according to *Esquire*—unbroken parade of violent movies? In talking to actors who'd worked with Peckinpah in the past to give some insight into the director, *Esquire* quoted actors from *The Getaway, Bunch,* and *Straw Dogs* and *only* those films.[41]

Even within the industry, Peckinpah had a tendency to be type-cast. In a combative 1984 interview, Brian DePalma, dealing with the same kind of feminist brickbats tossed at Peckinpah, defended himself in a comparison saying, "I like directing women. I'm not Sam Peck-inpah, you know, down in Mexico screwing the whores."[42]

On the contrary, the filmmaker displayed an interest in a variety of material, very little of which he was given the opportunity to bring to the screen. Peckinpah was as much a victim of his successes as of his demons, and, given the opportunity, he was as likely to make more introspective and frankly sweet films like *The Ballad of Cable Hogue* as the parade of *The Wild Bunch* pastiches, which became his only source of work following the debacles of *Pat Garrett and Billy the Kid* and *Bring Me the Head of Alfredo Garcia* and his subsequent ostrasization from mainstream Hollywood.

His critics, and even those in the movie trade, confused his private life with his professional possibilities, and it jaded their judgment of his work and capabilities. To his professional and critical detriment, Peckinpah often amused himself by further provoking controversy with his deliberately argumentative remarks. It was somewhat self-serving of feminist critics to lend too much credence to Peckinpah's flippant remarks as offering supposed insight into his work. Samuel Beckett had deliberately given misleading responses to questions about his work because he did not want to absolve his audience of the responsibility to think for themselves about a play like *Waiting For Godot*. Peckinpah may not have been a Samuel Beckett, and the motive behind his bon mots may have been less artistically altruistic, but the value of his commentary was equally dubious and even a half-hearted attempt to be more objective in analyzing his work would have shown it so.

His high visibility in the late 1960s and early 1970s and his outrageous responses to criticism helped make him a lightning rod for feminist critiques. Peckinpah was not the only filmmaker of the time to touch on feminist hot button issues, but a review of critical commentary of the time shows his work to have been singled out. Either by design or by reflex (understandable considering Peckinpah's provocative temperament), critics reacted much more harshly to controversial elements of his films than when those same elements appeared in the work of other directors.

In Bob Rafelson's *Five Easy Pieces* (1970), for example, Jack Nicholson, attracted to Susan Anspach, and assuming—correctly, as we discover—that she has a repressed yearning for him, breaks through her emotional resistance by physically forcing himself on her. The aggressive act quickly becomes one she accepts willingly (presaging Charlie Venner's attack on Amy in *Straw Dogs*). Critic Roger Greenspun did not label the act a rape in his review, nor confuse the subtext as was the routine with *Straw Dogs,* but called the act simply, "a sexual conquest."[43] The majority of reviewers shared the opinion set down in *The Motion Picture Guide* that the film was "wonderful" and one of the best films of the year.[44]

Paul Mazursky's *Blume In Love*, released the year after *Straw Dogs,* featured a scene where George Segal forces himself on his ex-wife. Again, the act evolves into one of acquiescence rather than force. In the three reviews selected by *Filmfacts* magazine to represent critical reaction to the film, there is no mention that the sex act is a forced one or argument about a woman character who welcomes the act of rape.[45]

Alfred Hitchcock's *Frenzy* was in release simultaneously with *Straw Dogs*. The film features the only graphic sex scene in Hitchcock's work: a rape/strangulation by a serial killer. Of the *sixteen* reviews canvassed by *Filmfacts,* only *one* was a negative, and the film was widely hailed by critics as a "return to form" by the director after several years of indifferent work! Vincent Canby's review read, in part, that, "*Frenzy* was the first good movie about a sex murderer since *Psycho.*"[46]

The same double standard can be seen regarding another supposed Peckinpah motif: "the heroes [in his films] rarely meet any women except whores."[47] Yet, in 1968, none of the four major reviews selected by *Filmfacts* of the Ted Post–directed *Hang 'em High* even mentioned that a significant amount of the film takes place in a bordello.[48] Robert Altman received critical acclaim for *McCabe and Mrs. Miller* (1971), a story about a brothel-keeper in the northwest. *The Wild Bunch* and the madam he enlists to manage the place.[49]

To go a step further, Peckinpah's works were pointedly exempt from an attitude harbored in some quarters that accepted prostitution as a viable cinematic device to depict women taking control of their lives. "Self-determination has often elicited admiration for hooker heroines from Julie Christie in *McCabe and Mrs. Miller* to Jane Fonda in *Klute,* and . . . Louise Smith in *Working Girls* and Julie Walters in *Personal Services.* What separates these girls working in celluloid from the traditional hooker is a common assumption that a girl's body is her own terrain to be rented to whom and for whatever price she may desire—ethics, romance, and dangers be damned."[50]

SAD TRUTHS

"I love outsiders," Peckinpah once said. "I go for the loners. I'm nothing if not a romantic, and I've got this weakness for losers on a grand scale."[51] This concept manifested itself time and again in his films. "[Howard Hawks and Peckinpah] founded communities of scarred and wounded badlanders. . . . [John Huston] and Peckinpah [liked] to populate their movies with colorful dregs, down-and-outers with a penchant for taking off on dangerously absurd trips to nowhere, for money or the dreams it can buy."[52]

It is certainly true enough of Peckinpah's Western men: the two aging gunfighters of *Ride the High Country,* their more visceral counterparts—as well as the men who hunt them—in *The Wild Bunch* and *Pat Garrett and Billy the Kid,* their spiritual colleague in *The Ballad of Cable Hogue*—all are men that are, in the words of the promotional poster for *Bunch,* "Out of step, out of place, and desperately out of time." Major Dundee is a variant, but essentially similar: a man belonging nowhere, failing at nearly everything he does, on a fruitless quest for dubious accomplishment to establish *some* sense of purpose and self-worth. Even Yellowleg, from Peckinpah's comparatively impersonal first film, *The Deadly Companions,* is of the same ilk: an outlaw, literally one *outside* the social system of law and order. They are all of a piece, these men: "the Westerner as a man no longer in control or even in the middle—a man totally outside, behind, and unnecessary to a civilization that Peckinpah felt lost its own soul when it lost its spiritual and geographical frontiers."[53]

The women of Peckinpah's period Westerns are of the same stripe. It is no surprise that whores appear so regularly in his period films. There is a factual basis for their being a recurring image in films respected for their realism, but aside from the historical rationalization, they are the natural co-inhabitants of the fringe world Peckinpah so often depicts. Still, we have seen that the claim that Peckinpah's heroes "rarely meet any women except whores" is a fallacy. Even a film immersed in the lives of die-hard outcasts as *The Wild Bunch* featured a variety of women.

It is selective criticism on Molly Haskell's part to dismiss the women in Peckinpah's early films as the product of "benign neglect" simply because they fail to fulfill the qualifications of her indictment. If the women in *The Deadly Companions, Ride the High Country,* and *Major Dundee* fail, it is not out of neglect but as a growing pain of Peckinpah's aesthetic, the films trying to encompass his own filmic ambitions while falling within predictable Hollywood archetypes and further restrained by autocratic producers. In all of Peckinpah's period Westerns, whether it is the dispassionate *The Deadly Companions,* the full-throttle Peckinpah flavor of *The Wild Bunch,* or the ambitious failure of *Pat Garrett and Billy the Kid,* Peckinpah offers a spectrum of women ignored by feminist and feminist-flavored criticism: Elsa Knudsen, the Teresas of *Dundee* and *Bunch,* the village innocents of the same films, Ida Garrett and Mrs. Baker from *Pat Garrett,* and, most important, *Cable Hogue*'s Hildy, who seems the cumulative sum of all the women, in small parts and large, Peckinpah had presented up to that point.

All of Peckinpah's Western women—whores, wives, widows, lovers committed and spurned, the innocent and the fallen, the selfless and the self-seeking—share a disenfranchisement more bitter than that of Peckinpah's Western men, for their powerless condition does not change with the times. It is a constant by-product of men's retention of the power of decision making, money, and physical force. It is a circumstance that ultimately exploits and/or victimizes, and provides women with scant options. Their productive instincts frustrated by the destructive ones of men, Peckinpah's women try to survive and escape down such paths as marriage, prostitution, and desertion.

Like some of Peckinpah's men, some of his women express few qualms about the actions they must take to survive. Peckinpah's men rob banks and railroads, they turn on one-time friends, they kill without compunction, they'll even betray their own sense of honor. Next to this, the whores of *Ride the High Country* and camp followers of *The Wild Bunch* seem all of a Western piece. If a Peckinpah woman is capable of shooting someone in the back, as in *Bunch,* then so are his men—and they do so in nearly every one of his Westerns! Opportunism and self-preservation know no gender boundary.

J. A. Cuddon, playwright, essayist, and editor of fiction collections of the macabre, in describing the ethos of the horror story, interestingly touches on the spine of Peckinpah's cinema fictions. Most of the filmmaker's work—and certainly all of his better films—deal with a certain kind of horror—the physical, psychological, and emotional destruction consequent to human failing, to resorting to more primal behavior rather than opting for evolving societal restraints:

> In the hands of a serious and genuinely imaginative writer the horror story . . . explores the limits of what people are capable of doing. . . . Thus he ventures . . . into the realms of psychological chaos, emotional wastelands, psychic trauma . . . the capacity for experiencing fear, hysteria and madness, all that lies on the dark side of the mind and the near side of barbarism . . . where some kind of precarious vigilance and control are kept by convention and taboo and by the repressive censors of feelings . . . the horror story . . . is part of a long process by which we have tried to come

to terms with and find adequate descriptions and symbols for deeply rooted, primitive and powerful forces, energies and fears which are related to death, afterlife, punishment, darkness, evil, violence and destruction.[54]

By that definition, a Peckinpah Western, when the director was on his game, such as in *The Wild Bunch,* is as much a horror story about humanity's dark side, as a tale of the Old West. There is no rational, logical reason to think that such human penchants are the provence of one gender or the other.

THE HIGH ROAD

Molly Haskell writes of "the big lie perpetrated on Western society": the idea "of women's inferiority."[55] Haskell alleges that that lie shows up on the movie screen in heroines that "could act on the same power and career drives as a man only if, at the climax, they took second place to the sacred love of a man."[56] Yet, in Peckinpah—one of Haskell's repeated targets—it is Heck who throws away his "career" (gunfighting) to follow Elsa's moral lead in *Ride the High Country;* Teresa rejects Dundee; Hildy leaves Cable Hogue when Hogue cannot leave *his* career (revenge) in the barren desert that spawned it.

For all the realism of his best films, Peckinpah was, in many ways, a romantic, particularly—and ironically—about women. He posited, in *The Wild Bunch,* that women were as capable of moral failure as men (the film is, in fact, the *only* Peckinpah Western where this is so), but more regularly granted them a moral ascendance. Women, in his eyes, had the same *capacity* for sin as men, but regularly opted for a higher moral road.

"[As] men in a patriarchal society have set women up on . . . pedestals," wrote film critic Robin Wood in explaining violence against women in films, "and thereby constructed them as oppressive and restrictive figures, they have developed a strong desire to knock them down again."[57] In Peckinpah's Westerns, however, it is the *men* who take the fall. Obsessive, destructive, and lost, Peckinpah's men—in those Westerns where he retained the most creative latitude—normally destroy themselves in one form or another: The

Bunch die, Cable Hogue dies, Steve Judd dies, Dundee's command is all but obliterated in its final battle, Pat Garrett kills his "better half"—his old friend Billy the Kid—spiritually killing himself.

The victimization of women in Peckinpah's West is, whatever auteur's psychology might have been at work behind it, presented not out of a gratuitous or a deserving punishment of womanhood, but as a product of the failure of men. Pat Garrett fails Ida; Dundee fails Teresa; Billy Hammond fails Elsa in *High Country;* Cable Hogue fails Hildy; Pike Bishop fails *his* Teresa. And in case the onus of blame is at first unclear, Peckinpah usually grants his men just enough insight to make them understand and be humbled by their respective failures. There is no sense of male satisfaction over the fate of these women, but of male self-recrimination. It is a theme that exists in its purest form in Peckinpah's period Westerns, but, as we've seen, what is at first explored in his Westerns extends through his other films. In *Bring Me the Head of Alfredo Garcia,* Bennie fails Elita; Doc's failing is his mistrust of his wife's sexual sacrifice on his behalf in *The Getaway;* Ace Bonner fails his wife time after time; David fails Amy in *Straw Dogs,* turning her from allied wife into enemy.

Peckinpah's women are defined both by the monopoly of power held by men, and also by the failings of men. Outside the perimeters of male power and within the space of male flaws, Peckinpah's women carve out niches for themselves. The unpalatability of those niches—such as prostitution—may, in effect, punish women, but for the sins of men.

★ ★ ★

"Art begins in a wound," wrote novelist and essayist John Gardner, "an imperfection . . . inherent in the nature of life itself—and is an attempt to learn to live with the wound or to heal it. It is the pain of the wound which impels the artist to do his work, and it is the universality of woundedness in the human condition which makes the work of art significant as medicine or distraction."[58] Carl Jung would qualify Gardner's position by saying that, "the personal life of the poet cannot be held essential to his art—but at most a help or hindrance to his creative task. He may go the way of a Philistine, a good citizen, a neurotic, a fool or a criminal. His personal career may be inevitable and interesting, but it does not explain the poet.''[59] All of which sums up the problematic exercise of putting Peckinpah's films through the prism of his life.

If Peckinpah's work was regularly misread, it was not a hard misread to make, the bias of the reader aside. The flaws in the man's personality—including his own energetic misrepresentations of himself—were so grandiose they begged, on the part of auteur critics, application to his work. Somewhere in the gulf between the skewed perceptions of the man and his films, and his own, skewed self-perception, lies the truth of his cinema tales.

When one compares the chaotic, abusive, self-destructive path that marked Peckinpah's personal way with the paths followed by the men and women in his films, one does see connections. Ironically, the ties between Peckinpah and his films are not between he and his heroes, but between he and his villains. The brawling, the self-indulgence, the debaucheries, and the personal violence of the Hammond brothers, Mapache, the more moronic members of Billy the Kid's gang, of the bounty hunters of *The Wild Bunch,* are all evidentiary traits that show up on almost any page of the director's biography. It is, perhaps, such up-close-and-personal acquaintance with the brutish side of human nature that makes such Peckinpah villains as the banditos cum Mexican soldiery, and the bounty hunters from *Bunch* come to repugnant life so vividly. So, what of his heroes? More to the point, what of his women?

Pike Bishop, Billy the Kid, Steve Judd, and Gil Westrum, and the other Peckinpah heroes in that line are, perhaps, aspirations. They are everything that Peckinpah the man claimed allegiance to and demanded of others, but was not: loyal, stoic, courageous, and philosophically resigned. When time runs out for Peckinpah heroes, they accept that—for better or worse—they have lived their lives as they've chosen, and manage to mark the end of that time with either grace *(Ride the High Country, The Ballad of Cable Hogue)* or apocalyptic majesty *(The Wild Bunch),* but in any case without whimper or regret. To betray their nature, as Pat Garrett and Deke Thornton do, is to put their remaining years under a dark cloud. Dundee, like Garrett and Thornton, will do what he has to do to remain a professional soldier; he does not have the insight of a Tyreen to know that the only fitting end for their type is to turn back toward an overpowering enemy and die a soldier's death.

If Peckinpah's men reflect the filmmaker's aspirations, then his women, in a blanket refutation of his cinematic misogynist label, reflect a near-holy ideal. In Peckinpah's period Westerns, there are no "bad" women. The dark side of their conduct is less an illustration of weakness in their sex than it is a reflection of and reaction to the misconduct of men. The aspects of Peckinpah's women that might turn us against them, such as shown by the prostitutes of *Ride the High Country*, blind to Elsa Knudsen's dilemma, or the back-shooting Mapache camp follower, are those characteristics they share most closely with men. Left to be women, as are Teresa, Hildy, Elsa, Mrs. Baker, they become the definition of inner strength, integrity, sympathy, and the courage to face life—this last more demanding, in Peckinpah's world, than the easy courage to face death as their men do.

That Peckinpah showed women regularly victimized by men was not a part of his personal misogyny. He revealed what remains an unpleasant and persistent truth: men victimize women. As perhaps Peckinpah's own behavior enabled him to so able render reprehensible characters like the Bunch's pursuing bounty hunters, that same behavior perhaps gave him a personal understanding of how completely men control and abuse women. Crippled by his own personal frailties, Peckinpah treated women on screen with a sympathy and respect he seemed incapable of in life.

Peckinpah may not have been obsessed with whores, but his nonjudgmental rendering of their circumstances could easily be tied to a sense of identification on his part. Even at the time of his greatest success he remained a director for hire and often referred to himself in prostitutive terms: "I'm a whore. I go where I'm kicked," he told *Playboy*. "I'm like a good whore. I go where I'm kicked," he reiterated to *The New York Times Magazine*.[60] It may have been a favorite quixotic allusion, some gutter poetry false modesty, but to review the circumstances of his career as we have here is to see more than a grain of truth to it.

*   *   *

Women have been romanticized in films from the beginning of the motion picture. Westerns have been no exception and are, perhaps, more guilty than other genres. The film Western derived its conventions from the Western literary models in which temporal social mores distorted historical truth to produce an "acceptable" construct. That product included such clichés as the virginal school marm, the dance hall girl with a soft center, the repressive matron from the East, and others. Peckinpah's films rejected that model.

"[He] depicted in final sardonic statement the bitter truth that there are no good guys . . . and that what has replaced the dead frontier is anything but a brave new world of civilization."[61] If the white-hatted hero and his flawless moral strength was a casualty of Peckinpah's revisionism, then so was the virgin as heroine and the sullied dance hall girl as someone who, at best, deserved forgiveness but not the hero.

Peckinpah granted his women nearly true—and brutal—equality. He reserved them the right to be better than his men, but showed them to be capable of being as opportunistic, self-seeking, self-preserving, double-dealing, and ruthless as their men, given a compelling set of circumstances. He showed that there are no heroes, or heroines, although some of the most unrepentant sinners are capable of heroic conduct. He showed that a whore and a gunman could have more integrity than the town matron and proper businessman. He showed that the lights and darks of human nature do not respect social class or gender.

He proved something of this paradoxical sort simply in making these films. Here was a man who abused his friendships but depicted majestic loyalty among certain of his characters. He despised the power brokers in his industry, yet forgave characters like Deke Thornon in *Bunch* and Pat Garrett who conceded defeat to the power brokers of the Old West, and could even find among their ranks certain admirable mavericks, like the banker who finances Cable Hogue. He physically and emotionally brutalized his women, but crucified the on-screen male characters who did the same in his films, and gave most of his women characters—from prostitute to innocent naif—a dignity he did not grant them in real life.

★   ★   ★

An opinion is an opinion, and a judgment about a creative work is nothing more or less than an opinion with all the subjectivity, bias, comfort level, and personal preference that informs *any* opinion. One might dispute the worldview Sam Peckinpah rendered in his films, sometimes weaving it around Hollywood conventions, sometimes supplanting them with it, but that view finds enough resonance in the real world to preclude one from dismissing it. There is no doubt that out of a desire for a better world, one can find much in Peckinpah's work that is objectionable, whether one's concern is about violence, sex, or any moral province.

What even a severely critical view of Peckinpah should be able to grant is that Peckinpah—whether auteur or simply "a good whore"—did not indulge gratuitously for the sake of pandering to box-office appeal. Even at his most egregious, with the rape of Amy in *Straw Dogs,* Pauline Kael berated Peckinpah not on the basis of being gratuitous, but for being "wrong-headed." Prime brickbat hurler Molly Haskell, throughout her book *From Reverence to Rape,* never accused Peckinpah of boosting the quotient of violence and sex—and violent sex—in his films for the sake of box office, but out of a machismo take on the world she considered symptomatic of a male-oriented industry serving a male-oriented society.

Out of a desire to right a social and cultural wrong, Peckinpah may have been done an aesthetic disservice. The feminist criteria that held him deficient was based not so much on whether or not Peckinpah was being honest in either artistic or real-world terms, but on the *palatability* of what he delivered on screen. Honesty and palatability are regularly incompatible partners.

"The artists are not making up obscenities," says actor/writer Eric Bogosian, "They are reporting on the obscene world in which they live."[62]

NOTES

1. Henry James, *The Bostonians* (New York: Vintage Press, 1991), 338.

2. Genaro C. Armas, "Road to Equality is Smoothest Up North," *The Star-Ledger* (November 16, 2000): 16.

3. "Audience Not in Tune with Era," *The Star-Ledger* [Newark, N.J.] (January 16, 1992, morning ed.): 2.

4. Leslie Laurence, "The Breast Cancer Academic: Women Aren't Just Scared, We're Mad," *McCall's* (November 1991): 28.

5. Dorchen Leidholdt, "Midsection—Pornography: Love or Death?" *Film Comment* (December 1984): 38.

6. Quoted in Lance Morrow, "Men: Are They Really That Bad?" *Time* (February 14, 1994): 57.

7. Morrow, "Men," 57.

8. Bridget Potter, Address to Indianapolis Professional Chapter of Women in Communications. (April 1988): 2.

9. Arnold Braeske, "It's Not a Ms-take: Steinem Ties Knot with Her Entrepreneur from S. Africa," People. *The Star-Ledger* (6 September 2000): 3.

10. Mark Baker, *Women: American Women in Their Own Words* (New York: Simon & Schuster, 1990), 284.

11. Marianne Schnall, "Interview with Gloria Steinem," *Ms.* (April 3, 1995): 2.

12. Schnall, "Gloria Steinem," 2.

13. Richard Lacayo, "Crusading Against the Pro-Choice Movement," *Time* (October 21, 1991): 28.

14. Alan M. Dershowitz, "Midsection Debate—Porn II: Love or Death?" *Film Comment* (December 1984): 34.

15. Leidholdt, "Midsection—Pornography," 37–38.

16. Barbara Rowes, *The Book of Quotes* (New York: Dutton, 1979): 92.

17. Braeske, "It's Not," 3.

18. Braeske, " 'Material Mom' Tires of Fans, Media, and Naked Ladies in British Papers," People. *The Star-Ledger* (September 14, 2000): 3.

19. Molly Haskell, *From Reverence to Rape: The Treatment of Women in the Movies* (New York: Holt, 1974): 38.

20. Robin Wood, "Beauty Bests the Beast," *American Film* (September 1983): 63.

21. Nancy Gibbs (reported by Ann Blackman, Priscilla Painton, and Elizabeth Taylor). "The War Against Feminism," *Time* (March 9, 1992): 53.

22. Gibbs, "The War," 51, 53.

23. Juliann Garey, "Sandra's Secret Side," *Redbook* (January 2001): 81.

24. Arnold Braeske, "Not Just a Pretty Woman but a Power Player," People. *The Star-Ledger* (December 6, 2000): 3.

25. Rebecca Ascher-Walsh, "Lady and the Chump," *Entertainment Weekly* (December 8, 2000): 34.

26. Christy Grosz, "The Power 50," *The Hollywood Reporter—Special Issue*. Ninth Annual Issue Women in Entertainment Power 50. (December 2000): 12.

27. Wolf Schneider, "Just Like a Woman," *American Film* (March 1991): 4.

28. "Sex Roles, Stereotypes, and Kids' Television: The Male Is In," *Hollywood Reporter* (October 25, 1991): 11.

29. Ben Horowitz, "People," *The Star-Ledger* (August 21, 2000): 3.

30. Frank Spotnitz, "Glenn Close," *American Film* (November/December 1991): 27.

31. Gibbs, "The War," 53.

32. Gibbs, "The War," 66.

33. Alan Silver and Linda Brookover, "The Ones Who Got Away," http://www.members.aol.com/_ht_a/screenie/Queen/noir.htm [accessed September 1, 2001].

34. Gibbs, "The War," 53, 80.

35. Betty Friedan, "The Dangers of the New Feminine Mystique," *McCall's* (November 1991): 80.

36. Schnall, "Gloria Steinem," 1.

37. Paula Saha, "Gun Control Becomes Issue for Campaign," *The Star-Ledger* (August 14, 2000): 20.

38. Marcia Pally, " 'Double' Trouble," *Film Comment* (October 1984): 13.

39. Ann Snitow, "Midsection— Pornography: Love or Death?" *Film Comment* (December 1984): 48.

40. "Cahiers du Peckinpah," *Esquire* (February 1972): 119.

41. "Cahiers," 119, 120–122.

42. Pally, " 'Double,' " 15.

43. Greenspun, quoted in *The New York Times Film Reviews: 1969–1970* (New York: New York Times and Arno Press, 1971), 211.

44. Jay Robert Nash and Stanley Ralph Ross, *The Motion Picture Guide: 1927–1983—E-G.* Vol. III (Chicago: Cinebooks, 1986), 862.

45. *"Blume in Love,"* *Filmfacts* XVI (1973): 167–69.

46. *"Frenzy,"* *Filmfacts* XV (1972): 120.

47. Philip French, *Westerns: Aspects of a Movie Genre. Cinema One* (New York: Viking, 1974): 64.

48. *"Hang 'em High,"* *Filmfacts* XI (November 15, 1968): 324–26.

49. *"McCabe and Mrs. Miller,"* *Filmfacts* XIV (1971): 189–93.

50. Karen Jaehne, "Hooker," *Film Comment* (May/June 1987): 25.

51. Joel W. Finler, *The Movie Director's Story* (New York: Crescent, 1985), 224.

52. Kathleen Murphy, "Sam Peckinpah: No Bleeding Heart," *Film Comment* (April 1985): 74.

53. Rita Parks, *The Western Hero in Film and Television: Mass Media Mythology. Studies in Cinema.* (Ann Arbor, Mich.: UMI Research Press, 1982): 115.

54. J. A. Cuddon, Introduction to *The Penguin Book of Horror Stories* (New York: Penguin, 1984): 12

55. Haskell, *From Reverence to Rape*, 1.

56. Haskell, *From Reverence to Rape*, 4.

57. Wood, "Beauty," 63.

58. John Gardner, *On Moral Fiction* (New York: Basic Books, 1978), 181.

59. Brewster Ghiselin, *The Creative Process: A Symposium* (Berkley: University of California Press, 1985), 231–32.

60. Quoted "Cahiers du Peckinpah," *Esquire* (February 1972): 121.

61. Parks, *The Western Hero*, 104.

62. "Expressing Themselves," *Star-Ledger* [Newark, N.J.] (October 29, 1991, morning ed.): 3.

· 6 ·

Coda

Straw Dogs was released in 1972. Ten years earlier, the slow-motion tumblings of bodies spurting blood and the—for its time—graphic rape of Amy would have been unthinkable. And yet, in 1972, the hair gel scene from the farce *There's Something About Mary,* the confrontational lyrics of rapper Eminem, and the "Christmas Poo" jokes from cable TV's animated series "South Park" would have been unthinkable *then.* "We all know how the laudable artistic and intellectual standards of one age become the limiting conventions of the next," wrote Margo Jefferson in a *New York Times* piece on arts criticism. "Readers and writers of the past . . . remind us how culture and taste change. And why."[1]

In a synchronous example, at this writing, the basic cable service American Movie Classics has licensed Sam Peckinpah's *The Wild Bunch,* debuting it under its "Tough Guys" umbrella in a December prime-time premier. To AMC's credit, it presented the more-or-less restored version of *Bunch.* "More or less" because while AMC runs films without commercial interruption, and, in this case, acquired the *Bunch* print that includes all the sequences deleted during the film's theatrical run, the film was still not completely intact. As a basic cable channel that skews toward an older audience with a line-up overwhelmingly composed of black-and-white entrées from studio libraries, when running more recent fare AMC routinely tempers edgier elements. In this case, the few, short scenes featuring brief glimpses of female nudity were cropped, and a number of epithets were bleeped—William Holden couldn't call Ernest Borgnine a "lazy bastard," and in one of their several spats as the Gorch brothers, Ben Johnson couldn't tell Warren Oates to "get off his ass and help once in a while." Yet every bit of on-screen violence—the slow-motion falls, bodies spinning violently under the impact of bullets, spurting blood—was left intact.

175

Taste and culture may change, but which changes represent adventurous art and which are simple crass attempts to draw an audience?
"Commerce being commerce," writes entertainment reporter Lisa
Schwarzbaum concerned over a rising coarseness she perceives in
mainstream entertainment, "pretty soon we may not be able to distinguish between the bestial and the best-selling." "The fence that separates the decent from the indecent has so many holes in it," says
Schwarzbaum, "that homophobes, racists, misogynists, and common
potty mouths step right through unchallenged. Smirking all the way
to the bank, they're indistinguishable from artists and innovators of
real, if disturbing, substance."[2]

While it is hard to disagree with Schwarzbaum, left unresolved in
her piece is the issue of who is to referee? And by what qualification?

Who decides what is innovation? What is substantial? What is
potty mouth verbiage? Jefferson's essay frankly confronted the fact
that critics are hardly objective judges: "Idiosyncrasy belongs as much
to criticism as to art. . . . It's interesting how often we critics believe
ourselves above and beyond the fallibilities of artists and audiences."[3]

Which is another way of saying that what Schwarzbaum might
find appalling, a filmmaker or producer may consider fertile and appropriate ground. "Having creative people doing what other people
might consider poor taste, the risk is worth it," says Darren Star, producer of HBO's "Sex and the City."[4] "It's great when creative people
have latitude to deal with more adult themes." Yet Star also holds
reservations: "At the same time, I think there is something called
good taste and I think that . . . it's like pornography: You know it
when you see it."[5]

Filmmaker Paul Verhoeven weighs in on the issue going a step
beyond Star: "I feel that I have no responsibility except to myself,"
he says, articulating a credo that most people who consider themselves
creative would probably subscribe to. "It's my moral judgement—
what I can tolerate. And that is what an artist is for—the antennae
of society. Art should not be something that's nice and friendly and
okay."[6]

The unspoken caveat emptor there, as inspiring a creative battle
standard as Verhoeven offers, is how credible the banner remains

when it's hung from poles like Verhoeven's *Basic Instinct* and *Show-girls*.

★   ★   ★

We are back where this volume started, with the same unanswered, elemental questions: Is bad art still art? Is unintentional art still art? Can the objectionable still be art?

They remain unanswered because they are unanswerable, and Sam Peckinpah provides a case in point. An artist working in extremes cannot help but be found objectionable to some, perhaps to many. Measured against artificial and arbitrary standards set to social agendas, what should be aesthetic judgments become social commentary, the consequence of which any creative talent worth his or her salt runs a regular risk of being considered a transgressor of some sort in some fashion. Judged within the oversimplified, narrow parameters of artistic concepts such as auteur theory, which flaunt the corporate nature of certain media like film and television, creators are praised and pilloried for accomplishments and sins that may be as much a product of happenstance as of artistic vision.

This reexamination of one element of Peckinpah's work will not put to rest feminist criticism of his films, nor should it. Those who still object to his work should go back, give it a second look, and *then* rebut if they find merit to a rebuttal. And then his fans should consider again what his detractors say, take still *another* look at his work . . . and so on. There is no endgame. There shouldn't be.

Hopefully, the case this exercise *can* make is that regular reevaluation of *any* creative work is part of an ongoing critical process, that it might persuade us to recognize how variable and transitory some standards of criticism really are. That issues about Peckinpah's work remain unresolved, that his films remain touchstones in so many categories of film appreciation and criticism, is a testament that there is work of worth here; that that work can still, after all these years, provide fodder for revisiting evidences that the work is more complex than both supporters and detractors initially proposed. What will stand along with the work is the work of those who seek to decrypt it.

"What will future readers make of us?" Margo Jefferson wrote of her fellow art critics. "It's foolish to hope they will find us infalli-ble. Let's hope they find us ferociously curious and eager to be edu-cated again and again."[7]

NOTES

1. Margo Jefferson, "Critics Judge, and Are Judged, Across the Centu-ries," *The New York Times* (August 21, 2000): E-2.

2. Lisa Schwarzbaum, "Lewd Awakening," *Entertainment Weekly* (Au-gust 11, 2000): 26, 22.

3. Jefferson, "Critics Judge," E-2.

4. Quoted in Schwarzbaum, "Lewd Awakening," 26.

5. Schwarzbaum, "Lewd Awakening," 22.

6. Quoted in Schwarzbaum, "Lewd Awakening," 26.

7. Jefferson, "Critics Judge," E-2.

Filmography

The Authentic Death of Hendry Jones (1957)
Screenplay by Sam Peckinpah (uncredited)
Based on the novel *The Authentic Death of Hendry Jones* by Charles Neider
Produced in 1961 as *One–Eyed Jacks*, directed by Marlon Brando

The Deadly Companions (1961)
Directed by Sam Peckinpah
Screenplay by A. S. Fleischman

Ride the High Country (1962)
Directed by Sam Peckinpah
Screenplay by N. B. Stone Jr.

Major Dundee (1965)
Directed by Sam Peckinpah
Screenplay by Harry Julian Fink, Oscar Saul, and Sam Peckinpah
Based on an original story by Harry Julian Fink

The Glory Guys (1965)
Screenplay by Sam Peckinpah
Directed by Arnold Laven

Viva Rides! (1968)
Screenplay by Sam Peckinpah and Robert Towne
Directed by Buzz Kulik

The Wild Bunch (1969)
Directed by Sam Peckinpah
Screenplay by Walon Green and Sam Peckinpah
Based on an original story by Walon Green and Roy N. Sickner

The Ballad of Cable Hogue (1970)
Produced and Directed by Sam Peckinpah
Screenplay by John Crawford and Edmund Penney

Straw Dogs (1972)
Directed by Sam Peckinpah
Screenplay by David Zelig Goodman and Sam Peckinpah
Based on the novel *The Siege of Trencher's Farm* by Gordon Williams

Junior Bonner (1972)
Directed by Sam Peckinpah
Screenplay by Jeb Rosebrook

The Getaway (1972)
Directed by Sam Peckinpah
Screenplay by Walter Hill
Based on the novel *The Getaway* by Jim Thompson

Pat Garrett and Billy the Kid (1973)
Directed by Sam Peckinpah
Screenplay by Rudolph Wurlitzer

Bring Me the Head of Alfredo Garcia (1974)
Directed by Sam Peckinpah.
Screenplay by Gordon Dawson and Sam Peckinpah
From a story by Sam Peckinpah and Frank Kowalski

The Killer Elite (1975)
Directed by Sam Peckinpah
Screenplay by Mark Norman and Stirling Silliphant
Based on the novel *The Killer Elite* by Robert Rostand

Cross of Iron (1977)
Directed by Sam Peckinpah
Screenplay by Julius Epstien, Walter Kelley, and James Hamilton
Based on the novel *Cross of Iron* by Willi Heinrich

Convoy (1978)
Directed by Sam Peckinpah
Screenplay by B. W. L. Norton
Based on the song "Convoy" by C. W. McCall

The Osterman Weekend (1983)
Directed by Sam Peckinpah
Screenplay by Alan Sharp
Adaptation by Ian Masters
Based on the novel *The Osterman Weekend* by Robert Ludlum

Bibliography

Armas, Genaro C. "Road to Equality is Smoothest Up North." *The Star-Ledger* (November 16, 2000): 16.

"Art Is Out." *American Film* (February 1979): 80.

Ascher-Walsh, Rebecca. "Lady and the Chump." *Entertainment Weekly* (December 8, 2000): 27+.

"Audience Not in Tune With Era." *The Star-Ledger* [Newark, N.J.] (January 16, 1992, morn. ed.): 2.

Bach, Steven. *Final Cut: Dreams and Disaster in the Making of* Heaven's Gate. New York: Plume, 1985.

Baker, Mark. *Women: American Women in Their Own Words.* New York: Simon & Schuster, 1990.

Bart, Peter. *The Gross: The Hits, the Flops—The Summer That Ate Hollywood.* New York: St. Martin's, 1999.

Basinger, Jeanine. "Ann Sothern." *Film Comment* (November/December 1999): 24–29.

———. "Ladies Matinee." *Film Comment* (November/December 1999): 27–28.

Baxter, John. *Sixty Years of Hollywood.* Cranbury, N.J.: A.S. Barnes, 1973.

Berman, Pat. "A Strange Fascination for Violence." *Columbia Record* [Columbia, S.C.] (February 1, 1975, Sun. ed.): 1–B+.

"The Best American Films of the Decade." *Take One* (July 1978): 27.

"Blume In Love." Filmfacts XVI (1973): 165–69.

Braeske, Arnold. "It's Not a Ms-take: Steinem Ties Knot With Her Entrepreneur from S. Africa." People. *The Star-Ledger* (September 6, 2000): 3.

———. " 'Material Mom' Tires of Fans, Media, and Naked Ladies In British Papers." People. *The Star-Ledger* (September 14, 2000): 3.

———. "Not Just A Pretty Woman but a Power Player." People. *The Star-Ledger* (December 6, 2000): 3.

Brooks, Tim, and Earle Marsh. *The Complete Director to Prime Time Network and Cable TV Shows 1946–Present.* 6th ed. New York: Balantine, 1995.

Brown, Helen Gurley. "Don't Give Up On Sex After 60." *Newsweek* (May 29, 2000): 55.

Bruno, Mary. "Bad Sports." *New York Woman* (November 1991): 64–66.

Bryson, John. "Sam Peckinpah." *American Film* (April 1985): 21+.

Buford, Kate. "Do Make Waves: Sandy—Alexander Mackendrick." *Film Comment* (May/June 1994): 41–43.

Byron, Stuart. "I Can't Get Jimmy Carter to See My Movie!" *Film Comment* (March/April 1977): 46–52.

————. "Something Wicker This Way Comes." *Film Comment* (November/December 1977): 29–31.

"Cahiers du Peckinpah." *Esquire* (February 1972): 119–22.

Carey, Gary. *All the Stars in Heaven—Louis B. Mayer's MGM*. New York: Dutton, 1981.

Carlson, Margaret (reported by Hays Gorey, Nancy Travers). "The Ultimate Men's Club." *Time* (October 21, 1991): 50–51.

Corliss, Richard. "Why Can't a Woman Be a Man?" *Time* (August 5, 1991): 66–67.

"Cross of Iron." Filmfacts XXII (August 1977): 203–5.

Cuddon, J. A. Introduction to *The Penguin Book of Horror Stories*. New York: Penguin, 1984.

"Daniel Melnick." *American Film* (March 1982): 13–20.

"The Deadly Companions." Filmfacts IV (January 16, 1962): 331.

Dershowitz, Alan M. "Midsection Debate—Porn II: Love or Death?" *Film Comment* (December 1984): 33–34.

"Dirty Pictures." People (May 29, 2000): 30.

Dougan, Clark, and Samuel Lipsman. *A Nation Divided. The Vietnam Experience*. Boston: Boston Publishing, 1984.

Dougan, Clark, and Stephen Weiss. *Nineteen Sixty-Eight. The Vietnam Experience*. Boston: Boston Publishing, 1983.

Edwards, Tamala M. "Flying Solo." Additional reporting Tammerlin Drummond, Elizabeth Kaufman, Anne Moffett, Jacqueline Savaiano, and Maggie Sieger. *Time* (August 28, 2000): 47–53.

Engeler, Amy. *"New York Woman's* Second Annual Roundup of Worst Places to Work." *New York Woman* (November 1991): 72–77.

Everson, William K. *A Pictorial History of the Western Film*. Secaucus, N.J.: Citadel Press, 1969.

"Expressing Themselves." *The Star-Ledger* [Newark, N.J.] (October 29, 1991, morn. ed.): 3.

Farber, Stephen. "Peckinpah's Return." *Film Quarterly* (Fall 1969): 5–11.

Fine, Marshall. *Bloody Sam: The Life and Films of Sam Peckinpah*. New York: Donald I. Fine, 1991.

Finler, Joel W. *The Movie Director's Story*. New York: Crescent, 1985.

————. *The Hollywood Story*. New York: Crown, 1988.

Fischer, Christiane, ed. *Let Them Speak for Themselves: Women in the American West 1849–1900*. New York: Dutton, 1978.

Folsom, James, ed. *The Western: A Collection of Critical Essays*. Englewood Cliffs, N.J.: Prentice-Hall, 1979.

French, Philip. *Westerns: Aspects of a Movie Genre*. Cinema One. New York: Viking, 1974.

"*Frenzy*." *Filmfacts* XV (1972): 117–21.

Friedan, Betty. "The Dangers of the New Feminine Mystique." *McCall's* (November 1991): 78+.

Gardner, John. *On Moral Fiction*. New York: Basic Books, 1978.

Garey, Juliann. "Sandra's Secret Side." *Redbook* (January 2001): 78+.

Gaydos, S. "After the Falls." *Hollywood Reporter* (February 10, 1992): S–10+.

Gentry, Curt. *The Last Days of the Late, Great State of California*. New York: Putnam, 1968.

"*The Getaway*." *Filmfacts* XV (December 1972): 627–30.

Ghiselin, Brewster, ed. *The Creative Process: A Symposium*. Berkeley: University of California Press, 1985.

Gianetti, Louis D. *Understanding Movies*. 2nd ed. Englewood Cliffs, N.J.: Prentice, 1976.

Gibbs, Nancy (reported by Ann Blackman, Priscilla Painton, and Elizabeth Taylor). "The War Against Feminism." *Time* (March 9, 1992): 50–55.

Goldberg, Robert. "TV: 'Black Venus' of the Roaring '20s." *Wall Street Journal* (March 18, 1991, morn. ed.): A12.

Goldman, William. *Adventures in the Screen Trade: A Personal View of Hollywood and Screenwriting*. New York: Warner, 1983.

Gottlieb, Carl. *The Jaws Log*. New York: Dell, 1975.

Greco, Mike. "Hard Riding." *Film Comment* (May/June 1980): 13–19.

Grosz, Christy. "The Power 50." *Hollywood Reporter—Special Issue*. Ninth Annual Issue Women in Entertainment Power 50. (December 2000): 12.

"*Hang 'em High*." *Filmfacts* XI (November 15, 1968): 324–26.

Haskell, Molly. *From Reverence to Rape: The Treatment of Women in the Movies*. New York: Holt, 1974.

————. "Molly Haskell's Guilty Pleasures." *Film Comment* (January/February 1997): 6–13.

Heston, Charlton. *Charlton Heston: The Actor's Life—Journals 1956–1976*. New York: Pocket, 1979.

Higham, Charles, and Joel Greenberg. *The Celluloid Muse: The Directors Speak*. New York: Signet, 1972.

Hine, Robert. *The American West: An Interpretive History*. Boston: Little Brown, 1973.

Hodenfield, Chris. "Last of the Real Ones." *American Film* (March 1990): 4.

Hodges, Ann. "*Baker* Gets Recipe Right." *Houston Chronicle* (March 10, 1991, Sun. ed., Television section): 1+.

Hoffman, Alice. "*Thelma & Louise.*" *Premiere* (October 1997): 69.

Horowitz, Ben. "People." *The Star-Ledger* (August 21, 2000): 3.

Jaehne, Karen. "Hooker." *Film Comment* (May/June 1987): 25–32.

James, Henry. *The Bostonians.* New York: Vintage Press, 1991 (1885).

Jameson, Richard T. "Sam Peckinpah." *Film Comment* (January/February 1981): 34–35.

————. "Lost Weekend." *Film Comment* (April 1984): 28–30.

Jefferson, Margo. "Critics Judge, and Are Judged, Across the Centuries." *The New York Times* (August 21, 2000): E–2.

Jennings, Gary. *The Movie Book.* New York: Dial, 1963.

Jones, Ken D., and Arthur F. McClure. *Hollywood at War: The American Motion Picture and World War II.* Cranbury, N.J.: A.S. Barnes, 1973.

Jones, Kent. "A Class Act." *Film Comment* (July/August 2000): 28–32.

"*Junior Bonner.*" *Filmfacts* XV (September 1972): 410–13.

Kessler-Harris, Alice. *Out to Work: A History of Wage-Earning Women in the United States.* New York: Oxford University Press, 1982.

Kirn, Walter. "One Man's Gripe: Women Keep Upgrading Their Formula for Mr. Right." *Time* (August 28, 2000): 53.

Kitsis, Jim. *Horizons West. Cinema One.* Bloomington: Indiana University Press, 1969.

Krich, Aaron, ed. *Four Fallen Women.* Introduction. New York: Dell, 1953.

Lacayo, Richard. "Crusading Against the Pro-Choice Movement." *Time* (October 21, 1991): 26–28.

Larson, Charles U. *Persuasion: Reception and Responsibility.* 5th ed. Belmont, Calif.: Wadsworth Publishing, 1989.

Laurence, Leslie. "The Breast Cancer Academic: Women Aren't Just Scared, We're Mad." *McCall's* (November 1991): 24+.

Leidholdt, Dorchen. "Midsection—Pornography: Love or Death?" *Film Comment* (December 1984): 37–39.

Leo, John. "On Society: When Rules Don't Count." *U.S. News & World Report* (August 7, 2000): 14.

Lester, Peter. "Actor–Writer Burt Young Has an Ex-Pug's Mug. But He Can Knock Out Scripts in Three Weeks." *People* (July 17, 1978): 71–74.

Lindgren, Ernest. *The Art of the Film.* 2nd printing, Collier ed. New York: Collier, 1972.

Lurie, Alison. Introduction to *The Bostonians.* New York: Vintage Press, 1991.

Macklin, Anthony F. "Pat Garrett and Billy the Kid." *Film Heritage* (Winter 1974–1975): 34–37.

"Major Dundee." Filmfacts VIII (July 1965): 105–8.

Mamet, David. *On Directing Film.* New York: Penguin, 1991.

Matranga, Stuart. "Sex Education." *Cable Guide* (September 1991): 6.

Maynard, Richard A., ed. *The American West on Film: Myth and Reality.* Hayden Film Attitudes and Issues Series. Rochelle Park, N.J.: Hayden Book, 1974.

"McCabe and Mrs. Miller." Filmfacts XIV (1971): 189–93.

Medved, Harry, with Randy Dreyfuss. *The 50 Worst Films of All Time (and How They Got That Way).* New York: Warner, 1984.

Mesce, William. *The Wild Bunch: A Filmguide to Research.* Unpublished research guide, University of South Carolina, Columbia, 1976.

"MidSection: Class of 1985." *Film Comment* (April 1985): 31.

Morgan, Marabel. *The Total Woman.* Old Tappan, N.J.: Fleming H. Revell, 1973.

Morrow, Lance. "Men: Are They Really That Bad?" *Time* (February 14, 1994): 53–59.

Murphy, Kathleen. "The Ballad of David Sumner: A Peckinpah Psychodrama." *Movietone News* (January 1972): 24–27.

———. "Sam Peckinpah: No Bleeding Heart." *Film Comment* (April 1985): 74–75.

———. "Blood of a Poet: The Cinema According to Sam Peckinpah." The Film Society of Lincoln Center, The Walter Reade Theater Program. (March 1995): 7–17.

Murphy, Kathleen, and Richard T. Jameson. *"Bring Me the Head of Alfredo Garcia." Film Comment* (January/February 1981): 44–48.

Murray, William. "Interview: Sam Peckinpah." *Playboy* (August 1972): 65+.

Myers, John. *The Westerners: A Roundup of Pioneer Reminiscences.* Englewood Cliffs, N.J.: Prentice, 1969.

Nachbar, Jack, ed. *Focus on the Western. Film Focus.* Englewood Cliffs, N.J.: Prentice, 1974.

Nash, Jay Robert, and Stanley Ralph Ross. *The Motion Picture Guide: 1927–1983—E-G.* Vol. III. Chicago: Cinebooks, 1986.

The New York Times Film Reviews: 1969–1970. New York: New York Times and Arno Press, 1971.

"1936–1986: Year By Year." *Life: 50th Anniversary Collector's Edition 1936–1986* (Fall 1986): 187–95.

Pally, Marcia. " 'Double' Trouble." *Film Comment* (October 1984): 12–17.

Parish, James Robert, ed. *The Great Movie Series.* Cranbury, N.J.: A.S. Barnes, 1971.

Parkinson, Michael, and Clyde Jeavons. *A Pictorial History of Westerns.* London: Hamlyn Publishing, 1973.

Parks, Rita. *The Western Hero in Film and Television: Mass Media Mythology.* Studies in Cinema. Ann Arbor, Mich.: UMI Research Press, 1982.

"Pat Garrett and Billy the Kid." Filmfacts XVI (February 1973): 86–89.

"Peckinpah's Cut of *Pat Garrett* Finally Emerges for a Screening." *Variety* (May 7, 1986): 110.

Phinney, Kevin. " 'Thelma,' 'Silence' Wow WGA." *Hollywood Reporter* (March 23, 1992): 1+.

————. "NOW Denounces *Basic Instinct.*" *Hollywood Reporter* (March 19, 1992): 3+.

"Pornography: Love or Death?" *Film Comment* (December 1984): 29–59.

Potter, Bridget. Address to Indianapolis Professional Chapter of Women in Communications. (April 1988).

Reese, Lori. " 'G' Rating." *EW Daily Online.* http://www.ew.com/ew/aol [accessed on August 17, 2000].

Reiter, Joan Swallow. *The Women. The Old West.* Alexandria, Va.: Time-Life, 1978.

"Ride the High Country." Filmfacts V (July 6, 1962): 137–38.

Rose, Phyllis. "Exactly What Is It about Josephine Baker?" *New York Times* (March 10, 1991): 31.

Ross, Nancy Wilson, ed. *Westward the Women.* New York: Random, 1944.

Rowes, Barbara. *The Book of Quotes.* New York: Dutton, 1979.

Saha, Paula. "Gun Control Becomes Issue for Campaign." *The Star-Ledger* (August 14, 2000): 17+.

Sarris, Andrew. *The American Cinema.* New York: Dutton, 1968.

Schecter, Harold, and Jonna Gormley Semeiks. *Patterns in Popular Culture: A Sourcebook for Writers.* New York: Harper, 1980.

Scherman, David E., ed. *Life Goes to the Movies.* 2nd printing. New York: Time-Life Books, 1975.

Schlafly, Phyllis. "School-To-Work Serves Industry, Not the Children." *Detroit News* September 14, 1998: A11.

Schnall, Marianne. "Interview with Gloria Steinem." *Ms.* (April 3, 1995). Eleanor Roosevelt National Historical Site.

Schneider, Wolf. "Just Like a Woman." *American Film* (March 1991): 4.

Schwarzbaum, Lisa. "Lewd Awakening." *Entertainment Weekly* (August 11, 2000): 20+.

Seitz, Matt Zoller. "All TV—Love and Bullets." *The Star-Ledger* (August 10, 2000): 59.

"Sex Roles, Stereotypes, and Kids Television: The Male Is In." *Hollywood Reporter* (October 25, 1991): 11+

Seydor, Paul. *Peckinpah: The Western Films.* Urbana: University of Illinois Press, 1980.

Shelton, Ron. "*The Wild Bunch.*" *American Film* (April 1989): 18–20.

Silver, Alan, and Linda Brookover. "The Ones Who Got Away." http://members.aol.com/_ht_a/screenie/Queen/noir.htm [accessed September 1, 2000].

Simmons, Garner. "Sam Peckinpah's Television Work." *Film Heritage* (Winter 1974–1975): 1–16.

———. "The Peckinpah Tapes." *American Film* (May 1985): 59–61.

Simon, Roger. "Philadelphia Story." *U.S. News & World Report* (August 7, 2000): 30–41.

Snitow, Ann. "Midsection—Pornography: Love or Death?" *Film Comment* (December 1984): 47–49.

Sochen, June. *Herstory: A Woman's View of American History.* New York: Alfred Publishing, 1974.

Spotnitz, Frank. "Glenn Close." *American Film* (November/December 1991): 22–27.

"Staying Sexy." *People* (July 31, 2000): 59–109.

Steinem, Gloria. "I'm Not the Women in My Mind." *Parade* (January 12, 1992): 10–11.

"*Straw Dogs.*" *Filmfacts* XV (February 1972): 1–5.

Terrill, Marshall. *Steve McQueen: Portrait of an American Rebel.* New York: Donald Fine, 1993.

Thomson, David. "Tuesday's Sisters." *Film Comment* (April 1985): 32–33.

"A Time of Tumult." *Life: 50th Anniversary Collector's Edition 1936–1986* (Fall 1986): 187–95.

Time-Life Books. *The Gamblers. The Old West.* Alexandria, Va.: Time-Life, 1978.

"Today's Almanac." *The Star-Ledger.* (August 10, 2000): 2.

Trachtman, Paul. *The Gunfighters. The Old West.* Alexandria, Va.: Time-Life, 1978.

"An Ugly Circus." *Time* (October 21, 1991): 34–35.

Wallace, Robert. *The Miners. The Old West.* Alexandria, Va.: Time-Life, 1978.

Warshow, Robert. "Movie Chronicle: The Westerner." In *Film Theory and Criticism,* edited by Gerald Mast and Marshall Cohen, 401–16. 2nd ed. New York: Oxford University Press, 1979.

Webb, Michael, ed. *Hollywood: Legend and Reality.* Boston: Little, Brown, 1986.

Webster's Ninth New Collegiate Dictionary. Springfield, Mass.: Merriam-Webster, 1987.

Weddle, David. "The Making of *The Wild Bunch.*" *Film Comment* (May/June 1994): 44–57.

Wheeler, Keith. *The Townsmen. The Old West.* Alexandria, Va.: Time-Life, 1978.

Wicking, Christopher, and Tise Vahimagi. *The American Vein: Directors and Directions in Television.* New York: Dutton, 1979.

"The Wild Bunch." *Filmfacts* XII (June 1969): 217–21.

"The Wild Hunch." *American Film* (June 1979): 80.

Wood, Robin. "Beauty Bests the Beast." *American Film* (September 1983): 63–65.

GENERAL BACKGROUND

Dr. Benjamin Dunlap, "Film Appreciation," University of South Carolina, Fall 1974.

―――――. "Advanced Film Appreciation," University of South Carolina, Spring 1975.

Dr. Naomi C. Liebler, "The Art of Drama," Montclair State University, Summer 1976.

Index

About the Author

Bill Mesce Jr., a native New Jerseyan and graduate of the University of South Carolina and Montclair State University, has worked for pay-TV giant Home Box Office for over 19 years, and is also a produced screenwriter and playwright, as well as a published novelist. His film work includes *Road Ends,* with Dennis Hopper, which was presented at the Mill Valley, Sante Fe, Sacramento and Breckenridge Film Festivals, and uncredited work on Brian DePalma's *Blow Out.* His play *A Jersey Cantata* was named one of the six best plays to premier in New Jersey during the 1997–98 season, and his debut novel, *The Advocate,* co-authored with Steven G. Szilagyi, was released in September 2000 to critical acclaim. A sequel, *Officer of the Court,* was published in all 2001.